WOMEN'S RETREAT

Voices of Female Faculty in Higher Education

Edited by
Atsuko Seto
and
Mary Alice Bruce

University Press of America,® Inc.
Lanham · Boulder · New York · Toronto · Plymouth, UK

Copyright © 2013 by
University Press of America,® Inc.
4501 Forbes Boulevard
Suite 200
Lanham, Maryland 20706
UPA Acquisitions Department (301) 459-3366

10 Thornbury Road
Plymouth PL6 7PP
United Kingdom

Library of Congress Control Number: 2013936410
ISBN: 978-0-7618-6113-3 (paperback : alk. paper)
eISBN: 978-0-7618-6114-0

Much appreciation to our husbands, Chris and John,
for their encouraging support throughout
our careers and specifically this collaborative effort.

We also thank our children, Emma, Chris and Carl
for the joy and meaning they bring to our lives.

And, we extend heartfelt thanks to our friends and colleagues
for the smiles and positive energy they offer to us.

Love and hugs all around!

Contents

Section Three: Cultural and Individual Identity

Section Four: Spirituality

Preface

Years ago, we attended a woman's retreat at an annual convention for Association for Counselor Education and Supervision (ACES). During that retreat, the group shared meals and rooms together, sang songs together, and took walks on a peaceful fall afternoon. Women from various personal and professional paths came together and connected with one another by sharing stories that brought moments of laughter, tears and silence. We left the retreat feeling rejuvenated, inspired, and purposeful, and the experience has become a fond memory which we all look back on and smile. An experience such as this retreat often becomes a vehicle for continued professional growth because we find a part of ourselves in others' stories and are genuinely touched by the people we encounter and stories we share. Perhaps, many, if not all of us, can think of times when collective sharing helped us become unstuck from an impasse, take a leap of faith, or see a roadblock from a slightly different angle.

A few of us from the retreat stayed in touch with one another and became good friends. It is comforting to have friends who can offer their shoulders for us to cry on, agree to disagree and still have our back, have an honest interest in our success, and "tell us like it is" because they care. Our friendships have helped us go through a number of personal challenges and helped to guide each of us in our professional endeavors. Although we seldom see each other, we have made the concerted efforts to have our own small retreat whenever we attend a same conference.

Academe can be a lonely, discouraging place without the support of colleagues whom we can also call friends. This book may not offer a same kind of support good friends can share with you. However, each contributor of this book shares with you a part of her journey, both ups and downs, in her chapter with the hope that something in her story speaks to you on a deeper level. Whether it is finding comfort, encouragement, or affirmation in a story, we hope that our collective sharing helps us connect with and inspire one another while also appreciating our own ability to direct our lives.

Acknowledgments

Thank you to all the contributors of this book. Their stories are of courage, perseverance, love and determination. This book exists because of their genuine sharing.

Section One

Career Development

Chapter 1

Parallel Play at the Mad Hatter's Tea House: Writing-In-Relation

Katrina Cook and Michelle Shuler

It was late in the evening, and I was sitting alone in a windowless office staring at the mostly blank Word document on the screen. After turning off the music I was playing because it disturbed the students in the classroom next door, the only sound I heard was their muffled voices. I searched through the drawer in case a long forgotten snack was still hiding there, but only found post-it notes and some tissues. The scattered and unconnected phrases on my monitor represented several hours' worth of non-productive work on a manuscript. The changing time was a constant reminder that the submission deadline was fast approaching. I was not having fun. Is this what my life in academia is going to be: night after night of loneliness and isolation while struggling to meet tenure guidelines for publication? Discouraged, I considered the possibility that choosing a new career as a counselor educator was not the right path for me after all.

Isolation in Academia

Ironically, as a new assistant professor in counselor education, I embraced the idea that my time would be divided among teaching, scholarship, and service. The requirement that much of my work week be devoted solely to the pursuit of writing is a gift I appreciate. However, I was not prepared for the sense of isolation that came with that gift as well as other aspects of life in academia. Generally, 40% of a professor's time is invested in writing, primarily a solitary activity; 40% in teaching, with its ancillary and often solitary activities of grading papers, designing exams and preparing for classes; and 20% on service, which might allow more opportunities for collegial interaction (Hill, 2009). Basically, this means that for most faculty members, a minimum of 40% of their time, roughly 2 or more days a week, is spent pursuing individual activities related to writing and teaching (Hill, 2009), a sharp contrast to my counseling career where much of my time was spent collaborating with colleagues. Decades ago, an undergraduate professor discouraged me from pursuing a doctoral degree by warning that loneliness and isolation are inescapable realities of academic life. The sense of isolation this English professor described appears to be a common experience among faculty. Driscoll, Parkes, Tilley-Lubbs, Brill, and Bannister (2009) used the phrase of "navigating the lonely sea" as a metaphor for their experiences as junior faculty seeking tenure (p. 5). Hill (2009) found that counselor educators often describe their experience as one of isolation, with pretenured counselor educators expressing more feelings of isolation than tenured counselor educators.

Compounding the isolation of academia is the solitary existence that writers often experience. From an early age, I bought into the mythic stereotype of a writer: a lonely person, usually male, who locks himself away for days or weeks at a time, pounding away on his typewriter into the wee hours of the morning, and whose only human contact is with his imaginary Muse. As an introvert, I have to admit that this stereotype of the solitary writer appeals to me. But somehow, the harsh reality of sitting alone in my office does not live up to the romanticized vision of a writer's life I had created. It became clear to me that writing as a solitary activity would become a dreaded chore for me, one that I avoided instead of pursuing, probably resulting in my falling behind my peers in writing productivity. Historically, female faculty tended to publish less often than their male counterparts (Candib, 2006; Roland & Fontaneai-Seime, 1996). Earlier findings seem true to me today. For example, the American Psychological Association Task Force on Women in Academe (2000) found that women had less time for research and writing than their male counterparts because they often have larger advising loads, and spend more time on campus committees. Female medical school faculty members published two-thirds as many articles as their male counterparts (Candib, 2006).

In the field of counselor education, men published more than women by a 2 to 1 ratio (Roland & Fontanesi-Seime, 1996), while female counselor educators were more likely to present at conferences (Ramsey, Covallaro, Kiselica, & Zila, 2002). As publication is a requirement for advancement, it is not surprising that many female faculty reach tenure more slowly than male faculty (August & Waltman, 2004).

The culture of academia has traditionally been based on a male-dominant orientation (Ramsey et al., 2002). To be successful, women found themselves trying to conform to the dominant academic culture, which is still mostly characterized by the male values of individualism, competition, and independence (Driscoll et al., 2009; Ramsey et al., 2002). But these attempts at conformity exact a high price from women, including feelings of isolation which can in turn inhibit their advancement (Benz, Clayton, & Costa, 1998; Driscoll et al., 2009). Female counselor educators report less job satisfaction than men (Alexander-Albritton, Hill, & Bastian Hanks, 2007), and much of that dissatisfaction appears to be related to feelings of loneliness and isolation (Magnuson, 2002). Mandleco (2010) suggested that the patriarchal system of academia contributes to female academicians feeling excluded and isolated. It would seem then that women are caught in a contradiction. Conforming to a male-dominated system in an effort to advance professionally can create feelings of isolation which hinders the advancement women seek.

The writing requirement for faculty adds another layer of women struggling to fit into the existing male-dominant institutional culture. Like academia, until recently writing has been an activity dominated by males (Candib, 2006). With few exceptions, women have only been writing within the last century (Candib, 2006). The stereotype of the solitary writer described earlier is a vision derived from my own automatic and unexamined acceptance of the male values of independence and individualism as the norm (Ramsey et al., 2002).

Writing-in-Relation

Jean Baker Miller, in her groundbreaking book Toward a New Psychology of Women (1976) introduced the concept that women are more relational in their approach. Women tend to be more preoccupied with connecting with others, and their sense of self revolves around maintaining relationships (Miller, 1976). Recognition of the importance of these relational experiences for women can foster their ability to participate in relationships that nurture growth (Miller, 1976). Female counselor educators have identified relationship and support issues as contributing factors in their job satisfaction (Hill, Leinbaugh, Bradley, & Hazler, 2005). Ramsey et al. (2002) speculated that women's preference for relational activities contributes to their lower publication rate, in that men tend to prefer the more solitary work traditionally associated with the writing process.

The paradigm for success in academia and writing is based on values that appear to contradict women's relational being. It is this relational aspect of being-in-relationship that may contribute to the feelings of isolation many female writers in academia experience (Candib, 2006). However, Candib (2006) suggested that women's relational competence, which appears to inhibit their success as writers and faculty members could actually become the impetus for creative and productive written work, transitioning to a different paradigm for the role of women in academia. She introduces the concept of writing-in-relation, a process like being-in-relation, characterized by female values of reciprocity and mutuality. Writing-in-relation with its focus on connectedness rather than independence could foster a more creative environment for female faculty. Women could begin to view writing as an interactional activity relying on cooperative strategies, instead of a solitary activity. The stereotype of the writer alone in his tower can shift to include female writers like Jane Austen as a model. Austen typically did most of her writing while surrounded by family (Smedley, 2011).

Strategies to promote writing-in-relation for female faculty suggested by Candib (2006) include making personal connections to foster their own and others' writing, writing for another person, or finding a writing partner. Female faculty members are encouraged to develop professional support systems with other female faculty (Magnuson, 2002; Roland & Fontanesi-Seime, 1996). Collaboration with peers has provided relief from feelings of isolation and loneliness (Driscoll, et al., 2009), and can provide supportive peer group environments (Grzybowski et al., 2003). However, formal mentoring programs for women initiated by university leadership appear to have mixed results (Driscoll et al., 2009). The dyadic nature of these mentoring programs can inadvertently reinforce a hierarchical power relationship and increased feelings of isolation and professional inadequacy (Driscoll et al., 2009). Although I never participated in a formal mentoring program, I informally sought out mentors within my department. The mentoring I received appeared to be more focused on the values of achievement, recognition, and competition than on personal enjoyment of the process. The fact that no one cared whether I enjoyed the scholarly work I was doing compounded the isolation I experienced. Peer mentoring, an alternate to dyadic mentoring is characterized by relationships focused on feminist principles such as mutuality, equal balance of power, appreciation for emotive expression and mutual interdependence (Driscoll et al., 2009). Peer groups designed around writing provide a nonthreatening environment that often facilitates increased publication (Grzybowski et al., 2003).

Stages of Social Interaction

When I think back to the experience of writing alone, what stands out the most for me was that I was not having fun. Certainly, the final product of writing, a published article or book chapter that represents one more step towards tenure, is important. Seeing my name in print is always exhilarating and a cause for celebration. However, for me, the process is just as important as the final product. If my writing experience is not enjoyable, then the accomplishment of publication seems hollow to me. What is the point of working so hard to get published if I am not enjoying the process of getting there? I wanted my work as a writer to be more like play, something I looked forward to with anticipation.

Interestingly, Mildred Parten's (1932) classic work identifying social interactions among children evolved from observing children at play. Through these observations, she identified stages of social interaction among children. *Solitary play* referred to independent play where children play separately from each other and have no involvement with what other children are doing (Parten, 1932). The definition of solitary play certainly seemed to accurately describe my experience of trying to write alone in my office. *Parallel play* involves children playing similar but separate activities. They are in proximity to each other, but each is involved in his or her own pursuits. *Cooperative play* involves working together as a team. This progression seems to mirror the description of a writing group's progression from isolated individuals working on their own to a collaborative group of writers, experiencing interdependence, and a collective voice (Driscoll et al., 2009).

Parallel Play

Katrina's Experience

Flash forward to the present time and a rewritten version of this chapter's first paragraph based on today's experience. It is mid-morning on a beautiful spring day with bright sunshine and a mild breeze. My laptop is set up on a table on the covered porch of Mad Hatters Tea House, an old house in San Antonio's historic King William District that has been converted into a funky little café. Enrique, the waiter, brings me a scone and excitedly tells me that he has been accepted to fashion design school and will be leaving for Manhattan in two weeks. Gina, the owner, drops by and proudly shows me drawings of the renovations they are planning. Some of my favorite Beatles tunes are playing in the background, and the voices of other patrons only add to the delightful ambiance.

Michelle, a friend from the days of our doctoral program, now a counselor educator in Oklahoma, sits across from me. The backs of our laptops lean against each other as we work on our individual projects. She looks up and asks "Can I read this to you and see what you think?" or I ask her "How does this sound to you?" I often affectionately refer to my time with colleagues at Mad Hatters as parallel play (Parten, 1932). We each work on similar but separate tasks, such as writing, grading papers, or preparing for classes.

For lunch, we share an appetizer of the famous Mad Hatters "wackymole" dip, and savor exotic teas, while we get caught up on each other's lives, and celebrate Michelle's most recent publication. Seamlessly, we move into Cooperative Play (Parten, 1932) as our conversation leads to a proposal idea for a conference presentation that we would later submit. I glance at the Word document on my computer and discover that most of the rough draft of my current project is completed, with plenty of time before the deadline. This time, I feel energized, and creative, and my "work" feels more like play. In the spirit of writing-in-relation, Michelle's description of her time at Mad Hatters follows.

Michelle's Experience

As a recent transplant to a small town in Oklahoma, coming home to San Antonio is a time I relish and look forward to all semester long. Being at Mad Hatters on this particular day visiting with Katrina, a trusted friend and colleague, could not be more fun. As we spend time getting "caught up," the stress and frustrations of the previous semester seem to float away leaving only a smile on my face.

I am reminded of the transition from doctoral student to counselor educator. During our time as doc students we spent hours upon hours at this very same place. Shortly after graduation a second transition began including a relocation of my family and me to an entirely new environment. Starting a new job, getting to know a new community, and leaving the support of friends and family seemed a daunting task. Transitioning from student to faculty seemed difficult enough. Little did I know I would be entering a department in full transition due to many recent and soon-to-be-retired tenured faculty. How I longed for those sunny days at Mad Hatters spending time with friends and colleagues sharing ourselves in creative play.

As I worked to become familiar with my new responsibilities, I became more aware of stressors in the academic setting. Not the least of these is the discrepancy between job demands and available time—a challenge often cited in literature that examines both new faculty experiences and occupational satisfaction throughout one's career (Lease, 1999; Olsen, 1993; Sorcinelli, 1994). Further compounding the work stressors were the needs to find balance between home, family life and the job (Sorcinelli, 1994). The combination of job expectation and family obligations at times felt overwhelming and at best felt more like just "getting by." Very seldom did I experience a sense of ease or satisfaction with work. More often I felt a longing to return "home" to join my group of friends and colleague in "play".

Unfortunately my experience with academia is not unfamiliar to many who report having difficulty managing to find balance in the demands of academia coupled with a lack of collegial relationship and support (Austin & Rice, 1998). Although literature suggests that female faculty members report a need for support and fair treatment as essential components of occupational satisfaction (Hagadorn, 1996), the experience of parallel play at Mad Hatters might indicate males also benefit from a similar experience. As I progress through moving from a new faculty member to a more "seasoned" academician, I realize that seeking this support is crucial to maintaining a sense of balance in life. Although maintaining long distance friendships with colleagues through email, joint projects, and occasional trips "home" takes time and effort from all parties, it is time well spent.

Spending time at Mad Hatters working on projects never resembles work in a traditional sense. Instead, as I reflect on time spent, a gentle calmness begins to flow over me as I picture in my mind's eye friends sharing space and time together. In this space and time, the means always seems to justify the end. The "end" may be a finished product or it may be a completely new idea without much form or structure, but an "end" that is always met with a sense of joy.

Summary

As an introvert, there are times when I (Katrina) prefer to work alone. However, the difference is that this occurs by choice, rather than something I force on myself because of mistaken notions that isolation is a requirement for life as an academician and writer. I found it interesting that Parten (1932), a female researcher at a time when women in academia were a rare occurrence, focused her research on the development of social interaction. Her work may have foreshadowed the discoveries that Jean Baker Miller (1976) and other feminist scholars made decades later about the importance of fostering connections, especially for women. I also find it interesting that Parten (1932) found that social interaction evolved from children's play. For me, writing-in-relation is play. From that perspective, writing becomes the joyful experience I wanted it to be. I have been writing-in-relation at Mad Hatters Tea House for some time now, and it is often affectionately referred to as my "other" office. As I meet and converse with other faculty, our conversations inevitably lead to the challenge of writing and sense of isolation many of us share, and I extend an open invitation to meet me at Mad Hatters. I have been fortunate that as many as 20 different colleagues have joined me at one time or another at this playground, expanding my constellation of colleagues and deepening our friendships. My current department chair, a male who recognizes the importance of relationship, has even joined me at Mad Hatters and encouraged me to spend more time in this creative environment. As a result, my writing productivity, as well as the writing productivity of many of the peers who join me has increased. We support and contribute to each other's writing efforts, and celebrate each other's successes.

Initially, I struggled to succeed in a structure that did not seem to be working for me. The solution was to embrace the relational aspect of myself and to stop accepting the notion that isolation and loneliness were inevitable parts of the job of being an assistant professor. Through connection with others, my creative nature thrives, and I am moving closer toward achieving my personal and professional goals, as well as my potential as a writer. The process of writing-in-relation facilitates the discovery of my own voice as I authentically express my identity as a woman in academia, and as a writer.

At times writing and working in academia feels more like trying to fit a "square peg" into a "round hole," than putting on a well-worn glove (Michelle). In this environment the individual can gain higher praise and recognition than those engaging in a collective effort. Discussions are held prior to engaging in writing projects to determine who will play certain roles (such as first author or second author). For those who find themselves in the world of academia learning to navigate which role to play, when to play it, and for whom, can be exhausting. Adding to such exhaustion is the constant wondering when the square peg will comfortably fit into the round hole of a socially imposed environment. In my experience this type of relationship with writing can at best get in the way and, at worst, stifle one's creativity. As a person who recognized long ago the propensity to be the "square peg" in a round world, I find writing-in-relation to be the "well-worn glove."

Like my good friend Katrina, I consider myself to be an introvert. And I suspect, many of you reading this also have a side which yearns for the comfort of an internal process in which your own is the only voice to be heard. The introvert in me enjoys time spent alone, while simultaneously needing to be "in relation." I find the true creative essence of my writing comes when I can allow for both the introvert and the one who needs relationship to work together. Parallel play at Mad Hatters has been time spent engaging with both the introvert and the relational self and allowing that partnership to engage with others. Writing-in-relation provides an opportunity to express the creativity often stifled by the constricting "round hole" we so often find ourselves stuck in.

We would like to express gratitude for the editors of this text, Dr. Mary Alice Bruce and Dr. Atsuko Seto. Together, they have modeled the concept of writing-in-relation by providing opportunities for women to write and share about their experiences in academia. By collecting chapters from women throughout the nation, we are indirectly engaging in a writing-in-relation experience with other female counselor educators that we do not even know yet. Each of us is contributing to the final project and hopefully enjoying the process at the same time. Parallel play and writing-in-relation can occur at a distance, not just in a shared physical space. We are grateful to both Dr. Bruce and Dr. Seto for giving voice to our experiences. We look forward to reading about the struggles and triumphs of the other contributors. In the meantime, join us at Mad Hatters Tea House! We'll be there!

Questions for Reflection

1. We often hear that female faculty members do not publish as much as their male counterparts. How well does this statement describe your experience? If it does fit your experience, what do you think accounts for the ongoing lower publication rate?
2. Where do you find support for your professional writing activities?
3. Do you agree that to be successful, writers must isolate themselves from family and friends? If so, how could that place women at an advantage or a disadvantage as writers?

References

Alexander-Albritton, C., Hill, N. R., & Bastian Hanks, B. (2007). *Women counselor educators: Level of job satisfaction while raising children.* Paper based on a program presented at the Association for Counselor Education and Supervision Conference, Columbus, OH.

American Psychological Association Task Force on Women in Academe. (2000). *Women in academe: Two steps forward, one step back.* Washington DC: American Psychological Association.

August, L., & Waltman, J. (2004). Culture, climate, and contribution: Career satisfaction among female faculty. *Research in Higher Education,* 45, 177-192. doi: 10.1023/B:RHE.0000015694.14358.ed

Austin, A. E. & Rice, R. E. (1998). Making tenure viable: Listening to early career faculty. *American Behavioral Scientist, 41,* 736-755. doi: 10.1177/0002764298041005009

Baker Miller, J. (1976). *Toward a new psychology of women.* Boston: Beacon Press.

Benz, E. J., Clayton, C. P., & Costa, S. T. (1998). Increasing academic internal medicine's investment in female faculty. *American Journal of Medicine, 105*, 459-463. doi: 10.1016/S0002-9343(98)00346-5

Candib, L. M. (2006). Writing troubles for women clinicians: Turning weakness into strength through writing in relation. *Families, Systems, & Health 24*(3), 302-317. doi: 10.1037/1091-7527.24.3.302

Driscoll, L. G., Parkes, K. A., Tilley-Lubbs, G. A., Brill, J. M., & Pitts Bannister, V. R. (2009). Navigating the lonely sea: Peer mentoring and collaboration among aspiring women scholars. *Mentoring & tutoring: Partnership in learning 17*(1), 5-21. doi: 10.1080?13611260802699532

Grzybowski, S. C., Bates, J., Calam, B., Alred, J., Martin, R. E., Andrew, R., . . . Berger, S. (2003). A physician peer support writing group. *Family Medicine 35*(3), 195-201.

Hagedorn, L. S. (1996). Wage equity and female faculty job satisfaction: The role of wage differentials in a job satisfaction causal model. *Research in Higher Education, 37*, 569-598. doi: 10.1007/BF01724939

Hill, N. R. (2009). An empirical exploration of the occupational satisfaction of counselor educators: The influence of gender, tenure status, and minority states. *Journal of Counseling & Development, 87*(1), 55-61. doi:10.111/1467-8454.00162

Hill, N. R., Leinbauch, T., Bradley, C., & Hazler, R. (2005). Female counselor educators: Encouraging and discouraging factors in academia. *Journal of Counseling & Development, 83*(3), 374-380.

Lease, S. H. (1999). Occupational and role stressors, coping, support, and hardiness as predictors of strain in academic faculty. *Research in Higher Education 40*, 285-307.

Magnuson, S. (2002). New assistant professors of counselor education: Their 1st year. *Counselor Education & Supervision 4*, 306-320.

Mandleco, B. (2010). Women in academia: What can be done to help women achieve tenure? Forum on Public Policy 2010 (5), 1-13.

Olsen, D. (1993). Work satisfaction and stress in the first and third year of academic appointment. *Journal of Higher Education, 64*, 453-471.

Parten, M. B. (1932). Social participation among preschool children. *Journal of Abnormal & Social Psychology 27*, 243 -269. doi: 10.1037/h0074524.

Ramsey, M., Cavallaro, M., Kiselica, M., & Zila, L. (2002). Scholarly productivity redefined in counselor education. *Counselor Education & Supervision, 42,* 40-57.

Roland, C. B., & Fontanesi-Seime, M. (1996). Women counselor educators: A survey of publication activity. *Journal of Counseling & Development, 74*(5), 490-494.

Smedley, R. (2011). The writing spaces: Far from Austen-tatious. *Fuel Your Writing.* Retrieved from http://www.fuelyourwriting.com/the-writing-spaces-far-from-austen-tatious/

Sorcinelli, M. D. (1994). Effective approaches to new faculty development. *Journal of Counseling and Development, 72,* 474-479.

Chapter 2

Passionate About Teaching

MARION CAVALLARO

I love to teach, and this joy has stayed with me throughout my career. Every September is an opportunity to meet new students and share in their journey toward becoming counselors. Staying passionate about teaching over thirty years has required personal and professional reflection as well as a commitment to continue growing at every stage of development as a counselor educator. Some years are more challenging than others, but every difficult time has been an opportunity to learn how I can change and improve as a teacher. As with any long-term relationship, teaching for many years has its peaks and valleys. While I have learned that sometimes I have no control over the valleys in front of me, I do choose how to face them. I suppose I can say that I actively decide each year to stay passionate about teaching and that certain themes emerge in this quest to stay committed to what I do.

For the past thirty years I have been fortunate to be living the life of a counselor educator. I have shared this work with devoted, talented, and supportive colleagues at an institution that emphasizes teaching and values faculty members as teacher/scholars. Over the years I have met incredibly wonderful students of many diverse backgrounds and have been privileged to contribute to their growth as counselors. Each year I continue to be awed by the many obstacles some of these students overcome in order to reach their goals. They are truly an inspiration to me.

My greatest passion as a counselor educator is to teach and nurture these prospective counselors.

Identifying My Own Model of Teaching

In one of the courses I have taught for nearly thirty years, Counseling Theory and Techniques, I encourage students to develop their own theoretical model of counseling. As counselors, our model serves as a guide to our work and continually evolves as we learn more about the field of counseling and ourselves as counselors. I have found the same to be true in my work as a counselor educator. Roger's person-centered approach (Cooper, O'Hara, Schmid & Wyatt, 2007; Rogers, 1961, 1977, 1980), the feminist therapy model of the importance of egalitarian relationships (Daniels, 2012; Hill & Ballou, 2005; Worell & Remer, 2003), and a bit of ancient Chinese wisdom, have all formed the foundation for my work as a teacher.

When I was a first-year graduate student I was strongly influenced by the writings of Carl Rogers, particularly *On Becoming a Person (1961),* and over the years have found his guiding principles of forming a counseling relationship to be just as helpful in the classroom. In order to be effective as a teacher of counselors, I have found that the core conditions of a therapeutic counseling relationship, (i.e., authenticity, empathy and nonjudgmental acceptance), have also been the critical ingredients in fostering a positive teaching environment for students.

Authenticity

Authenticity, being genuine in the relationship, is considered by Rogers (1961, 1977, 1980) to be the key ingredient in a therapeutic relationship and seems just as crucial when teaching. One of the surprising aspects of teaching for me has been discovering that a part of me comes out in the classroom that is often hidden at other times. In essence, being in front of a group of students somehow allows me to express a certain gregariousness that I find difficult to share one-on-one or when I am a member of a group. Students often do not believe me when I tell them that when I was a graduate student I was one of the quietest in the class. Other students gave feedback encouraging me to share more of my thoughts and feelings with the group. In fact, as a student I thought individual counseling would be the best career path for me because of my quiet and sometimes reserved nature. Fortunately I had the opportunity as a graduate student to teach some undergraduate psychology courses and found myself enthusiastic and outgoing in the classroom. As I reflect upon this personality transformation in front of the students I realize that I actually allow myself to share more of my feelings, thoughts and reactions in front of a group than when I am actually a member of a group. In the latter situation I usually tend to listen to others and focus on their experiences rather than my own. My expectation that a teacher is to lead helps overcome some of the inhibitions I would have if I were just a member of the class; it frees me to express myself openly and genuinely with the students.

I have also found that being authentic in the classroom has often led to some of my most powerful teaching moments. Many years ago when my father was dying of cancer over a prolonged period of time, I could not help hide some of my emotions. I would find myself welling up with tears if we were discussing existential issues such as death and loss, and I shared some of my feelings with the students. Many reacted with compassion and nurturance and shared some of their own moments of pain and sorrow. These times generated deep and introspective discussions on topics such as boundaries in counseling, self-care as a professional, and what it means to be real in a relationship. Over the years there have been other times when students have witnessed my emotional responses to situations and have been equally as caring and giving. Once I was called out of the classroom because my husband had to be rushed to the hospital for an emergency heart procedure, and students saw my anxiety and fear as I left in a rush. Fortunately my husband was fine after the procedure, and in our next class many students willingly shared some of their own fears and anxieties. Then we had a meaningful discussion on how these emotions could potentially impact them as counselors. It seems that I have received some of the best ratings from students during the semesters when I was experiencing the most personally upsetting events, that is, the times I was my most vulnerable self in the classroom.

Empathy and Unconditional Positive Regard

Empathy, as defined by Rogers (1961) requires that we see the world from another's subjective experience. In fact, the concept of empathy as a critical component of the counseling relationship has endured since Rogers first introduced the concept in his seminal book (Bohart &

Greenberg 1997; Cain, 2002; Egan, 2009). As an instructor I have found it helpful to look at the overall course and each class from the students' perspective. I was much better at this when I was not as far removed in age from my own graduate studies, so I must constantly remind myself to do that now. I ask myself questions all the time such as: *"Is this too much material to absorb at once? Are there too many assignments grouped together? Are they interested or bored right now? Do they feel valued and respected?"* I also ask the class these and other questions to obtain a sense of their experience. Some of my best ideas on modifying class material and assignments have come from students who are usually more than willing to share their ideas. My best clue, though, continues to be my own awareness of what I am experiencing during the class. Most likely when I feel bored, overwhelmed, and/or confused, the students are feeling the same way.

Conveying unconditional positive regard to others is an essential element in forming a strong working relationship (Cooper, O'Hara, Schmid & Wyatt, 2007; Elliott, Watson, Goldman & Greenberg, 2004; Rogers, 1961, 1977, 1980), and I have found this to be another critical element when teaching. As do most counselor educators, I care about my students, value their contributions, enjoy their presence, and respect wherever they may be developmentally in their growth as counselors. Students often lack self-confidence in their developing abilities as counselors and seem to thrive on acceptance, especially when receiving constructive feedback. There have been a few times in my career when I felt that I did not convey this strongly enough to a student, and I have always regretted afterwards that I was not attentive enough to this very important aspect of the relationship.

For example, one time I gave a student very specific feedback on how to enhance counseling skills but in doing so failed to acknowledge the student's strengths and developmental need for support, acceptance and encouragement. Later in the week the student came to see me to discuss the feedback. During that meeting I realized that I had not attended to the essential process of conveying my unconditional acceptance during the class and that the student had left the class feeling judged and hurt. I tried to repair the relationship by listening closely to the student's feelings, validating the student's experience, and apologizing for not acknowledging during class the many positive skills the student had demonstrated. Throughout the remainder of the semester I closely monitored my own behavior and frequently checked in with the student after class. I was fortunate to have a student who was willing to share with me personal reactions to my feedback and to learn such an important lesson about the never-ending need to be nonjudgmental with my students.

Self-disclosure

From the feminist therapists (Daniels, 2012; Hill & Ballou, 2005; Worell & Remer, 2003) I have learned the value of appropriate self-disclosure as a way of fostering an egalitarian relationship with my students. Sometimes I share my immediate experience in the classroom, such as *"These existential theories are the most confusing to me of all the counseling theories, and I am worried that I will not be able to explain them clearly to you. Does anyone else share my confusion?"* Whenever I comment in this manner students seem more likely to share their honest opinions about the class material.

Students seem to be the most responsive when I share stories from my own experiences and struggles in learning to become a counselor. Whenever we are studying Meichenbaum's (1977, 1986, 2008) theory of cognitive-behavior modification, I always tell the following story of how my faculty adviser, Dr. Betz, used this theory to save me from nearly failing the oral portion of my doctoral exam. Unfortunately I have the tendency to cry when under stress. As my oral doctoral exam began in front of a committee of four faculty members, including Dr. Betz, I began to cry while answering the questions. Dr. Betz had the wisdom to ask me to explain Meichenbaum's (1977) cognitive-behavior modification theory regarding performance anxiety. In the process of explaining the major tenets, such as how individuals under stress are telling themselves negative messages and need to substitute positive coping messages, I began to use myself as an example and explained to the committee that I needed to substitute my negative self-statements such as *"You are crying and will fail this exam"* with coping self-statements such as *"Just take a deep breath, focus on the question. You know this material."* Miraculously I stopped crying, answered the remaining questions and passed the exam. Students really connect with the themes of anxiety, lack of confidence and resiliency in this story, and some alumni that I meet years later tell me they still remember it and use the theory now with their own clients.

Some Chinese Wisdom

There is an ancient Chinese proverb *"Tell me and I'll forget; show me and I may remember; involve me and I'll understand"* (Chinese Proverbs, n.d.a) which forms the foundation of how I approach each class. Our counseling theories and career counseling courses, which I have taught for many years, are content-rich and lend themselves to many experiential activities. I rarely lecture more than 20 minutes at a time before breaking into some activity that encourages students to apply the material in some way. Whether the students are analyzing their dreams, role-playing a Gestalt empty chair dialogue (Frew, 2008; Passons, 1975; Paivio & Greenberg, 1995, Perls, 1992; Strumpfel & Goldman, 2002; Woldt & Toman, 2005) or interpreting their Self-Directed Search (Holland, 1994) results with one another, they are actively engaged in exploring and/or applying the theories. While it is a great tool for the students, selfishly it keeps me interested in teaching the same content areas each year since student material and responses are refreshing and always changing.

Another Chinese proverb *"He who talks too much errs often"* (Chinese Proverbs, n.d.b) reminds me to stop talking and listen to my students. When standing in front of a class I sometimes can get lost in the content of the material and rush to make sure I cover all the notes I have planned for the day's lecture. Through the years, though, I have learned to reduce the amount of content for each class and focus additional time on student reactions and comments. When I spend a great deal of time talking I am modeling that content is more important than process and thus erring in my role as a counselor educator. Taking the time to engage students in conversation by asking questions such as *"What personal reactions do you have to these ideas?,"* *"When have you seen this concept operating in real life?,"* or *"What aspect of this theory will be helpful to you as a person and as a counselor?"* seem to help students understand and internalize course content and make it relevant to their lives and future work as counselors.

The Chinese proverb *"A journey of a thousand miles must begin with a step"* (Chinese Proverbs, n.d.a) is a wonderful reminder to me as a teacher that students are learning counseling concepts and skills for the very first time and I must have realistic expectations of what they can master in the time we spend together. As best I can, I try to structure the class so that skills are learned as incrementally as possible. For example, when teaching skills based on Albert Ellis's Rational Emotive Behavior Therapy (Ellis, 1994, 2004, 2008), first I have students identify irrational beliefs in a list of client statements, and then I have them engage in a class debate in which they have to refute each other's irrational beliefs. Once students are comfortable with that process, I role play how to help a client identify and refute his or her own irrational beliefs and finally have students role play as counselor a similar task. Since I have been in the counseling field for over thirty years, I may sometimes forget my early struggles in learning to become a counselor. In addition to structuring the content of the course to make the learning process as sequential as possible, I also find it helpful to ease some of the students' anxieties about the learning process by sharing some of my beginning frustrations when learning these skills. When I tell students that after my first time practicing Gestalt therapy experiential exercises as a counseling student, I went home and cried because they seemed so difficult, students seem willing to voice some of their struggles in learning the material and feel validated by the process of hearing others discuss their experiences as well.

Having Fun

While I am very committed to doing the best job possible, I want to have fun doing it as well. I think we all enjoy learning when some fun is added in, and I try to keep myself interested in my courses by making them enjoyable for my students and myself. I am always looking for ways to add humor to the learning process, such as taking excerpts from movie comedies to illustrate various counseling issues and theories. The movie *What About Bob?* (Ziskin & Oz, 1991) is an amusing look at therapeutic boundaries and generates great class discussions on how to handle situations when clients seek personal relationships. The comedy, *Meet the Parents* (DeNiro, Roach, Rosenthal, Tenenbaum, & Roach, 2000), has a funny scene which illustrates the roles of social prestige and gender stereotyping in career choice and is a great tool to use in my career counseling course to demonstrate Gottfredson's (2002, 2005) theory of circumspection and compromise. These movies and other videos as well as YouTube clips help make counseling theories less dry and more alive.

Another way I keep myself enthused about courses I have taught for so many years is to incorporate my own interests into the class material. For example, I practice yoga on a regular basis and find it one of the best ways for me to relax. When teaching Behavior Therapies I have introduced a unit on stress management strategies in which I lead the students through a series of deep breathing, deep muscle relaxation, meditation, and guided imagery exercises that I have learned primarily through my yoga practice. Many of these strategies find their way into other courses as well, such as using these tools to help students keep calm during the weeks before their master's level comprehensive exam.

I take my work seriously, but I have found that I better not take myself too seriously while doing it. Laughing about my mistakes, especially when I am in front of a group of students, has helped me survive the errors that I am always bound to make. One time I noticed that the students were furtively staring at my feet. I finally asked them what was so interesting about my feet, and one student honestly told me that I was wearing two different shoes. After we were all done laughing, we had an interesting conversation about how we handle embarrassing moments as counselors.

Content and Process

When I first began teaching I was really concerned with the content and getting it "just right." In time I realized that the content aspect of teaching was easier for me to master than the process element. However, I still continue to devote a considerable amount of time to updating course content. In order to refresh myself, I do not teach summer classes, but devote myself to my family, friends, and personal interests. I also work on my courses, seeking to add new material, develop assignments, and create learning and experiential activities. Much as a car needs an oil change every 3000 miles, my courses are on a self-created schedule in which I revise each component on a three-year cycle. To keep myself energized when teaching the same courses each year, I am always looking for ways to add new content or experiential exercises. I mine interesting and valuable course material from all the rich experiences my life affords, whether they are professional—such as attending a conference or reading a work-related book, or personal—such as watching a good movie, traveling, or interacting with family and friends.

While I usually have control over the content aspects of my courses, it is the process elements of teaching that I can never predict, and therein lies the reality that each time I teach one of my courses it is a new experience. As I am teaching, I try to attend to each student as an individual and also recognize that together they form a group with its own identity. The dynamics of the class need constant monitoring, which I do by asking myself if each student feels respected and valued by me and the other students, checking if there is an imbalance of power among the students and determining how to handle it, and assessing and addressing if some students feel marginalized in any way. As in a counseling setting, I use my own awareness of what I am feeling in the moment to help me understand the students' inner experiences. Unfortunately I know I can't be 100% successful at this each time I am with a class, but I am always striving to improve my ability to create a healthy, safe, and nurturing learning environment.

In addition to focusing on my inner voice and feelings to gauge the process aspects of the learning environment, I also try to help students become aware of their own inner experiences and how to use that awareness as an essential tool in their work as counselors. I frequently role play in class, with myself as the counselor, to demonstrate various counseling strategies. Throughout these role plays, I will stop and share with them my feelings and internal dialogue at the moment to model for them how to focus on process. I will also ask students to imagine how they would feel and think in the counselor role and how it would impact their relationship with the client and what they would say next to the client. I also discuss with the student in the client role what he or she is experiencing as the client, and we reflect on our inner dialogue together. When students engage in role plays in the counselor role, I also have them stop throughout the role play to focus on what they are experiencing and to talk with their "clients" about their inner experiences as well. Frequently asking students to give voice to their intuitive beliefs and how these beliefs could guide them as counselors seems to build their confidence in attending to the process aspects of counseling and trusting their inner voice.

Helping students to focus on process when learning counseling skills also includes helping them let go of traditional academic norms of grades, mastery of content and "getting it right." Giving them permission to make mistakes is an important aspect of this process, and discussing how we learn from mistakes eases them into this different way of thinking. Once again I try to model this flexibility as much as possible when I am not sure of what I am doing, or I feel that I have made a mistake and need to do something different. For example, when I demonstrate the counselor role I will tell them as an aside something like "*I am not sure of what to say here"* or *"I don't think I made a very good empathic response this time, I need to try again in a different way."* Comments such as these validate their personal struggles, help them talk about their feelings, and learn from one another. In addition, since as the teacher I do have to evaluate student progress, I share with students that I base the grading as much as possible on their willingness to try new skills, learn from their mistakes, engage in the process and reflect on what they have learned.

The process elements of teaching also include working on my own personal development as a teacher, something that has continued during the different stages of my career. When I first began as a new faculty member at the age of 26, I was younger than some of my students. At that time my "process" work focused on gaining confidence in myself and the trust and respect of my students. However, since I was also close in age to many of my students I was able to easily connect to their life experiences. Thirty years later I am aware that I not only view myself differently but that students do so as well and sometimes assume I am more wise and expert than I really am. My "process" work now focuses not on gaining their respect but on understanding their perspectives, struggles and challenges and helping them feel comfortable with some-one from a previous generation and at a much different life stage.

Role Models Everywhere

During my graduate studies at Ohio State University, I was fortunate to have some wonderful teachers who inspired me to learn and to believe in my ability to pursue my dreams. I still reflect on them when I teach my courses and try to emulate their commitment and dedication to the counseling profession. In particular I admired my professors who had the highest standards for themselves and for their students. They demon-strated this commitment to excellence through their in-depth knowledge, thoroughness, professionalism, painstaking preparation, and fascinating, challenging classes. I found real inspiration in the fact that so many of my professors modeled the concepts that they were teaching—both in and outside the classroom. For example, I learned not only the content of existential-humanistic and feminist therapies in class, but more impor-tantly experienced some of these concepts by the way classes were held. Professors honestly wanted us to share our experiences in class, fre-quently validated our feelings, openly acknowledged their appreciation for our contributions and created as egalitarian a relationship as possible in the classroom. I learned the value of being real and genuine as a teacher from professors who would honestly share their own reactions and feelings during classroom discussions and would not hesitate to role model their struggles and vulnerability. Some of my professors also taught me the value of how to use humor and real life stories in the classroom through their often entertaining lectures and/or sharing of personal experiences connected to class material. However, the unconditional support and encouragement I received from my professors and their belief in my ability to become a counselor, even when I doubted it, are the qualities I try to emulate as much as possible with my students now that I am privileged to be in the role of a counselor educator.

Over time I have also worked with many dynamic faculty members and have learned by watching them. In particular, faculty who have provided me with lifelong mentorship have also taught me the immeasurable value of consistent, specific, and long lasting encouragement. Due to their support I am inspired to do the same with new faculty in the department. In addition, the new faculty remind me of the value of enthusiasm, the willingness to try new things and not be stagnant, and the joys of being a counselor educator. Also, whenever I go to a conference or workshop, I am learning from the presenters more ways to inspire, motivate, and encourage learning. As I sit in the audience it also helps me better understand my students' perspective and reminds me to attend to their learning styles, physical needs, and personalities.

Students Are My Best Teachers

Over the years I have been privileged to have students in my classes who have lived rich, diverse lives. Many of them experienced traumas but modeled resiliency and strength in the face of those hardships. When I step into the classroom I may be an expert on counseling theories, but many of my students are the experts on dealing with the existential issues of life such as loss, aloneness, or death or have grappled with difficult challenges such as overcoming addiction, rearing an autistic child, navigating life while blind or physically disabled, or surviving hidden wounds of abuse or neglect. Some students are parents and/or have worked as teachers, police officers or in the human services field and have practical and relevant ideas on how to handle various counseling situations. As much as possible I try to design the courses so that students can voluntarily share their life experiences and use their accumulated wisdom as a foundation for their growth as counselors.

For example, when teaching existential theories, I break the class into small groups to discuss issues such as personal freedom, anxiety, critical boundary situations in their lives, and how these experiences help them grow as persons and as counselors (Corey, 2009). In the career counseling class I encourage students to learn from their accumulated wisdom through the use of narrative counseling activities such as the Life Chapters Exercise (Cavallaro, 2005; Niles & Harris-Bowlsbey, 2009) in which students think of their lives as a book, divide the book into chapters each representing a stage of their lives, and create titles for the book and each chapter. In small groups students discuss the important life lessons learned in each chapter and what chapters they want to live in their future. As in all class discussions, however, students are given the option to discuss only those experiences they wish to share with others and a written class policy reviewed at the beginning and throughout the course reminds students to respect the confidentiality of other students.

I think I have learned the most about human courage and have been most deeply touched by those students who have chosen to pursue their counseling studies while also facing a serious and/or terminal illness. Unfortunately there have been a few students who have passed away during my years as a counselor educator, and I witnessed their incredible spirit and determination in pursuing their dreams. While those times have been very painful for me as their teacher, I learned some of life's best lessons, such as to never underestimate a person's willingness and ability to dream and strive for a goal despite the odds. I have also been inspired by the goodness and compassion of their fellow students who bore the pain of watching a classmate suffer and pass away. Working with students who were ill or students who witnessed the illness or death of another student has challenged me as a teacher and as a person. In cases where a student's illness was known only to me in confidence, I tried to convey my caring and support by respecting his or her need for privacy and checking in with the student after class on a regular basis and asking what could be done to make the course as comfortable and nurturing as possible. In some situations, however—such as after the death of a student—allowing the grieving students in the class to share feelings of loss, treasured memories of their classmate, and ways they might like to honor that student's meaning in their lives, helps them process that difficult experience.

Final Thoughts: A Cycle of Connection

The connections forged with my students over the years have been the most personally rewarding aspect of my work. It has been gratifying to receive notes and e-mails from former students as they share some of their joys, such as the birth of a child or their professional successes, such as a new job or acceptance into a doctoral program. As each class graduates, I have learned how to process my own feelings of termination and loss by taking a picture of my internship class and placing it in a frame in my office. As I sit at my desk I am surrounded by pictures of the many wonderful students I have taught and have a way to remember each of them. I have experienced great professional fulfillment in visiting a school or agency where one of my current students is interning and be greeted by a former student who is now serving as the intern's site supervisor. Much as a parent who basks in the joy of watching a child mature into adulthood, I find great reward in seeing the cycle of counselor education continue as my former students mentor the next generation of counselors. Experiences such as these have sustained me through the years and nurtured my passion for teaching new counselors.

Questions for Reflection

1. What can I do to support students in bringing their personal experiences into the classroom discussion?
2. How can I integrate some of my own interests into my teaching experiences in ways that are meaningful and relevant to class material?
3. What can I do to renew and nurture my own passion for teaching over the years?

References

Bohart, A. C., & Greenberg, L. S. (Eds.). (1997). *Empathy reconsidered: New directions in psychotherapy.* Washington, DC: American Psychological Association.

Cain, D. J. (2002). Preface. In D. J. Cain & J. Seeman (Eds.), *Humanistic psychotherapies: Handbook of research and practice* (pp. xix-xxvi). Washington, DC: American Psychological Association.

Cavallaro, M. (2005). The life chapters exercise. In C. Minor & M. Pope (Eds.), *Experiential activities for teaching career counseling classes and for facilitating career groups* (Vol. 2, pp. 20-21). Tulsa, OK: National Career Development Association.

Chinese Proverbs. (n.d.a). Great-Quotes.com. Retrieved Wed Jan 18 09:41:55 2012, from Great-Quotes.com Web site: http://www.great-quotes.com/quote/

Chinese Proverbs. (n.d.b). Wikiquote.org. Retrieved Wed Jan 18 09:45:52 2012, from Wikiquote.org Web site: http://en.wikiquote.org/wiki/Chinese_proverbs/

Cooper, M., O'Hara, M., Schmid, P. F., & Wyatt, G. (Eds.). (2007). *The handbook of person-centered psychotherapy and counseling.* New York: Palgrave Macmillan.

Corey, G. (2009). *Student manual for theory and practice of counseling and psychotherapy* (8th ed.). Belmont, CA: Thomson Brooks Cole.

Daniels, J. (2012). Feminist counseling and therapy. In A. Ivey, M. D'Andrea & M. Ivey (Eds.), *Theories of counseling and psychotherapy A multicultural perspective* (pp. 451-493). Thousand Oaks, CA: Sage.

DeNiro, R., Roach, J., Rosenthal, J., & Tenenbaum, N. (Producers), & Roach, J. (Director). (2000). *Meet the parents* [Motion Picture]. United States: Universal Studios.

Egan G. (2009). *The skilled helper: A problem management and opportunity development approach to helping* (9th ed.). Belmont, CA: Brooks/Cole.

Elliot, R., Watson, J., Goldman, R., & Greenberg, L. (2004). *Learning emotional-focused therapy: The process-experiential approach to change.* Washington, DC: American Psychological Association.

Ellis, A. (1994). *Reason and emotion in psychotherapy revised.* New York: Kensington.

Ellis, A. (2004). *Rational emotive behavior therapy: It works for me—It can work for you.* Amherst, NY: Prometheus.

Ellis, A. (2008). Rational emotive behavior therapy. In R. Corsini & D. Wedding (Eds.), *Current psychotherapies* (8th ed., pp. 187-222). Belmont, CA: Brooks/Cole.

Frew, J. (2008). Gestalt therapy. In J. Frew & M. Spiegler (Eds). *Contemporary psychotherapies for a diverse world* (pp. 228-274). Boston: Lahaska Press.

Gottfredson, L. S. (2002). Gottfredson's theory of circumscription and compromise. In D. Brown, L. Brooks, & Associates (Eds.), *Career choice and development* (4th ed., pp. 85-148). San Francisco: Jossey-Bass.

Gottfredson, L. S. (2005). Applying Gottfredson's theory of circumscription and compromise in career guidance and counseling. In S. D. Brown & R. W. Lent (Eds.), *Career development and counseling: Putting theory and research to work* (pp. 71-100). Hoboken, NJ: Wiley.

Hill, M., & Ballou, M. (2005). *The foundation and future of feminist therapy.* New York: Haworth.

Holland, J. L. (1994). *Self-Directed Search.* Odessa, FL: Psychological Assessment Resources.

Meichenbaum, D. (1977). *Cognitive behavior modification: An integrative approach.* New York: Plenum Press.

Meichenbaum, D. (1986). In F. H. Kanfer & A. P. Goldstein (Eds.), *Helping people change: A textbook of methods* (pp. 346-380). New York: Pergamon Press.

Meichenbaum, D. (2008). Stress inoculation training. In W. O'Donohue & J. E. Fisher (Eds.), *Cognitive behavior therapy: Applying empirically supported techniques in your practice* (2nd ed., pp. 529-532). Hoboken, NJ: Wiley.

Niles, S., & Harris-Bowlsbey, J. (2009). *Career development strategies in the 21st century.* (3rd ed.). Upper Saddle River, NJ: Pearson.

Paivio, S., & Greenberg, L. (1995). Resolving "unfinished business": Efficacy of experiential therapy using empty-chair dialogue. *Journal of Consulting and Clinical Psychology, 73,* 419-425.

Passons, W. R. (1975). *Gestalt approaches in counseling.* New York: Holt, Rinehart & Winston.

Perls, L. (1992). Concepts and misconceptions of Gestalt therapy. *Journal of Humanistic Psychology, 32,* 50-56.

Rogers, C. (1961). *On becoming a person.* New York: Houghton Mifflin Company.

Rogers, C. (1977). *Carl Rogers on personal power: Inner strength and its revolutionary impact.* New York: Delacorte Press.

Rogers, C. (1980). *A way of being.* Boston: Houghton Mifflin.

Strumpfel, U., & Goldman, R. (2002). Contacting Gestalt therapy. In D. J. Cain & J. Seeman (Eds.), *Humanistic psychotherapies: Hand-*

book of research and practice (pp. 189-219). Washington, DC: American Psychological Association.

Woldt, A., & Toman, S. (Eds.). (2005). *Gestalt therapy: History, theory, and practice*. Thousand Oaks, CA: Sage.

Worell, J., & Remer, P. (2003). *Feminist perspectives in therapy: Empowering diverse women* (2nd ed.). New York: Wiley.

Ziskin, L. (Producer), & Oz, F. (Director). (1991). *What about Bob?* [Motion Picture]. United States: Universal Studios.

Chapter 3

A Photograph of Women in Academe: "Dr. Mom"

BARBARA C. TROLLEY

A s female doctoral students begin their journey en route to academe, they find it much like Dorothy's travels on the yellow brick road, gathering courage, maintaining heart, and searching for intellectual knowledge. But much like Dorothy's later encounter with the magical Oz, women in academe may find many disappointments and obstacles during their professional expeditions, making it seem more like falling through the dark hole in *Alice in Wonderland*. The many joys and professional growth associated with teaching in higher education are often overshadowed by its inherent difficulties.

Personally, I reached the "pinnacle" of my academic success when I became a full professor a few years ago, in my fifth decade of life. In this chapter I share my personal journey en route to this goal, an excursion much akin to a rollercoaster ride. Next, I offer a review of the literature in which my specific experiences as "Dr. Mom" are intertwined with a broader view of others' similar experiences. At the end of this chapter, I share some recommendations that may be helpful to others who are embarking on this career path and raise some questions as 'food for thought.'

An Overview of My Journey in Higher Education

My academic journey started over two decades ago. Prior to coming to academe, I worked in agencies and private practice, providing direct clinical service and performing administrative work. My academic passage began when a former professor invited me back to the state university to teach in a full-time, non-tenured line. Since that time, I have progressed to the status of tenured full professor at a smaller, private university. I am also the mother of five children, ages nine to twenty two. The following are some of the critical incidents which shaped my professional career in academe.

State University

When I began the full-time position, I was told I could treat it as just a full-time, non-tenured line job, or I could pursue research and service endeavors, in preparation for a possible tenure-track opening. The dream of a secure tenured position was enough of a carrot that I intensely began several research projects. I was fortunate enough to have a former professor who mentored my research development. He had a wonderful way of indicating my novice mistakes in a constructive, non-threatening manner, co-authored some of my first empirical works, and was accessible for any inquiry. This mentor, now deceased, told me in the beginning not to focus on only one research project at a time, as there would be lulls in each study. As a very compulsive, focused professional, I initially found this to be disconcerting but eventually began to understand the advantages of such an approach.

Throughout the eleven years at my alma mater, several additional interactions and events shaped my development. Three times I applied and interviewed for a tenure-track position related to the work that I was doing. The first two times, the line was pulled due to state budget cuts. This news arrived the second time in the middle of my interview presentation. I persevered, taking on more work, at times not knowing until late summer if I would be renewed for the fall. A male colleague and friend, who was chair of the department, at one point jokingly said I needed to mess up a bit more, as the more I did well, the more tasks I would be assigned. This same professional, toward the end of my work there, indicated that I may not be a 'good fit' at the university. While these words delivered a lasting sting, with time and perspective I have come to understand them. Overshadowed by the focus on research and national presentations, mentoring and program advocacy are not always the highest-valued goals in academe. While I was pumping out research all along, my focus was on the student body as well as program advancement and enhancement.

A few additional interactions shaped my journey. After one of the budget cuts to the tenured line, I was at the copier when a female colleague approached me. This colleague was an exemplary role model of hard work and accomplishment as an academician. She made a comment to me that indicated no matter what happened with the tenure line, I still had my children. As with the chair's comment above, I was initially upset, feeling that while I loved my family dearly, having a family did not negate all the hard work I had put into my achievements at the university. Again with the passage of time, I look back and see this comment potentially as an attempt at comfort, from a woman who put her entire self into the job, and was not able to be a mother—a role she had explored.

The mention of family evokes another critical event in my journey. During one of the accreditation visits, I was unable to be present as I was adopting my second child from Korea. I had received approval from the chair for the absence, especially considering I was not in a tenured line. After the visit, I became aware of several male colleagues' resentment that I wasn't there. Further exploration revealed a breakdown in communication between administration and program faculty. Ironically, it was during a later accreditation visit that a woman faculty member from another state, who was on the review team, said to me that colleges and universities usually don't like to hire their own graduates. This was definitely a wakeup call for me! A tenure position for my line was listed for a third time. At this point, I had begun exploring other options but decided to give it one more try. During this period, our woman dean at the time, who has since passed, bolstered my spirits and shared tips as to how to show everyone "how good I truly was." This application was the most difficult of all, as there had been rumors that a candidate, who had already interviewed, was the prime choice, and I had not even done my presentation.

In this situation, trust was a big factor, but so were paranoia, frustration, and self-doubt. I had decided to leave and had sent my vita to several universities. One happened to be advertising a full-time, tenure-track position. I indicated I still had a part-time commitment to finish out that year, but if anything should come up in the future, I would like them to let me know. The program director contacted me; we had lunch, and I was hired part-time the first year. While it was hard to let go of my original dream with the state university after shedding blood, sweat, and tears for over a decade, it was evident that, in many ways, the decision was not as much personal as one of my status of being an alumnus and a homogenous female. I have now gotten past feeling "strung along." I value the experiences and opportunities I had during the 11 years I worked there. They helped me begin to build a national reputation for research, learn a great deal about university dynamics, and work with some wonderful mentors.

Private University

After I had worked half time at the private university for a year, I was interviewed for the tenure-track position and obtained it. It was a university environment that emphasizes the value of teaching, a philosophical standpoint that fits well with who I am professionally. The male program director at the time I was hired was very understanding, supportive of my family life, and remained a wonderful mentor and colleague throughout my time there. I was able to obtain tenure on my first attempt but mistakenly applied for promotion at the same time, an often-discouraged move, I later discovered. The lesson learned is that it is important to talk with trusted senior colleagues and administrators who will share practical applications of university regulations and nuances.

Our former dean, who is now assistant provost, has been a tremendous source of support throughout my advancement process. One day I came to her with two huge binders of materials I had prepared for my promotion application to full professor. I had been working on our main campus, as well as spending much time teaching and informally overseeing our weekend program located some distance away. She was able to hear all that I was doing on both campuses and agreed to review all my materials, laying aside an isolated perception that had been shared with her regarding my need "to be more present on the main campus before being promoted." Interestingly, I *was* physically present and actively involved in teaching, advisement, and committee work on the main campus. I cannot think of anyone I admired or respected more than her at that time. For someone to say, "Yes, I will openly review your materials and reserve judgment until that time," seemed to me the epitome of fairness. She wholeheartedly supported my application. I persevered and reached full professor status a few years later.

A Broader Picture of Female Experiences in Higher Education

The prior discussion is a family portrait of my journey to full professor. The tenure and final promotion have given me a sense of personal peace and accomplishment. In this section, I share a picture of what literature reports that female academics often experience. Specifically, I focus on climate and biases; position and assignments; role balancing; recruitment, retention, and advancement; as well as salary and evaluation.

Climate and Biases

In 1982, Gilligan asked why men and women are not more similar. This question describes in very few words one of the main challenges women in academe face: an environment historically defined by a male culture (Fouad, Brehm, Hall, Kite, Hyde & Russo, 2000; Twombly, 1998; Young, MacKenzie & Sherif, 1980). While many positive changes have occurred since the time when females were not allowed in the Harvard library, women faculty are still confronted with biases and stereotypes. As Morahan, Gleason, Richman, Dannels and McDade (2010) indicated as recently as 1993, it took 15 years to develop an advancement program for women faculty in academic health centers.

Subtle examples of my differential treatment include having a male colleague talk over me in a staff meeting, then hearing my ideas being voiced by a male colleague. There also was muted resentment over my obtaining grants and advancing before my male counterparts. Fox (2001) found that women faculty members were less likely than men to feel that they were being taken seriously and respected. Aquirre (2000) stated that women and minority faculty were deemed less competent than the white male faculty members. At times, the university environment has been seen as toxic for female faculty, leaving them to feel second class citizens. Wilson (2004) went further in asserting that these toxic environments can hamper women's research, and suffocate their enthusiasm.

Some female faculty deal with such treatment with the help of women's networks on campus and the support of their mentors. Others assume the role of an 'androgynous' staff member, playing the female or masculine part, depending on the circumstances (Armenti, 2004a). Furthermore, Koenig, Eagly, Mitchell, and Ristikari (2011) pointed out the *Catch 22* women face in their need to adopt male roles required by leadership positions to survive when the roles are deemed inappropriate for them. I can recall multiple times when I wanted to share joyful news such as the addition of another child to the family but spent agonizing moments deliberating how this news might be received (Note: all of my children are adopted so expected additions had not been physically obvious.) Would they see me as less available or competent on any level? The converse was also true. A specific instance comes to mind in which I was sitting in a staff meeting with my phone on vibrate, waiting for a call from home, and then having to make up some excuse—such as going to the bathroom—in order to return the call.

Although the "old boys' club" notion is still alive and well in many university settings, there are also many changes that support women faculty. These include women who are administrators in higher education, have noteworthy publications, and who have obtained national recognition for their service. Yet even with all of these accomplishments, subtle discrimination may exist as demonstrated in communication patterns, work recognition, and even something as simple as male-dominated lunchtime physical activities.

Positions and Assignments

As already mentioned, women have achieved much in the three traditional university roles: teaching, research and service (Denker, 2009; Fouad et al., 2000; Henry & Closson, 2010). However, it has long been deemed that women are the teachers, and advisors/mentors, while men are the researchers (Armenti, 2004a). One major difficulty with this differential role assignment is that most universities prioritize scholarly work above teaching in tenure and promotion decisions. While the publication gap between the genders is lessening, such a divide still exists. Even in the present decade, this gap remains a topic of exploration. Productivity comparisons between the genders are made, research incentives are compared, and the smaller number of publications by women is held up beside those of men, despite the women's having spent greater time in administrative and professional activities (Chen, Gupta, & Hoshower, 2004; Curtis, 2004; DesRoche, Zinner, Rao, Iezzoni & Campbell, 2010; Gallivan & Bebunan,-Fich, 2006).

Reasons for this gender differential in publishing vary. Denker (2009) found that women faculty members' ability to do research is oftentimes hampered by heavy teaching loads, lack of female research mentors, large advisee assignments, and multiple service commitments. The research topics of female faculty members may also be dismissed as irrelevant, as when my former male program director indicated my research topic would make a "nice summer project."

In regard to service, women have been known to have difficulty in saying *no*, with resultant excess service responsibilities taking time from research pursuits. Nevertheless, service activities can facilitate exposure to other university members and involvement in policy-making, which are important variables for advancement. In choosing committees to join or lead, I have found that it is important to consider one's passion, schedule convenience, ability to have an impact, and university focus.

Role Balancing

In addition to the wide range of needs they meet on campus, women faculty members also need to look at the impact of childbearing and rearing. This is perhaps one of the most voluminous areas of research pertaining to women in higher education. Interesting gender differences have been noted in this work. First of all, in a Canadian study, pre-tenure women have been noted to have more difficulty balancing work and family activities than men (Armenti, 2004b). Hewlett (2002) further found that academic women were much more likely to perform childcare duties than their male counterparts or husbands, while Wilson (2003) found that 48% of men in academe versus 91% of female faculty members had spouses who worked full time. Loeffler, Ely and Falrety (2010) indicated that childrearing must no longer be seen as a detriment to granting tenure.

In lieu of a career, women may decide to avoid having children. Comer and Stites-Doe (2006) indicated that female faculty members were twice as likely to be as childless as their male counterparts, and those women in academe were less likely to have children than women in other professions. Starting a family may be delayed until tenure is achieved, hoping any needed fertility treatments will be successful. For those who do have families, biases run rampant. There is a widespread canard that women cannot handle both a career and a family (Gerten, 2010; Demerling, 2011; Jaschik, 2011). As Wilson (2001) stated "You can't do a credible full-time job and be a full-time mom" (p. A11). While this statement may seem dated, unfortunately I believe its impact is still sometimes experienced. Women have felt there is a need to hide pregnancies, or to have 'May babies' to avoid being deemed non-committed (Armenti, 2004b; Denker, 2009). There may be also perceptions of disparity and resentment from colleagues if women ask for time off or lighter workloads to take care of their children (Comier & Sites-Doe, 2006). Henry and Closson (2010) addressed the issue of the 'Sandwich Generation' for older faculty women who have both grown children, and the responsibility for care of aging parents. I experienced this firsthand when my mother came to live with us 6 years ago and stayed with us 3 years until her death. While taking her in was the best decision for all involved, there were numerous times of stress and guilt, and of feeling overwhelmed in the roles of daughter, wife, mother, and faculty member. Despite regrets on all levels, the ability of my children to have precious moments with their grandmother, to watch someone dying naturally at home, and to see their mother model the crucial importance of family, could not ever be replaced.

A final consideration is that of the diverse work hours associated with an academic position. Many aspects of the position allow female faculty members to work at home and care for their family. However, this issue of working at home can also be associated with "no work boundaries," with work tasks always in the foreground (Comer & Sites-Doe, 2006). There have been so many times when my younger children have said, "But Mom, you said, 'Five minutes at the computer,' and it's been thirty! Are you really just checking your emails?" My oldest daughter who is 22 is often sympathetic to the work demands on me, and how non-competitive academic pay is compared to that in other fields such as technology. I take these comments to heart, try to model that women can do both, and simultaneously make adjustments. I also tend to remind my children, "If Mommy had a five-day-a-week job from 9 to 5, I would not be here to give you snacks when you get off the bus and then to help with homework!"

Recruitment, Advancement, and Retention

Another domain that has received much attention is the area of numbers and ranks of female academicians. According to the American Association of University Women (AAUW, n.d.), while over half of the instructors and lecturers are women at four institutions, only 27% of the tenured faculty members are women, and nationally, only 33% are full professors (2005). However, Aguirre (2000) indicated that while the numbers of women faculty members in academic positions have been increasing, they remain underrepresented relative to their numbers in the U. S. population. Even the first part of Demerling's article in 2010, *Where are all the women?* speaks to this disparity. As Gerdes (2006) indicated, *The more things change, the more they stay the same.* These statements suggest that while women are increasingly more visible in higher education, they may not be in the majority of 'permanent' residents. One explanation for the lower percentages of women faculty in four-year institutions is that such professionals may be more attracted to two-year, community colleges where the focus is more on teaching, leaving more room for family life (Wolf-Wendel, Ward & Twombly, 2007).

The competition and struggles women encounter on the promotion path may also add to their reluctance to pursue advancement opportunities at four-year institutions. In addition, policies associated with workloads—key variables in the advancement process—may be unclear or too broad, leaving much discretion to individual department heads, and uncertainty in promotion expectations (Barrett & Barrett, 2011). The chancellor of the University System of Maryland indicated that while tenure remains a cornerstone at universities, its policies and principles are outdated (Wilson, 2005).

Salary and Evaluations

Fouad found that, in psychology fields, salary disparities exist in favor of male faculty, regarding resources such as research funds and teaching stipends. When salary and other sources of income are combined, women are receiving 49% of what men do in higher education (Fouad et al., 2000). At Worcester State College, women continue to earn an average of five to ten thousand dollars less than their male colleagues (Worcester State College Information, 2009). This discrepancy may exist in part due to the fact that universities are still male dominated, and thus it is the male population deciding the salary scale. Another explanation is the lower ranks that women generally hold.

What Have I Learned?

There have been many lonely episodes on this journey, as well as times of frustration, and even anger. While I have been aware of the notion of male bonding, I naively didn't recognize it at first nor the very subtle sex discrimination that existed. I have learned that I can work and gain satisfaction in spite of inequality at times. It has taken me a while, but I have also progressed in learning which projects to take on, and whom to choose as collaborators who will not be team members in name only. I doubt myself less and keep good boundaries when it comes to family life. While male colleagues along the path may have children, when they had to cross over into work (e.g., bringing them to class), they were more openly received than the female colleagues. I have observed one too many times when a female colleague who brings her child to work is anxious, while her male counterpart is laid back. This speaks volumes. The universal, recognized time for this to occur for all faculty members was *Take Your Child to Work Day* in April. I have personally been often reminded by a male colleague that I chose to have five children, and everyone has life issues. With time, I have become aware of differential investments in program and in student issues—and which I am able change. Some of the obstacles arose from my own passion and unquestioned belief in others' commitment. I have needed to alter my expectations and learn where real support and collaboration can be obtained.

In addition to the challenges, I have been rewarded a hundred times over by students whom I have taught, the numerous books and articles I have written alone and with colleagues, national opportunities and respect, and lifelong friendships I have made. I treasure many instances of feedback from my students reporting that while I demand a lot, I am also understanding and helpful. In addition, it is exhilarating when students positively indicate they liked and learned from a newly created assignment. For instance, the *Critical Review of the Counseling Field Portfolio* is an assignment I developed for students to find and critique a dozen examples of counseling in the media and their personal lives.

While the journey has been a long one and at times an extremely rocky one, I would not change career paths if I had the chance to start over. It is important to note that I would not have managed to survive and progress without the physical and emotional support of my husband. As a dentist, he has some flexibility in his schedule, and he is a very *hands-on* father. My children at times have indicated I work too hard, or that I am on the computer too long. However, I see myself as a role model in that I have homework, and I need to be organized and responsible. I am very involved in their lives at school and home and have found ways to balance work time and family time. The element that is most frequently short changed is time for myself.

How to Survive and Succeed

Clearly, a faculty position for women is a multi-faceted job that carries with it both challenges and joys. Armenti states this over-arching need: ". . . (I)t is time that universities acknowledge the importance of a home and family in a balanced life" (2004b, p. 228). This is true for *all faculty members* but especially in regard to women. Frechette (2009) argued for more research in which the fit of women faculty in universities be further explored. This particular statement hits a special nerve with me since a chair had indicated early on that I might not be a good *fit*. Yet, although I did alter some of the ways I conveyed my passion or reactions to issues—such as the need for the mentoring of students—I did not lose the essence of who I am. Female faculty members are definitely molded in many ways by the male-dominated culture. However, this does not mean that we have to sacrifice treasures we offer like our capacity for nurture. Rather, it means that we may need to become sophisticated as to how to better convey our thoughts in order to be received, and go beyond the stated policies to learn the nuances of our position. We also may need to find additional or alternative ways to connect with our male colleagues, such as having lunch, rather than just joining in athletic social times.

Generally speaking, Barrett and Barrett (2011) indicated the need for further focus on career planning, workloads, and diversity in policy making, and the development of equity training programs, specifically targeting management. Helpful policies could be implemented related to tenure deadline extension, job sharing, review of workload allocations, dual career recruitment, support of outside clinical practice, reduced teaching load, provision of mentors for new hires, and assignment of graduate assistants (Armenti, 2004b; Barrett & Barrett, 2011; Helfat, 2002). More individualized attention from women academicians who have already met their professional goals is also an essential aspect of support for new protégés. Availability of mentors as a means of facilitating advancement for women has been echoed in the literature, and may be particularly needed for those entering the academic world at a later age (Henry & Closson, 2010).

Female faculty members must also take ownership of their career development. Women must serve as compatible, collaborative colleagues within their department, thus avoiding competitive interactions and working alone. Women need to support each other and drop the defensive guards that have been set in place for alleged survival. Even as recently as this past semester, I said to a colleague, "I am looking forward to working together and let's be up front if any differences arise." Paradoxically, those of us in the counseling profession are sometimes those that are most gun shy about addressing process issues in our meetings.

Women faculty members need to continue to establish their self-confidence and competence, as well as their ability to professionally assert their needs and limits. Recently in a discussion with a female colleague with children, we agreed that most of the time, we do a great job at work and at home, but our own time for rest and enrichment is frequently minimal or non-existent. It may also be beneficial for women to alter their response and coping mechanisms. As my husband has often said, "You need to be more like Teflon and let things slide off you, rather than taking it all in like a sponge."

Summary

Despite all of the obstacles women face in academe, they are generally satisfied both with their careers and their motherhood roles (Wolf-Wendel et al., 2007). There is nothing more gratifying than when a student has an "aha" moment, demonstrates professional growth, or takes the time to say *thanks*. Indirectly, seeing the career advancement of alumni is another source of extrinsic reward for a professor. Even the blood, sweat, and tears that go into publication are easily forgotten upon the arrival of a published book or a journal which contains an authored manuscript. Additionally, providing service to the university community and broader spectrums has an inherent value. My own work in the area of autism was richly rewarding—seeing teachers engaged in professional development opportunities, and knowing that the support group provided just a glimmer of respite for parents on overload.

Many aspects of an academic position are inherently rewarding: flexible work hours, diversity of tasks, intellectual stimulation, impact on student careers, and contributions to the profession. Women faculty members must determine the things that are within their control, and those that are not. In the process, they also need to distinguish between institutional-caused obstacles and those that are intrinsically determined.

At times, I have recently found comfort in the lyrics created by recording artist and songwriter Katy Perry, who wrote encouraging lyrics about the amazing qualities of people who let themselves uniquely shine, just as fireworks sparkle in an awesome fashion.

Questions for Reflection

1. Can you develop a hierarchy of tasks that need to be done at your institution for tenure and promotion? How will you balance these tasks with those required of your day to day work, such as teaching?
2. How would you handle professional, ethical concerns somewhat beyond your control in the academic setting which also comprise your personal health and family needs?
3. Can you identify your professional mentors as well as your support systems within your institution?

References

American Association of University Women (n.d.). *Tenure statistics.* Retrieved from: htttp://www.aau.org/laf/library/tenure.cfm

American Psychological Association (1998). American Psychological Association Committee on Women in Psychology and Commission on Ethnic Recruitment, Retention, and Training in Psychology. *Surviving and thriving in academe: A guide for women and ethnic minorities.* Washington, DC: Author.

Aguirre, A. (2000). Women and minority faculty in the academic workplace: Recruitment, retention, and academic culture. *ASHE-ERIC Higher Education Report, 27*(6), 91-110. San Francisco, CA: Jossey-Bass.

Armenti, C. (2004a). Gender as a barrier for women with children in academe. *Canadian Journal of Higher Education, 34*(1), 1-12.

Armenti, C. (2004b). May babies and post-tenure babies: Maternal decisions of women professors. *Review of Higher Education, 27*(2), 211-231.

Barrett, L., & Barrett, P. (2011). Women and academic loads: Career slow lane or cul-de-sac? *Higher Education, 61*, 141-155.

Chen, Y., Gupta, A. & Hoshower, L. (2004). Faculty perceptions of research rewards. *Journal of College Teaching and Learning,1*(12). Retrieved from: http://journals.cluteonline.com/index.php/TLC/article/view/2013

Comer, D., & Sites-Doe, S. (2006). Antecedents and consequences of faculty women's academic-parental role balancing. *Journal of Family and Economic Issues, 27*, 495-512.

Curtis, J. W. (2004). AAUP research director reports on gender gap. *Academe*, May-June. Retrieved from: http://www.aaup.org/AAUP/pubsres/academe/2004/MJ/AW/RptGndrGap.htm

Demerling, R. (2010). Where are all the women? How traditional structures of academia hinder female university professors. *The Socjournal*. Retrieved from: http://www.sociology.org/gender/women-traditional-structures-academia-hinder-female-university-professors/

Denker, K. (2009). Doing gender in the academy: The challenges for women in the academic organization. *Women and Language, 32*(1), 103-112.

DesRoches, C., Zinner, D., Rao, S., Iezzoni, L. & Campbell, E. (2010). Activities, productivity, and compensation of men and women in the life sciences. *Academic Medicine*, 85(4), 631-639.

Fouad, N., Brehm, S., Hall, C., Kite, M., Hyde, J. & Russo, N. (2000). *Women in academe: Two steps forward, one step back.* American Psychological Association Task Force on Women. Washington, DC: APA.

Fox, F. M. (2001). Women, science and academia: Graduate education and careers. *Gender & Society, 15*(5), 654-666.

Frechette, J. (2009). Women, leadership, and equality in academe: Moving beyond double binds. *Forum on Public Policy Online, 2*, 1-26.

Gallivan, M., & Benbunan-Fich, R. (2006). Examining the relationship between gender and the research productivity of IS faculty. In *Proceedings of the 2006 ACM SIGMIS CPR Conference on Computer Personnel Research*, (103–113). New York: ACM Press.

Gerdes, E. (2006) Women in higher education since 1970: The more things change, the more they stay the same. *Advancing Women in Leadership, 21*. Retrieved from: http://www.advancingwomen.com/awl/summer2006/Gerdes.html

Gerten, A. (2011). Moving beyond family-friendly policies for faculty mothers. *Affilia, 8*(1), 47-58.

Gilligan, C. (1982). *In a different voice: Psychological theory and women's development.* Cambridge, MA: Harvard University Press.

Helfat, C. (2002). Work-life issues in academe and business: The current state of affairs. *Journal of Management Inquiry, 11*(3), 329-331.

Henry, W., & Closson, R. (2010). Women faculty post-50 years of age in tenure earning positions: Opportunities and challenges. *NASPA Journal about Women in Higher Education, 3*(1), 236-260.

Hewlett, S. (2002). *Creating a life: Professional women and the quest for children.* New York: Talk Miramax Books.

Jaschik, S. (2011). Hiring women as full professors. *Inside Higher Education*, 3/21. Retrieved from: http://www.insidehighereducation.com/news/2011/03/21/mit_issues_new_report_on_status_of_women

Koenig, A., Eagly, A., Mitchell, A., Ristikari, T. (2011, July). Are leader stereotypes masculine? A meta-analysis of three research paradigms. *Psychological Bulletin, 137*(4), 616-642.

Loeffler, D., Ely, G. & Flaherty, C. (2010). *Parenting on the tenure track: Exploring gender differences in perceptions of collegial and supervisor support.* Retrieved from: http://www.academicleadership.org/article/Parenting_on_the_tenure_track_Exploring_gender_differences_in_ perceptions_of_collegial_and_supervisor_support

Morahan, P., Gleason, K., Richman, R., Dannels, S. & McDade, S. (2010). Advancing women faculty to senior leadership in U.S. academic health centers: Fifteen years of history in the making. *NASPA, Journal About Women Higher Education, 3*(1). Retrieved from: http://journals.naspa.org/njawhe/vol3/iss1

Twombly, S. (1998). Women academic leaders in a Latin American university: Reconciling the paradoxes of professional lives. *Higher Education, 35,* 367-397.

Wilson, R. (2001). A push to help new parents for tenure reviews. *Chronicle of Higher Education, 48*(11), A10-A11.

Wilson, R. (2003). How babies alter careers for academics. *Chronicle of Higher Education, 50*(15), A8-A14.

Wilson, R. (2004). Where the elite teach, it's still a man's world. *Chronicle of Higher Education, 51*(15), A1.

Wilson, R. (2005). Report calls for a more flexible tenure process. *Chronicle of Higher Education, 51*(25), A13.

Wolf-Wendel, L., Ward, K., & Twombly, S. (2007). Faculty life at community colleges: The perspective of women with children. *Community College Review, 43*(4), 255-281.

Worcester State College Information, U.S. University Directory "State Universities, Online University Degree Search and College Rankings." Retrieved from: http:www.stateuniversity/MA/ Worcester_State_College.html

Young, C., MacKenzie, D., & Sherif, C. (1980). In search of token women in academe. *Psychology of Women Quarterly, 4*(4), 508-525.

Chapter 4

Mentoring: Authentic Connections and Pathways

PENNY DAHLEN AND NANCY FORTH

When we first considered this book contribution, we spent a great deal of time talking with each other about our own journeys. We soon realized that it is not a matter of reading all the journal articles and presenting at conferences that keeps us up to date in the field and continues our personal growth. Rather, what keeps the passion in our careers is developing and nurturing mentoring relationships and helping students develop into effective professionals (Casto, Caldwell, & Salazar, 2005). In our process of becoming counselors, we too have had mentors who have played very significant parts in our lives.

There were also a few students in the process of becoming counselors, with whom we have had a deeper connection, a genuine authentic relationship and a more open process of communication. We asked those students to respond to three questions about their experiences and now encourage the reader to ponder these same questions tailored to being a counselor educator: 1) Prior to and during your process of becoming a counselor, what life challenges did you encounter? 2) What were key moments in your growth during your counseling program? 3) What about your mentoring relationship assisted in your personal and professional growth?

Listening to these stories, we found that several themes emerged: wanting to please and be accepted; anxiety about sharing of self when working with clients; feeling the need for personal growth; overcoming personal obstacles; developing trust and self-acceptance; and a lack of confidence. We noticed that there was more to mentorship and supervision than skills development and conceptualization. "Mentoring can support all aspects of women's professional (and often personal) lives as students, educators, researchers, practitioners, and leaders in the counseling profession" (Casto, Caldwell, & Salazar, 2005, p. 331). It was with these genuine encounters that a deeper transpersonal process took place.

Penny: I have been reflecting on my career and writing this chapter in a way that might have some meaning for others in the field. My journey to becoming a counselor educator probably began early in my life. I grew up inside myself, always pondering the meaning of life and death while other kids were playing *Duck-Duck-Goose*. Early on, I was an observer and always interested in the inside of people and their life stories. All of this pondering led me into the field of counseling.

I found my first mentor in my master's program at Colorado State University when I was in my early 20s. Nathalie embodied kindness, genuine caring, and wisdom. I never felt judged by her, and she helped me to become more compassionate. I can't think of what exactly she said to me that helped me grow. I think it was mostly who she was. Of course, I wanted to please her because that was the way I was at that time. It was who she was and how she taught from a place of presence and compassion that I remember most. From that time, I knew I wanted to teach someday. I took three years off between my master's and doctoral work. When I was ready, Nat and I traveled to my first ACA conference and she introduced me to ACES. I had found my home. Nat has been an integral part of my growth throughout my life and career including witnessing the birth of my son.

Anxiety and wanting to please emerged during this experience. Natalie's acceptance and our deeper relationship helped me get over much of my "need to please." Nat's relationship with her first mentor, Molly, was a very genuine encounter that helped her heal after her divorce.

Natalie: Penny was one of my first students when I started teaching in the counseling program at a university. I remember her as a bright light and a very hard worker. She was one of those students who would go the extra mile with every assignment and would share ideas and resources with me as much as I shared with her. She was very professional, and I remember thinking she seemed to have the world by the tail at such a young age: husband, home, career focus. How did she do it? Well, I should have remembered that, from an external perspective, I too seemed to have it all together when I was her age. Yet the anxiety and discontent going on inside of me was brewing just beneath the surface. Then mentors came into our lives to rescue us from ourselves, our perfectionist scripts, and our illusions of having it all together.

My first mentor, the person who rescued me from myself, was Molly. We both were in the counseling program at a university for the same two-year period in the late 70s, she a professor and I a master's student. Molly helped me realize that I could make choices in my life and that I could, and should, periodically re-evaluate those choices. She called forth the counselor and teacher in me and, like Penny, I found my home as a counselor educator.

But what distinguished these mentoring relationships—mine with Molly and Penny's with me—was the level to which we opened up to each other as people. Molly and I still laugh at the hours we spent running in the Rockies, bandanas over our faces to beat back the Wyoming wind, as I cried, and Molly counseled me through a difficult divorce. And I remember how honored I was when Penny asked me to serve as her unofficial doula at the birth of her first child, and then, after so many hours of difficult labor, to be able to be with her during the Caesarian section that brought her lovely son into the world. It's difficult, amid the busy-ness of academic life, to make room for nurturing and sustaining such wonderful relationships. Yet, Molly and Penny and I are forever connected by this web of mentorship where life's learnings continue to be passed back and forth, no longer between teachers and students, but now colleagues and friends. I feel so fortunate to have been given a profession where I am paid to pass on to the others the lessons I've been given from my teachers and mentors. I really can't ask for more than that.

As seen from Penny's, Natalie's, and Molly's connections, powerful role modeling, encouragement and support can provide the groundwork for powerful internal transformations (Bruce, 1995). Furthermore, mentoring relationships can also be fostered beyond academia.

Penny: While I was a faculty member at the University of Wyoming, I met Nancy Forth, a very bright doctoral student. Nancy was a very kind and intuitive person who probably wanted to please me as much as I wanted to please Nat, but that is not what brought us together. It was Nancy's incredible intuition that I was drawn to as her supervisor. She had insights that were deep about master's students and clients. These insights were never presented with judgment. She could confront a client from such a place of compassion and empathy that we started calling it *carefrontation*. I am not sure we really came up with that word. It could have been out there someplace, but it sure worked for Nancy's style. Nancy went on to become a counselor educator. In an interview for a department chair position, I was asked to relate one of the most meaningful experiences I had had in my career. It immediately came to me when I said "I had a doctoral student who went on to become an amazing counselor educator, and she asked me to present with her." Over the years, we have processed our careers as well as the births and deaths of those close to us.

Nancy: Like Penny, I too was a young observer of others, wanting to understand and to help. I struggled with learning and expressing myself in school. With terribly low grades, my desire to be a nurse was not to be realized. I settled for a technical degree as an x-ray technician, where I worked for nearly 20 years. Although skillful at my job, I felt a deep longing to do more than help people with their physical health. I decided I needed to make a serious change in my life, but what would it be? Join the circus, or go back to college? I realized that helping people with their mental health might fill the void.

While I loved learning, during college I discovered I was still struggling with that process as well as with expressing myself. Frustrated, I made an appointment with a counselor at my community college who suggested I be tested for a learning disability. Discovering that I was learning disabled was empowering for me.

While completing my graduate degree in counseling there was one faculty member, JoLynne, who shared with me that she saw I had the ability to become a counselor educator. I was surprised, encouraged, and after working as a professional counselor for a brief time, I came to believe her and made the move to another university for my doctoral work. It was there I met Penny Dalen, a faculty member who seemed to know me better than I knew myself. Penny's old soul and free spirit was, and still is, the epitome of client-centered theory. For the first time I experienced unconditional positive regard and acceptance as a unique individual. Through this time of self-transformation, I learned to value, trust, and accept myself. Penny's spirit and role modeling are a constant companion of mine. So many times when struggling with personal or professional issues I ask myself, what would Penny do? And the answer always comes.

Like Penny, I found a home in being a counselor educator and have been privileged to feel connected with students who continue to touch my heart and help me in my own growth (Casto et al. 2005). Audrey was one of those students with whom I was honored to work during her internship. Audrey struggled with anxiety, trusting and believing in herself, and feeling competent. We spent quite a bit of time in supervision exploring these matters. I had similar struggles and found that in working with Audrey, I became able to trust myself as a counselor educator on a deeper level. The following is her story in her own words.

Audrey: When I began upon my journey in the counseling program, I was extremely apprehensive and unsure of myself. I often worried about saying the wrong things and would sit in class in a sweat, panicked that I would say something silly or *non-counselor-like*. Deep down, I knew that I had it in me to be an effective counselor because it was very natural for me to care about others and want to help them. However, I didn't have the confidence to believe in myself and truly trust the process. Although I had always tried my very best and hoped for a good outcome, I never really had enough self-confidence to feel very safe or comfortable with my decisions and actions.

Through the counseling program, I learned that it is okay to believe in myself and that I can in fact be an effective counselor. At first, it was often hard for me to hear positive comments from my peers when receiving feedback on my counseling sessions and skills. I became extremely nervous accepting that attention, and I was often envious of how comfortable others were during these sessions of our class. Dr. Forth, my professor, noticed this, and I still remember her calling me out on it in class. I didn't realize it was so noticeable to others, and I won't forget the day I realized how hard it was for me to accept positive feedback. Through our numerous talks in supervision, I learned that it was okay for me to believe in myself and that I should not doubt myself so much. I still remember many key phrases that she told me that really made me stop and think about how I was treating myself. I still use those phrases with students today when I notice they are doing the same thing. I will carry her guidance with me always. Dr. Forth helped me gain confidence in my own skills as a counselor and as a person.

As you can see from Audrey's, Nancy's, and Penny's experience, there was a great deal of personal growth that took place which included learning to believe in and trust themselves, and developing self-confidence (Walker, 2006). It is also evident how the web of connectedness from Molly to Nat to Penny to Nancy to Audrey continues.

Penny: Kittie was a student I met in a master's program. She had a fascinating life story of self-discovery and was very empathetic and insightful with her clients. I was so honored to be included in her journey to becoming a counselor. I will let Kittie tell her own story, but want to share here my experience with her. Kittie and I met her first year of master's studies. She was a single mom and transitioning from a career in finance to counseling. She was wise enough to take a little bit of extra time with her program. Kittie was one of those rare students who looked at herself and her own reactions to clients. I will never forget a pivotal moment in counseling when she shared her deep insight with her client, and they connected on such a deep level for those few moments that it transformed the client instantly. I was so honored to share in that and other experiences with Kittie.

Kittie: I believe that people come into our lives at exactly the right time and under the right circumstances. Certain individuals show up in an extra-special way, and Penny is one of those people in my life. I remember the first time I met Penny we were at an orientation session for first-year counseling students, sitting in a circle on the grass outside the university's community counseling clinic. When we were asked to share a little bit about ourselves, I was nervous. At that point in my life I had begun to find my voice, but was not yet comfortable sharing with strangers. I decided to tell the group the real reason I was in the counseling program rather than gloss it over with a superficial response. I explained that I felt very strongly that this master's program was my destined path. I was passionate and drawn to work with people to facilitate both healing and authentic living. My own journey of self-exploration and growth was propelling me forward and I wanted to share with others the freedom that I felt. However I was scared to have opened up so boldly with this group of fellow student counselors. When Penny instantly validated what I had shared with the group, I knew the two of us would share a special connection.

With Penny I always felt safe being myself, which included all my imperfections or my *humanness* as I like to call it. Feeling safe to explore, learn, and experiment was crucial for my growth as a counselor. I learned from Penny that the most important thing I can bring to a client's counseling experience is being present and authentic. She taught me that who I am in the room is more important than any staged technique. It is the relationship between the client and the therapist that leads to change and healing. After working with clients for four years in the master's program and now three years post grad, I still remind myself daily that the corrective emotional experience that clients have during our work together and our relationship itself lead to their transformation and healing (Bridges, 2006; Palvarini, 2010). I feel honored and blessed to witness my clients' lives. We have so much to offer the world simply by having the courage to be who we are. That is a lesson that Penny helped me discover for myself during supervision. There was this one moment where she had me close my eyes and check in with myself about the client/counselor relationship. I was able to see clearly that I was right on track so I stopped questioning myself. Penny believed in me, and I trusted her to be vulnerable; I moved through my insecurities at a good rate during that semester.

As seen from Kittie's experience, and as mentioned in Tara's story that follows, mentees often see that the mentor-mentee relationship is parallel to their own relationships with clients.

Nancy: Tara was an astonishing, passionate student I had the great honor to work with during her education specialist degree. Even though she struggled with her own personal issues, she was always able to put those aside and to be a true advocate for her clients. It is through her passion and dedication that she is known across the state as an expert in the area of grief and loss with children. Here is her story.

Tara: I was nearing the end of my school counseling program when I learned that our department would be hiring a new professor to take the place of one who was leaving the department. When I heard a new professor would be coming on board and would be leading my internship class, I was feeling quite nervous. I just knew this person could not be as good as the professors who were already in the program. I couldn't believe I was going to have to do some of my toughest work as a counseling student under someone that was coming in so late in my program.

When I showed up for the first night of my internship class, I was excited, yet nervous. I really didn't know what to expect. When I left, I was frustrated. This woman was expecting us to identify the theories from which we were working. What? I struggled in my theories class, and I was definitely not confident with this part of it. She talked about what we would do throughout the semester. I left wondering, who does she think she is coming in here at the end of my program when I'm supposed to know everything and she's making me realize that I don't!

I have since learned that the relationship between counselor educator and student parallels the journey a counselor takes with her client (Bridges, 2006; Campbell, 2000). There's anxiety initially. Why would this person care about what I do? She's just here to do a job. I'm just another student. I definitely resisted, as a client might. The trust wasn't there right away, and she expected us to do things that took me out of my comfort zone.

Despite my fear, Dr. Forth was there to guide, push, support, and encourage. Even though I might have resisted, that didn't faze her. Eventually, as many clients will, I got motivated to dive back into the process again because, at some point, it had become safe. Sometimes things got quite personal and very difficult. It was at those times, I now realize, that we were in that "magic" place, a place that cannot be described to an outside person with words that they will fully understand. It's in that place that I discovered things about myself that I did not know or believe possible. Why did Dr. Forth believe I was important enough? Now I know it wasn't just me, but it was her way of mentoring and supporting that allowed me to feel as if I were the only student she had. After graduating, it was scary to go out into the world on my own, but Nancy was there nodding her head and smiling. She knew I could do it.

Kittie's and Tara's stories indicate the importance of feeling accepted and safe, in enabling them to find their voices (Gilligan, 1977, 1982/1993). It is clear that the genuineness modeled in the mentoring relationship is then recreated by the mentees for their clients. We will now explore how powerful mentoring can be through some difficult times (Walker, 2006).

Nancy: Jenny was a dedicated student who, due to a personal crisis, had taken a leave of absence from her education. We both seemed to share self-doubt and the need to please others. Being a part of Jenny's journey has been amazing, as she has inspired my own growth.

Jenny: I could have been anything. That's what they all told me, and I believed them. And, if you had asked any of them—my parents, my teachers, or my friends—they would have told you that I planned to become the first woman president of the United States. Against the adamant persuasions of my mother, I discerned during my undergraduate years that I would forgo any political aspirations and become a teacher. Even then, I hoped that the next stop on my professional journey would be to serve in the role of a high school counselor. Could it be true that I would be forced to keep on learning for the rest of my life?

It was in 2006 that the unthinkable happened. My mother, who had been diagnosed with an aggressive breast cancer, was bombarded with the news that the cancer had spread to her bones. Within weeks, she died. I became severely depressed, and the last thing on my list of concerns was finishing my master's education, which had become an ominous cloud looming over my head. I took a year off from school, hoping that I'd be able to get refocused. I was three years into the degree, and more importantly, I'd made a promise. I promised my mother, and subsequently myself, that I would not quit. I had learned long ago that perseverance was a quality to embrace. Yet, I was so anxious! Had my friends and professors forgotten about me? In a program that was all about connections, had I lost all of mine?

During my sabbatical, Dr. Nancy Forth was hired and had established strong relationships with many students in the program. What would she think of me? I had such a personal need to be liked by my instructors, coupled with a professional desire to excel. I remember seeing her for the first time on Day One of my two-semester internship. She seemed nice, unassuming, and confident. She seemed real. Looking back, I had no idea that she would become one of the most influential people in my life. Nancy became my surrogate mother, my friend, and my constant consultant. I could call her in the middle of my work day during a student crisis, and she would empower me. She never gave me the answers, which was, at times, infuriating! Rather, she encouraged me to come to them on my own, and in my own time. She knew that competence was a characteristic that fueled me. Would others see me as good enough? Could I see myself as good enough? Nancy helped make the answers seem clear. Through class activities or weekly supervision, through emails, texts, and phone calls, Nancy filled the role of encourager, cheerleader, and mentor.

Although our relationship has evolved over the years, I still see her as my teacher. When I'm feeling professionally stagnant, I'll find the motivation to publish an article or present at a conference. She welcomed me not only into that classroom, but into her life—into her realm of knowledge and of friendship. She believed in me, and continues to do so, and for that, I am forever grateful.

Jenny's story is similar to the stories of mentors like Molly helping Nat through a divorce and Nat helping Penny have a child. Nancy helped Jenny through her grief to become an incredible counselor who now serves as a powerful mentor for others. Once again, the web of connectivity continues.

Penny: A student whom I shared a deep soul connection with was named Jill. She questioned the ideas of counseling without spirituality at a very deep level. Her enthusiasm for counseling and life was contagious. She was a runner and would come to supervision after a good run with the most amazing ideas and insights about life and her clients. She also worked on herself continuously. Her family history was very interesting; she needed to leave home and family to really be herself. As she journeyed along this thoughtful path, I was honored to share in her intuitions. I appreciated that when she had had some powerful dream, she would call me and we would dive into it. She would actually get advice in her dreams about her clients. I guess that was the higher supervision! What I most honor about Jill is her ability to flow with the present and stay open to her changing journey. We continued our connection after her graduation when she came and was a nanny for me for a few weeks. She still has dreams about my dogs. I invite her to tell her story here.

Jill: As soon as I looked into Penny's bright blue eyes I knew there was some kind of connection that I had to follow. Little did I know that my relationship with Penny would forever change my life and set me free from living a life that was not authentic. She taught me some of the deepest spiritual messages and left me yearning to find my own path.

I was lucky enough to have Penny as a supervisor at the beginning of my graduate school program. As soon as I walked into her office, she conveyed complete love for who I am and where I was in my journey Yet I also felt vulnerable, in a way, when I was challenging the deepest parts of myself. Penny has the ability to see right through a person. While most professors in the program were very "clinical" and distant, Penny cut right to the heart where a sacred, authentic relationship was formed. She modeled for us the kind of therapeutic relationship that we were all striving for with our clients. The relationship with Penny conveyed unconditional love and support while challenging long-standing belief systems that no longer served me.

When I first met Penny I was coming from a very evangelical tradition where women had no authority or voice. Inside I was very angry, but women "weren't supposed to be angry" and I felt powerless. For most of my life I had been ramming my head against a wall trying to fit my parent's spirituality to my own so that I could please them. At the time, I did not realize that the quiet voice inside telling me that my parent's path was not my own was, in fact, valid and wise. Penny taught me to honor that voice and recognize it in all its forms. I started listening more to my dreams, and I noticed more when I got "gut feelings" about people. Not only was I able to start using the voice inside me with clients, but I encouraged them to start doing the same for themselves.

I realized that listening to the voice inside me was one of the kindest things I could do for myself. It all seemed to boil down to a connection with and love for who I am. I had spent a lifetime trying to please others, thinking that this was the only way I could be loved, but I realized all the love I wanted was already inside of me. What an incredible truth to learn! The clients I saw seemed to have the same yearnings. Penny saw that spark inside of me and set it ablaze.

A professor once told me, "You can only take your clients as far as you have gone." Supervision with Penny was such an insightful experience because Penny had done so much of her own work and was open for more. I came to find that any kind of counseling and supervision is a two-way relationship where one person is not any higher than the other, but they cooperate for their mutual healing and growth.

Jill's story is similar to Tara's story which demonstrates how she experienced unconditional love and acceptance and was able to find her voice and trust herself. It is apparent throughout these stories how the mentoring relationship provides for the genuine development of the counselor as a person and professional (Casto et al., 2005).

Conclusion

When we started this process, we decided we wanted to write from our hearts. As we engaged with each other as mentors and mentees in writing this chapter, we all found that to put into words the importance of our genuine connection brought tears to our eyes. There is really no way to conclude a chapter like this one, as each student will move on to mentor someone else, and the web of connectedness will continue. However, as we close this part of the story for now, we want to thank Natalie, Audrey, Kittie, Jill, Tara, and Jenny.

Questions for Reflection

1. Prior to and during the process of becoming a counselor, what life challenges did you encounter?

2. What were key moments in your growth during your counseling program?
3. What about your mentoring relationship assisted in your personal and professional growth? Perhaps the relationship web is also full of unconditional love and provides those in the future with unconditional acceptance so that the web continues. For it is through these connections, our lives are made fuller, and our pathways more authentic.

References

Bridges, M. R. (2006). Activating the corrective emotional experience. *Journal of Clinical Psychology, 62*(5), 51-568.

Bruce, M. A. (1995). Mentoring women doctoral students: What counselor educators and supervisors can do. *Journal of Counselor Education and Supervision, 35*(2), 139-149.

Campbell, J. M. (2000). *Becoming an effective supervisor*. Philadelphia: Accelerated Development.

Casto, C., Caldwell, C. & Salazar, C. F. (2005). Creating mentoring relationships between female faculty and students in counselor education: Guidelines for potential mentees and mentors. [Special issue]. *Journal of Counseling and Development 83*(3), 331-336.

Gilligan, C. (1977). In a different voice: Women's conceptions of self and of morality, *Harvard Educational Review, 47*(4), 481-517.

Gilligan, C. (1982/1993) *In a different voice*. Cambridge: Harvard University Press.

Palvarini, P. (2010). Is the concept of corrective emotional experience still topical? *American Journal of Psychotherapy, 64*(2), 177-194.

Walker, J. A. (2006). A reconceptualization of mentoring in counselor education: Using a relational model to promote mutuality and embrace differences. *Journal of Humanistic Counseling, Education and Development, 45*, 60-70.

Section Two

Balancing Personal and Professional Life

Chapter 5

Dancing Backward in High Heels: Balancing Traditionally Male Academia within Feminine Life

LORI ELLISON AND CAROL M. SMITH

> *"Sure he was great, but don't forget Ginger Rogers did everything he did backwards . . . and in high heels!"*
>
> —Bob Thaves,
> "Frank and Ernest" [cartoon],
> 1982 © NEA Inc.

Balancing professional and personal life in academia is like dancing backwards in high heels. While the movies of Fred Astaire and Ginger Rogers display the artistry of a fabulous couple dancing fully in sync, Rogers' role presented an added and formidable challenge. She is required to anticipate, balance, and reverse in a mirror image, maintaining all the while an air of floating grace and effortless fluidity. Like dancing backwards in high heels, female faculty are challenged to balance the same academic loads as their male counterparts while omnisciently nurturing others at home, anticipating needs with grace and effortless patience.

We are both young professors and mothers. Lori is in her third full-time year after 7 years as an adjunct and a doctoral student, and 19 years as a clinician. Carol is in her fourth full-time year after 6 years as an adjunct and part-time clinician. We are both licensed professional counselors, but neither is actively building a practice. We are in "the Sandwich Generation." We are both married with school-aged children and care—long distance—for frail, aging parents. It is disingenuous for us to *advise* on balancing personal and professional lives, but circumstances have qualified us to *wrestle* with this topic. In pondering the challenge, we hope to share insights on our journey: the joys and frustrations of what we're learning.

We will never catch up. Unlike the perfect balance of the ballroom, pursuit of tenure can heartlessly consume *all* waking hours without assurance that things are going according to the choreography. When some aspect of job performance misses tenure-track expectations, the dark cloud of tenure review looms overhead and job satisfaction falls precipitously (Magnuson, Black, & Lahman, 2006). On the other hand, personal life can also require comprehensive and continuous effort despite gathering self-doubt. The ideology of "intensive mothering"—apparently the dominant view in the United States—implies that a mother's focus should be on nurturing her children to the exclusion of employment (Medina, 2007). Mothers in academia are not immune to this ideology. In fact, it has become the standard of "the good mother," even while on the tenure track (Medina, 2007). Such an ideology represents a Catch-22: One cannot focus exclusively on one's children and their needs while wholeheartedly pursuing a successful career in academe. Caught in this double-bind, it is no wonder that we invite more stress about both commitments.

Multiple roles stretch our personal resources to the breaking point as we seek to nurture those around us and simultaneously maintain a professional edge. If we put our families first, we fall behind on the tenure track. However, when precedence is given to academia, family life suffers. Either way, the only "expendable" seems to be self-care. We accumulate self-sacrifice to meet the demands on our time. What happens then, to the stressed out academician/mother who desperately tries to achieve all and be all to both her family and her institution?

Gambles, Lewis and Rapoport (2006) observed that, since the late 1950s, employment for both genders has overshadowed every sphere of life, undermining the value of familial care and community or social involvement. The resulting isolation and over-commitment to corporate expectations has left relationships and individuals impoverished and "running on empty." Gambles et al. (2006) concluded that, unless rigid gender roles adjust, work-life balance for both sexes was likely to remain elusive, even with substantial and progressive work policies in place.

Women entering a male-dominated field face more challenges in fulfilling multiple roles (Van Anders, 2004). While it may be illusory, men seem to be better balanced, less stressed, less concerned about multiple roles. Women, on the other hand, seem to have swallowed the fallacy that they can do it all, if only they manage time better and "improve themselves" enough. Female counselor educators, in our unscientific opinion, seem to be the worst self-blamers. They feel more angst than their male counterparts, who, arguably, have fewer roles to begin with (Van Anders, 2004). Women in academia, especially those with young children, are often at a disadvantage to their male counterparts in keeping up with their tenure requirements because of the expectation that women will also continue to maintain the household and do most of the child-rearing (Hunter & Leahey, 2010; Stack, 2004). Even when domestic help is available, female professionals often feel guilty that they *should* be doing more. The assumed aspiration of "superwoman" endures, despite decades of articles about being "good enough."

For me (Lori), this "shoulding" comes from growing up watching a "superwoman" (my mom) do it all and never quite feeling, though I was always wanting to, that I could live up to her legacy. Perhaps for others, it may come from a different sense of obligation to self or family or a desire to become for their own families what someone significant could not be for them. Somewhere on that continuum there is pressure to succeed at everything we put our hands to.

Medina (2007) found that many women find great fulfillment professionally, but tend *not* to feel accomplished when it comes to familial duties. Academic mothers may decide the tenure track is not worth the struggle. They may move to non-tenured or part-time positions or they may leave academia altogether, amid the shaking heads of their associates ("What a waste of her education!") and choose to be stay-at-home moms (Crone, 2008). Many, when faced with the choice between successful mothering and successful career building, will leave academia rather than endanger their maternal role (Stack, 2004). Others will merely find ways to compensate for their parenting obligations. They will "collaborate more often, avoid having as many children as they may have preferred, and limit activities unrelated to work or family" (Hunter & Leahey, 2010, p. 435). In a way, we female counselor educators expect ourselves to be "better" mothers than other professional women, because our training and expertise in child development and family dynamics "should" make us more adept at it (Medina, 2007). Since we presumably know how the healthy family *should* operate, how adept parenting *should* be performed, how couple time *should* be prioritized in the family, we *should* have both an optimally healthy family *and* a successful career, right? If we aren't busy blaming ourselves with this unworkable self-talk, our children, spouses, or parents could quickly pick up the refrain, confirming our self-doubts with external criticism or unsolicited advice.

Reality dictates that we would benefit by looking at ourselves, careers, families, and responsibilities through more compassionate eyes. We need to approach self-regard with *grace*, the same grace we afford others. For example, while perfectionism condemns, *grace* says things like, "It's okay if you didn't do this perfectly" and, "Your child will not be permanently scarred if you were a little late picking her up from school," or "The walls of your house will not fall if you didn't do the dishes before bedtime." In sum, we need to find *balance*.

Balance

Balance can be defined as a state of personal equipoise—successful management of two or more role domains—and is often equated with success and personal satisfaction (Gröpel & Kuhl, 2009; Gupta, 2011; Kalet, Fletcher, Ferdman, & Bickell, 2006). Balance is the *summum bonum* of empathetic, congruent, genuine, professional counselor educators. Managing personal and professional life *is* like dancing backwards in high heels. It requires balance, coordination, and fluid transitions. However, an unrelated metaphor also applies. The scene that comes to mind is of a performer who places plates, one by one, on several tall, thin poles and proceeds to spin them to maintain their balance. The ensuing entertainment is watching this performer run among the poles to produce enough velocity to keep each plate's precarious position on top. The life of a female academician can feel like "spinning plates" at times. We run between poles (or "roles") and do a fine job of spinning—until another is added, then another, and another. The more plates, the more likely one will come crashing to the floor. We are, as mothers and professors, expected to balance our roles as adeptly as the performer spinning plates in perpetuity with equal energy, time, and attention.

Why do both metaphors—dancing backwards and spinning plates—apply to the challenge of balancing professional and personal life? Both metaphors apply because balancing professional and personal life is exactly like excelling simultaneously at disparate and unrelated tasks. Whether home life represents dancing backwards and professional life is like spinning plates, or vice versa, our roles are widely varied and pregnant (no pun intended) with unrelated and unforeseen challenges. We women in academia are either "hormonal" or "gifted" for attempting to take on such dichotomous roles. We are all the more unbalanced (or matchless) for doing so with grace and fluid patience.

For example, my "To Do" list from last Tuesday included five professional development goals, six course development tasks, three advising goals, five errands for my son, six household tasks, two errands for my husband, and ten tasks for my father, including efforts to reconfigure his home to accommodate new cognitive and physical restrictions. The list included tasks like "do the dishes" and "learn the neuroanatomy of the limbic system." I presume readers are nodding and imagining their own overloaded, unending, challenging, and mundane task lists. During chapter revisions this afternoon, I was interrupted by three calls, seventeen e-mails, and two doorway conversations. In addition, I retrieved my son from camp when the other car-pool parent had a last-minute conflict, got him snacks, helped with a DVD that didn't work, and admired the "tree fort" he constructed with blankets throughout the living room. Meanwhile the cat vomited half a bird on the porch, a neighbor crushed our garden wall with her car, and my husband came home with a fever and virus. I learned my Dad's heat pump couldn't be repaired, and he needed new air conditioning right now in the summer heat. Dad is 81, lives alone in a rural area 5 hours away, and is recovering from major surgery. There is no one nearby to help. By 4:30 pm, the notions of "matchless grace" and "fluid patience" were pretty unrealistic. My options were to melt down, or breathe out and laugh.

In reality, *balance* can represent yet another luminous expectation we consistently fail to meet, despite heartfelt effort. Failure to achieve—much less maintain—the elusive transcendence of *balance* provokes guilt and the "imposter phenomenon," (Clance & Imes, 1978; Parkman & Beard, 2008). This refers to the belief that we've mistakenly been allowed in to the hallowed halls of academe in which we don't really belong. We don't seem to be able either to spin plates or dance backwards very well at all. We seem to be "stuck" between the unattractive options of endless striving or the personal failure of "falling on our faces" (or watching plates crash around us). Weaver (2008) urged those of us who wage this war with ourselves to choose carefully how we use our time in both pursuits.

Perhaps we aren't dancing the right dance or spinning the right plates. Perhaps we aren't even asking the right question. Perhaps a smarter strategy would be the development of purposeful priorities (Weaver, 2008). Perhaps we could learn to recognize the signs when a plate is about to fall and respond accordingly. Perhaps we could stop a plate or two and place them back on the shelf for later. Maybe we could concentrate on the most efficient way to keep spinning the plates that remain. Maybe we need to kick off the high heels and start "dancing as if no one were looking." While we haven't figured it all out, here are a few things we're learning along the way.

Double-edged Flexibility

We in academia both benefit and suffer from schedule flexibility. On the one hand, we have more freedom than our corporate counterparts to attend to family responsibilities as they arise, even when they intrude on our workday. On the other hand "work expands to fill the time available for its completion" (Parkinson, 1955, p.1). Time flexibility can mean we commit *all* waking hours to the tenure track, because the opportunities are endless. I (Carol) tried this approach during my first 18 months of full-time employment. As a result, I was constantly irritable with family members due to my academic preoccupations. Worse, I impatiently "harrumphed" through workdays while distracted by family concerns. To excel professionally, I emphasized work ahead of my family. I left my son at after-school care until nearly 6:00 p.m. daily, ignored most of my share of the house work, grimly prepared pre-packaged school lunches, rushed through dinner and bedtime story, and stayed up until 2:00 a.m. most nights trying to "fix" all the "problems" I saw in my courses, and in my students' work. Sensing my family was more patient than my department, I allowed them to "bear the brunt" of my aspirations. I berated myself for "weakness" at the tears that welled up whenever I bothered to "foster mindful awareness" of just how much stress I was generating for myself and my family. I was too proud to admit that I needed a classic cognitive "reframe." Counselor, heal thyself.

It only took about 18 months, but it dawned on me gradually that 8 or 9 hours a day (okay, sometimes 10-12) was *enough* commitment to work. Similarly, within that work-day, I'm learning to set limits on "maintenance tasks." For example, I attend to the "e-mail monster" for an hour in the morning, and an hour in the afternoon. I do my best to commit the rest of the day to priority projects. I gave myself permission to stop attending to *every* detail, to be gentle with myself, repeating "enough is enough." I finally remembered that my home, family, and relationships are gifts to be cherished, not re-scheduled. Planning ahead and kind smiles require no more time than sighing and impatient reactions. As dumb and simple as it sounds, I made a different choice. I chose to emphasize what was going well. I chose to smile and make eye contact with my son, and really listen, rather than tense my shoulders and rush him. I chose to leave the office at a more reasonable hour, and to spend real time with my son. I learned (again) that he has only one childhood, and my every mood affects his sense of "place" in the world. I chose to join my husband in his activities (like watching baseball games, reading, prowling through antique stores). I chose to learn to "work smart" (I'm still working on this one). I chose to do one or two really important things each day, rather than everything I *could* or *should* be doing. I chose to be grateful for daily accomplishments rather than stress about things left undone. The Counseling Department continues to function, students continue to learn, no one cares whether the house is spotless, and the world continues to spin on its axis *despite* my failure to achieve *superwoman* status, spin *every* plate, or even to dance (backwards and in high heels) very gracefully at all.

Progress: A Noun and a Verb

Like *balance, progress* is defined phenomenologically. There is no perfect "professional" or "parent" or "spouse." The joy is in choosing to be purposeful, to progress (verb) then celebrate the progress (noun). In some ways it is easier to see professional progress in academia because we have relatively clear guidelines for success. While not all expectations are as clear as we would like, we still know what their fulfillment looks like (numbers/types of publications, national presentations, teaching evaluations, and so on). Understanding our expectations, obtaining support from colleagues and mentors, and seeing our students learn and grow as professionals all help to push us forward in our own professional growth. Assuming all of these things are present, success can be expected to follow, and satisfaction with our positions in academia will increase (Magnuson et al., 2006).

Progress in our personal lives is less quantifiable. We don't have tasks or quotas of activities to define "success" like our promotion and tenure policies. How then do we know we are successful? Do we judge ourselves by a spotless home, a beautiful yard, wedded bliss, above-average children, or communal connections? If familial success is driven by such intangibles as our beliefs, values, and priorities, then it is also more difficult to determine when success has been achieved. For example, personal, familial success, for me (Carol) is peace in conversations at home. Success consists of shared quiet time, a meal without stressing about perfect nutritional balance, walking around the neighborhood, watering the porch plants, petting the cat, enjoying a meaningless TV show, chatting with the neighbors, calling our parents, making a small dent in our ongoing efforts to de-accumulate, playing with our son, enjoying him for who he is, and, occasionally, a hot bath, spiritual self-care, and guiltless puzzle games on the computer. I realized my stress originated internally, through my own unreasonable expectations. I appreciate more than ever the easy-going temperaments of my husband and son. They maintain their own inner peace naturally, and were just happy to see me being more peaceful, too. I'm learning to trust my abilities, practice gratitude and be pleased with what *is*. We benefit from defining balance in terms of "good enough," and success in terms of "progress."

Core Values

After months of exhaustion, self-doubt, and irritability, we are now clarifying our core values. While imperfect, we try to focus only on the most important things at work and at home. While this sounds obvious, significant challenges lurk in the specifics of prioritizing. I (Carol) found I settled for accomplishing easier tasks—for immediate gratification—rather than digging into the more important, complex tasks about which I was less confident. Looming deadlines produced an anxious and paradoxical retreat to familiar, less risky tasks, fostering a vicious spiral into hard work with little to show for myself. Priority is a combination of phenomenological and fearlessly honest weighting of intrinsic (not extrinsic) values, nearness of deadlines, and projected consequences. This algorithm requires frequent recalibration with self-statements that provide motivation rather than guilt. Reaffirming basic motivations provides needed perspective. For example, a basic motivation in my (Carol's) life is "comfort." I used to believe *comfort* required a completed task list. Now that task list completion is unattainable, I am obliged either to remain unsatisfied, or to redefine *comfort*. Now I am satisfied by working in good faith, and stopping at a reasonable time, rather than at the end of the task list. I maintain internal encouragements like "sufficient for the day is the trouble therein," "this too, shall pass," and "this will do," with approval rather than resignation.

We entered our academic careers with a sense of purpose, a calling, if you will, that focused our passion on the specific goal of educating new generations of counselors. When I (Lori) entered the classroom for the first time, I worried that I had nothing to offer these fresh faces. However, when I realized that they were eager to receive the experiences and instruction I had to offer, it was like a runner's high of endorphins. Suddenly, my previous work and experience took on a purpose beyond what I could accomplish as a lone practitioner. I was hooked. Now, as Weaver (2008) described, my desires to be a successful wife and mother as well as a successful academician have become inexplicably and inextricably intertwined.

Healthy Boundaries

We are (ta-dah!) recognizing that we have limitations and that boundaries are good. We are getting closer to that "sweet spot" that finds equal fulfillment and satisfaction in both roles. How? Part of the answer is being benevolent with ourselves when we fall short. Despite our desires to be "Supermom" and "Superprof" we're learning to be less driven to *perfection* and more driven to *purpose*. When we buy into the myth that we "can do it all," we set ourselves up for frustration, failure, guilt, and compromised physical health. A healthy sense of "boundaries" between work life and private life helps prevent burnout. We are learning to share time between home roles and professional roles, even when each role interrupts the other, and better, to be *okay* with the interruptions. We are learning, on occasion, to take a plate from its pole and let it rest or, perhaps, hand it to another to carry on. For example, last fall, I (Lori) found myself in an increased state of stress over getting everything done. Course preps, conference presentations, developing a new certificate program for our students, and, of course, two teenage kids heavily involved in their high school competition band (with my husband and me right in there with them) kept me in high gear just about all of the time. In September I was asked to present a supervision CEU workshop at the November conference of one of our state organizations. I accepted at the time, thinking I would be able to work in the preparation for that without any problem. By early-October, the time commitments to my work and my family just seemed to multiply, and I realized that making this a quality presentation was not going to be possible. I stressed myself out over my sense of obligation to complete the task I had agreed to perform and my inability to get the materials together in time to work up a presentation that I could feel proud of. I finally resigned myself to the notion that it was okay if I was not able to do this; there were other professionals in the state who could step in and present in my place. So I contacted the organization and asked them to please take my name off of the program. They did so and were able to find someone in plenty of time to present for them. When I did this, I felt such a relief. I could place that plate back on the shelf for another time when I had the energy and time to do the task well.

Time Management

We are learning to overestimate time needs, and "under-schedule." Things always take more time than anticipated because it's impossible to anticipate the unknown. Babies will "urp" on one's best suit as one walks out the door in the morning. Computers will crash just before the presentation. We are limited human beings, with finite reserves of time, energy, and resources. While our circumstances are idiosyncratic, we can pad time estimates for the troubles we can anticipate, and we can be flexible when unanticipated troubles occur.

I (Carol) routinely fail to anticipate problems or interruptions in completing tasks. I am learning to concede that things will go wrong and that more complex tasks have more interruptions and delays. I am also learning how to "backtrack time" (Nelson, 2011), adding time for transitions between tasks. For example, it's a good idea to add time for commuting, parking, gathering materials, etc. *prior* to an appointment or class meeting time. For example, I (Carol) live close to the university, and can park very near our building (a rare privilege in higher education). It takes exactly eleven minutes to commute (assuming no traffic). However, it is smarter to allow for traffic (five minutes), transitions between house, traffic, and office (another five minutes), and time to double-check class materials and technology (about 15 minutes). It also helps to be available for students (another 10 minutes). If I want to maximize my stress, I can wait to leave the house fifteen minutes before class. If I'm prudent, and want to model self-actualization to my students, it makes sense to leave the house 30-40 minutes ahead. And if I'm really smart, I'll arrange child care and meals well ahead, usually the week before.

When bombarded with requests for collaboration and service, we are learning to say, "No" or "Not now." Opportunities for service, inquiry, publishing, and projects in academia are endless. Sometimes saying "no" involves foregoing opportunities that are personally interesting, significant, or politically advantageous. Nevertheless, we are learning to focus our commitments (research and teaching) upon topics about which we are most passionate in our field. Even service opportunities can be tailored to one's passion. Finally, it helps to enlist department members to foster accountability to one's passionate commitment. For example, if Lori's e-mail asks, "How is that chapter coming?" my productivity increases. We agree to specific deadlines, and make ourselves accountable. I have learned to inflate my time estimates, because every project takes longer than planned, and every plan is interrupted. When I arrive, I tend to poke my head into any colleague's office just to say, "Hi, just getting here; how are you doing'?" We share snacks (yes, it's that simple), and check in with each other when we leave for local meetings "(I'm going over now; you coming?"). Our program director recognizes contributions by name in faculty meetings. We are comfortable enough to joke and to "give each other a hard time," with some gentle verbal repartee. Our new dean takes pains to wander the building, checking in with faculty, and occasionally surprises us with unannounced treats like hot chocolate and homemade cookies (I am not making this up). If we need her, she makes time, listens carefully, and answers thoughtfully and truthfully. We reciprocate by trusting her, minimizing our requests, and by "sticking to the knitting" when we do talk, respecting her schedule.

Productivity

We are learning to do our best work, whether writing, preparing for courses, or managing grants, when we're "on our A-Game." For Carol, that's early in the morning, and any time before her son's school lets out for the day. For Lori, it's in the mid-morning to afternoon, after personal errands have been run. We are learning to capitalize on available productivity tools. For example: in the information age, it just makes sense to synchronize email, calendar, and tasks with all devices. We can set multiple reminders and have calendars handy to reduce double-bookings. However, it is easy to let our devices, lists, and reminders overwhelm us. There is wisdom in turning off the "connectivity" in order to foster "productivity." We can prioritize tasks and make a chronological to-do list so that we can let go of what needs to happen tomorrow and relax for the remainder of today. I (Carol) have learned to give myself permission to stop, saying, "I have done enough for one day, and now it's time to rest." Sounds silly, but this self-talk allows me to be gentle with myself, and settle down for a decent night's sleep.

Making Fully-conscious Choices

Sometimes dancing involves hard questions and difficult choices. So what is a woman to do when she is doing her best with the dance and finds herself stumbling over a difficult step? Recently I (Lori) have felt challenged to maintain my professional identity in the face of competing familial roles. The angst I felt at moving my family 1000 miles from home for my first academic appointment was unparalleled in my life. According to Van Anders (2004), women tend to experience more stress than men when faced with relocation for a job. While at peace about accepting the job, I struggled with leaving two parents in fragile health and uprooting my children from the only home they had known. This made the transition very challenging indeed. However, difficult choices are inevitable in adult life. Feeling torn between roles seems "par for the course" for most women. I don't know if this applies to all men, but I've learned that it does for all the men I (Carol) know. Hunter and Leahey (2010) reported that it is generally less so for men than women, however.

Since settling into our (Lori's) new home we've had a few bumps. Although we are acclimating to the new environment, and my parents' situation is improving, I struggle with nagging guilt. "I should be doing more." "I should be more involved in my parents' care." "I need to be home with my family more." "Should I really take this conference trip?" These are all questions that plague me, even as I prioritize my schedule to participate in my children's activities and spend time with my family. I still second-guess, "Am I doing enough?" The choices I have made about career and family have not been easy ones, but I am learning to face the outcomes as they arise. I have learned to lean on my husband for help when I can't do it all, and he faithfully helps me without complaint. This spousal support is one condition that Weaver (2008) stated as integral to the success of any mother in academe and one with which I am truly blessed. For those women who are out there doing it on their own, Hill (2004) found that the value of supportive colleagues is also immeasurable. Perhaps this could provide that needed buttress if a supportive spouse is not available.

Mentors

Magnuson et al. (2006) noted this idea that counselor educators tend to handle the stress of academic demands better when they have the support of colleagues. We are finding extraordinary women in our institution and are learning that they're delighted to encourage us in our search for balance. I (Lori) sought out a mentor in my first year at my university through a program for new faculty. Though we are on different campuses, from different disciplines, and teach a different demographic, she is able to encourage me as I work toward tenure and advise me on university-wide issues that I'm too new to know much about. We have developed a good relationship and try to connect in person at least once every month or two. We talk about university life, but also life in general, and how to be a successful woman in academe. Her support and knowledge of the ways of the university (she's been here 20+ years) are invaluable. In addition to academic mentors, we also look for support outside academe to nurture the other roles in our lives. As examples, a faith community, a support group for mothers of young children, an interest group (art, music, cooking) or the like, can be invaluable to those who feel overwhelmed. We are learning to resist the temptation to "be an island" for we do not function at our best alone.

Self-Care

We are learning to be gentle with our self-talk and expectations. For example, I (Carol) engage in mindful self-care in the small moments of life: in the shower, at stoplights, in line, waiting for my son to gather his stuff. Techniques we use to help our clients also work for us (e.g., breathing, music, breaks, silence or meditation, whatever works best in the circumstances). We each practice at least one simple, self-indulgent activity each day. For Carol, it's Spider Solitaire. For Lori, it's any of a number of puzzle games on the computer. However, we set indulgence limits, so they don't become counterproductive.

Eat right. Drink lots of water. Take a walk. Did we say *exercise*? For us in academia, it's almost a dirty word, evoking more guilt and failure. But honestly, some kind of physical movement is not only the right, good, and healthy thing to do, it also increases blood flow to the brain, fosters insight, creativity, and memory (Archer, et al., 2011) (and what's not to like about *these*?).

It is evident that personal success, balance, and happiness are based much more on internal choices than on external variables. As we treat our clients with grace and positive regard, we benefit when we are gentle with ourselves as well. We may find that, paradoxically, the more we remove ourselves from impossible expectations (imposed by others or ourselves), the more energy we have, the more resilience we have, and the more spontaneity we have. Energy, resilience, and spontaneity provide fertile ground in which we can plant the seeds of joy in our care at home and in our work in higher education. Whether spinning plates or dancing backwards in high heels, we join with and salute our sisters in academia.

Questions for Reflection

1. What are the primary sources of the stress you feel in your divergent roles? What is at the core of that stress? Family of origin values? Self-talk? Disorganization? Lack of support? Ambiguity?
2. What would constitute "balance" for you? Make a list of all that it would entail.
3. Who are among your primary support people? Your family? Your co-workers? Another group? How could you enlist their help in achieving greater equilibrium in your life?

References

Archer, T., Fredriksson, A., Schütz, E., & Kostrzewa, R. (2011). Influence of physical exercise on neuroimmunological functioning and health: aging and stress. *Neurotoxicity Research, 20,* 69-83. Retrieved from EBSCO*host.*

Clance, P. R., & Imes, S. A. (1978). The imposter phenomenon in high achieving women: Dynamics and therapeutic intervention. *Psychotherapy: Theory, Research and Practice, 15,* 241-247.

Crone, M. (2008). One of the boys. In E. Evans & C. Grant (Eds.), *Mama, PhD* (pp. 159-167). New Brunswick, NJ: Rutgers University Press.

Gambles, R., Lewis, S., & Rapoport, R. (2006). *The myth of work-life balance: The challenge of our time for men, women, and society.* Chichester, England: Wiley.

Gröpel, P., & Kuhl, J. (2009). Work-life balance and subjective well-being: the mediating role of need fulfillment. *British Journal of Psychology, 100,* 365-375. Retrieved from *Medline.*

Gupta, V. (2011). How Hindus cope with disability. *Journal of Religion, Disability, and Health, 15,* 72. doi: 10.1080/15228967.2011.540897

Hill, N. R. (2004). The challenges experienced by pretenured faculty members in counselor education: A wellness perspective. *Counselor Education & Supervision, 44,* 135-146.

Hunter, L. A., & Leahey, E. (2010). Parenting and research productivity: New evidence and methods. *Social Studies of Science. 40,* 433-451. doi: 10.1177/0306312709358472

Kalet, A. L., Fletcher, K. E., Ferdman, D. J., and Bickell, N. A., (2006). Defining, navigating, and negotiating success: The experiences of mid-career Robert Wood Johnson clinical scholar women. *Journal of General Internal Medicine, 21,* 920-925. doi: 10.11 U/J. 1525 1497.2006.00524.x

Magnuson, S., Black, L., & Lahman, M. (2006). The 2000 cohort of new assistant professors of counselor education; Year 3. *Counselor Education and Supervision, 45,* 162-179.

Medina, S. (2007). The impact of motherhood on the professional lives of counselor education faculty: A phenomenological study (Doctoral dissertation) Available from ProQuest Direct Database. (UMI No. 3273842*)*

Nelson, J. (2011. March 17). Late (again) this morning? How to kick the habit. [web log article]. Retrieved from http://today.msnbc.msn.com/ id/42093131/ns/today-today_health/t/late-again-morning-how-kick-habit/

Parkinson, C. N. (1955). Parkinson's Law. *The Economist*. London: The Economist Newspaper Limited, November 19, 1955. Retrieved September 1, 2011, from page 1, paragraph 1, sentence 1 at http://www.economist.com/node/14116121

Parkman, A., & Beard, R. (2008). Succession planning and the imposter phenomenon in higher education. *CUPA-HR Journal, 59*, 29-36. Retrieved from EBSCO*host*.

Stack, S. (2004). Gender, children and research productivity. *Research in Higher Education, 45*, 891-920.

Van Anders, S. M. (2004). Why the academic pipeline leaks: Fewer men than women perceive barriers to becoming professors. *Sex Roles, 51*, 511-521.

Weaver, N. (2008). Coming to terms at full term. In E. Evans & C. Grant (Eds.), *Mama, PhD* (pp. 77-79). New Brunswick, NJ: Rutgers University Press.

Chapter 6

Professional Expectations and Partnership: Perspectives from the Beginning, Middle, and End

REBEKAH J. BYRD, AMANDA C. LAGUARDIA, AND KELLY EMELIANCHIK-KEY

In this chapter, we seek to provide thoughts, insights, and a framework for reviewing expectations related to balancing the roles of productive working professional and partner in an intimate relationship. Traditional gender roles and the meaning of work for both genders in westernized cultures are discussed. The impact of patriarchy and cultural expectations within the United States on the internal struggle related to women's roles is reflected upon as we, the authors, share our experiences. This chapter is dedicated to the preparation of counselor educators during their doctoral work and is written from the perspectives of three new counselor educators reflecting on their respective journeys. We contribute our thoughts and experiences to this book to give voice to women who are working to pursue their educational and career goals, because we believe students and developing leaders are vital to the future of the profession. To provide an overview, Kelly addresses struggles consistent with beginning a partnership and planning a marriage while starting and completing doctoral work. Amanda discusses concepts related to maintaining a marriage/partnership while completing doctoral work and how personal dynamics influence the job search. Rebekah reflects on the process of ending a partnership while completing her doctorate.

Women, Academia, and Career

We have observed the environment of academia across the country at many institutions, and we have been aware of the personal and professional demands on all students and faculty, but especially female students and faculty. The inter-relatedness of the personal and professional is articulated by Wilson (2008):

> In many ways, young professionals learn to treat work and family as either/or choices at the very beginning of their graduate professional educations. The intense time demands and pressures of graduate professional education teach students early on to place professional obligations over personal. (p. 95)

According to the U.S. Department of Labor (2009), 46.8% of the total US labor force is women. The number is expected to rise by the year 2018. Research also indicates that although a rise in women in the workforce occurs, women are still expected to do the majority of domestic/house work, and they are also expected to have primary responsibility for caregiving (Cha, 2010). As the number of women working outside of the home has increased, so too has the number of women present in educational institutions. The number of women entering undergraduate and graduate education has significantly risen in the past 35 years (Mason & Goulden, 2004; National Center for Educational Statistics, 2008).

In terms of graduate education and pursuit of career advancement, "the fact that women still assume primary responsibility for domestic work can undermine their ability to devote themselves to the requirements of career advancement" (Ezzedeen & Ritchey, 2009, p. 271). This could be because women have fewer opportunities to excel in the workplace or because, unlike many men, women oftentimes must consider other life priorities and responsibilities over and above moving up in the work world (Pruitt, Johnson, Catlin & Knox, 2010). "As a group, men are not put to a choice between work and family in the same way that professional women are" (Wilson, 2008, p. 98). Examples of this dual burden can be seen in research that qualitatively highlights the voices of tenured associate professor women pursuing full professorship. Many have indicated that they felt discouraged due to conflicting career and family obligations (Pruitt et al., 2010).

Accordingly, when women reduce contributions to their career, this may have negative effects on their jobs. Conversely, reducing contributions and responsibilities at home also has negative impacts and contradicts societal expectations of wives (Allan & Crow, 2001; Cha, 2010). For some, this could feel like a double-edged sword. Wilson (2008) described this conflict in that "society loses when professionals are forced to choose family over work, society also loses when the most accomplished and productive are forced to say no to family" (p.101).

Healey and Hays (2012) found that the gender with which one identified served to predict a person's level of professional identity development and engagement within the counseling field. In addition, Healey (2009) found issues of role conflict emerging for women in counseling in a qualitative study of new practitioners, doctoral candidates, and tenure-track educators. Many expressed concern related to balancing work and family, with many experiencing a general lack of support at their jobs. Women in this study expressed this conflict as a disparity between what they valued, what they thought the profession valued (as based on the counseling philosophy), and what was actually expected of them. Many women in this study attempted to find a balance, looking for ways that their professional obligations and interests could help them meet the expectations of their personal lives. However, participants found this process difficult as they perceived institutions de-valuing the unique issues women face, stating ". . . this is how our university's going to reward us—if we exhaust ourselves" (p. 184).

Regardless of partnership status or family/children responsibilities, women in academia are less likely than men to receive tenure, and women in tenure-track positions are more likely to be unpartnered (Mason & Goulden, 2004). Research seems to imply that success in the labor market makes relationships difficult for women and discusses instances of divorce among those successful few. "Ladder-ranked faculty women have a 144 percent greater probability of being divorced than do ladder-ranked men" (Mason & Goulden, 2004, p. 87). Also, in terms of career advancement and family planning, women with children ages 0-6 were the least likely recipients of a tenure-track faculty position (Mason & Goulden, 2004).

We, as women entering the world of academia, navigated the system as best we could while always seeking that balance between conflicting aspects of our personal and professional lives. Using a framework based on the goal of balance and wellness as a way of achieving personal happiness and fulfillment, we present our stories.

The Beginning

Common questions for which people seek a simple answer often include, *what is the secret to a long-lasting and stable relationship?* This question will never be universally answerable due to the complexities inherent in individual partnerships. Many people have different thoughts about what makes strong and lasting relationships. Within any relationship, there are bound to be pitfalls and areas of negotiation. Each partner has to learn about the other's expectations, needs, and desires while finding a way to integrate two worlds for the improvement of both. This is not an easy task to accomplish in the best of circumstances.

Kelly's Story

As a single female entering a doctoral program, I had high expectations for myself and for my future. At that time, I knew my professional goal was to find a position as tenure-track counselor educator. However, I knew what the research said about the challenges of starting intimate relationships in conjunction with the challenges present for female faculty members in academia. Women typically are obtaining their PhD's around the age of 34, an age when family planning is a significant consideration. Women in their thirties often begin to develop long-term family goals, which can include settling into a committed partnership and having children (Acker & Armenti, 2004).

When examining the relationship quality of female faculty members, the conflict that can exist between balancing family and personal relationships is connected to some *less than ideal* outcomes. The impact that daily decisions have on one's career progression and personal life can be significant and must be taken into consideration. Forster's (2001) research conducted with women in academia indicated that half of all participants made career changes or adjustments for the good of a relationship, and a third of all participants made career sacrifices for their family or relationship. Unfortunately, looking at the results of studies such as this one accentuates many limitations and reasons that prevent relationship and career success of women, specifically women in academia (On Campus with Women, 2008; Philipsen & Bostic, 2008).

Forming Relationships

All of this research makes me ask myself, why would a career-driven female pursuing a life in academia choose to enter a new relationship, a long-distance relationship at that? As our economic culture becomes increasingly globalized, such arrangements are becoming more and more common among romantic partners. Long-distance relationships have been around for years. Commonly seen in the military, they are now depicted in the media, prevalent on college campuses, and recurrent among dual-career couples (Stafford, 2005). With all of the potential factors that play a role in building and maintaining a lasting relationship, one might question the potential longevity of long-distance relationships. Further, physical distance and lack of proximity of such partners have been connected with lowered relationship fulfillment (Van Horn et al., 1997), stress (Pistole, Roberts, & Chapman, 2010) and constancy (Lydon, Pierce, & O'Regan, 1997). Other studies have also revealed that long-distance relationships result in increased depression (Guldner, 1996) and possible instability when reunited (Stafford & Merolla, 2007). Entering into a new, long distance-relationship while beginning my doctoral degree was a difficult decision that required special attention, but I decided to jump in head first.

Career Conflicts

There were many bumps along our journey that eventually led to marriage, but it was our careers that appeared to present the largest hurdle. From the start it was clear that my partner and I were goal-oriented, career driven, and not willing to let go of our high expectations and aspirations for ourselves. Nonetheless, we both took the leap to try and build our relationship while pursuing our work in different locations. Thus we learned the art of compromise, communication, and commitment. Our greatest challenges included both time management and career-related decisions. My partner was a new business owner, and I was trying to complete my degree, write my dissertation, and accomplish the "requirements" (publishing and presentations) expected of a potential faculty candidate; many disagreements focused on which person's career was to be regarded as more important. The disagreements went the same way each time. He was often the one to leave work and travel to see me, which in his eyes meant that he was expected to put my career first. All the while, I felt that I put my work and career aspirations aside to devote all of my time to him when he traveled to see me. Gender roles were also unconsciously present in this continuing disagreement. Looking back, these arguments seem silly. We now realize that none of those discussions were really about the importance of career; rather, they were about valuing and respecting each other and what the other person was willing to compromise or sacrifice for the good of the partnership.

As our relationship grew, we began to have a sense of shared accomplishment and mutual appreciation for each other's career advancements. I began to take a great interest in his work as he did in mine. Our successes were no longer viewed as *yours* and *mine*, but they became *our* accomplishments. His business success felt like my own in a way that was deeply meaningful. In turn, he often states that he is very proud of my dissertation and doctorate and feels as if he achieved it in some way as well. These feelings are supported by Aron and Aron's (1986) self-expansion model which suggests that when people become involved in a romantic relationship, self-concept inflates to include the other person's resources, perspectives, and characteristics (Aron & Fraley, 1999; Slotter & Gardner, 2009).

Although we faced many challenges in the beginning, I feel that an appreciation for one another and each other's careers was the key to the success of our courtship. When I was pursuing my doctorate, my partner would attend all program events when he could fit them into his schedule. Currently, he comes to at least one state or national counseling conference with me every year to learn more about what I do in my profession and engage with me in my professional life. I also make time to attend seminars and other events that he sponsors in his office, and always take an interest in what is happening at his work. We still face a long road ahead as newlyweds and anticipate years of bliss and bumps. But looking back, I am amazed at the challenges that were thrown our way and the hurdles that we overcame. If we had focused on the obstacles and barriers inherent in doctoral work and academic careers we might not have been as optimistic about the longevity of our relationship. I am glad that we took the risk of entering a new relationship despite the potential challenges. As a new faculty member and counselor educator, my partner and I are looking ahead with the hope of a newly-married couple.

The Middle

As women work towards educational or career-related goals, issues related to creating a balance between personal and professional expectations become increasingly ubiquitous. Traditionally, women have been expected to maintain domestic responsibilities, while men have been expected to attain success outside of the home in order to support the financial welfare of the family. These expectations seemed to play a role for me as I left home to pursue my doctorate in that my partner did not always take on domestic responsibilities while I was away—a source of many arguments. As western societies have changed to include women in what were once traditionally male economic roles, the roles expected of women within the home have not totally changed and, therefore, women who choose to work often seek a balance between family and career. This concept of the *double day* defines the double burden many women face when deciding what roles take precedence on a day-to-day basis (Cobble, 2003). The tension between household responsibilities and career advancement can contribute to disparities between men and women's pay and promotion, as well influence women's general sense of well-being. For instance, Shelton and Firestone (1989) demonstrated in their study of household labor and earning disparities that women's labor time in the home had a direct effect on earnings outside of the home even when years of work experience, hours worked outside of the home, occupation, and educational level were controlled for (Kjeldal, Rindfliesh, & Sheridan, 2005). Wage disparities are still evident today, especially in academia (National Center for Education Statistics, 2009).

Statistics on gender in comparison to the attainment of tenure in 4-year, Title IV institutions currently shows that women account for only 35% of all faculty becoming tenured—a 5% decrease since 2007—but comprise 43% of faculty across disciplines—up 10% from 2007 (National Center for Education Statistics, 2007, 2009). The percentage of females represented as faculty continues to decrease as status changes from assistant to full professor in comparison with their male counterparts. Women who do manage to attain the status of full professor still face more than a $10,000 salary disparity overall in 4-year public institutions (National Center for Education Statistics, 2007, 2009). In assessing salary and role within the profession, it is important to keep in mind the gender role expectations of our culture, institutions, and individuals since these beliefs and values will influence self-perception, relationships, the value ascribed to one's work, and institutional policy. While my partner says he is proud of my accomplishments, money is often a source of conflict between us. He is affected by cultural messages—as are all of us—whether or not he would like to admit it. And because he is from England, our perceptions of these messages sometimes differ. He still feels the pressure to be the *bread winner* and often reveals it—in months when he is able to make more money than I—by emphasizing, "It's not really *that* important."

Gender Role Expectations

Gender role attitudes are generally beliefs and values that serve to define behavior based on an individual's overt biological sex. Harris and Firestone (1998) found in their longitudinal analysis of women's sex role ideologies that women (White, Black, and Hispanic) are generally moving towards adopting more egalitarian gender role beliefs regardless of their individual characteristics. Of specific note, they found that participation in the labor force, income level, and higher educational attainment were also positively associated with higher agreement with egalitarian gender beliefs. In contrast, being foreign-born or a member of a fundamentalist religious group greatly influenced one's agreement with more traditional gender role beliefs (Scott, Corra, & Carter, 2009). As culture changes, and women and men's gender roles begin to overlap in a way affirmed by society, each group faces differing transitional issues that may influence the man-woman relationship.

Mandy's (Amanda's) Story

When I think about my journey through education and academia, I know that relational support has been vital to my success. Due to our financial situation, my partner could not quit his job and move with me when I decided to pursue my doctorate in counselor education. During my three years away, we found ways of maintaining our relationship together and supporting one another. We had to make time for phone conversations, plan trips to see one another, and ensure we shared our daily struggles, successes, and concerns openly. This was difficult at times, especially when my workload demanded increasing amounts of attention. Sometimes he watched TV, and I did my work while we were on speaker phone, just so we could feel connected to one another. My partner supported my decision to pursue my education and was willing to move wherever I needed to go once I began looking for a job in academia. This support was very important to my ability to focus on my work. I wasn't working for me only, but I was working to make both of our lives better. I found a way to balance my personal and professional goals, which helped me to balance my daily obligations.

In addition, I also had mentors with whom I frequently communicated. They let me vent my frustrations, share my accomplishments, and e-mail whatever crazy things came into my mind at two in the morning while I was working on various projects. They never judged me and always supported me; knowing I was my own worst critic, they encouraged me to focus on my strengths. My mentors, my partner, and the friends I made as I worked towards my doctorate served as constant sources of reassurance. They provided a base for me without which I wouldn't have been able to do what was necessary to succeed. While mentoring may play a role in supporting women and marginalized people as they work towards their professional and personal goals, the full influence of mentors in academia has not been fully assessed with regard to burnout prevention or attainment of success within the field of counselor education. Mentoring has been found to be extremely beneficial in improving confidence, supporting professional identity development, and increasing feelings of belongingness—all of which may help women surmount obstacles they may face in academia (Briggs & Pehrsson, 2008; Kurtz-Costes, Helmke, & Ulke-Steiner, 2006). Finding a mentor who is both personally and professionally encouraging can be critical for success in any field, and it is certainly so in counselor education. Feeling support from personally meaningful sources is something I found to be important for me, even essential, as I strove towards my life goals and attempted to move successfully through difficult times.

Success is subjective, but in order to attain it, one also needs to recognize the cultural and institutional expectations associated with objective assessments of success. Balancing the two is an individual process that involves careful reflection on one's goals, barriers (internal and external), as well as one's values and beliefs. Professional time requirements have also been found to play a particularly important role for women. Meeting life's obligations, including domestic and vocational demands, requires women to balance personal and professional responsibilities to manage potential role conflict (Hill, Leinbaugh, Bradley, & Hazler, 2005; Mason & Ekman, 2007; Medina, 2008; Simon, 1995). My career is particularly important to me because I have a personal investment. I worked in the mental health system for years, and I recognized that there were many systemic issues that needed to be addressed to improve the lives of children and families. This desire to help facilitate change has become a personal priority, and my partner shares in recognizing its importance.

The End: Rebekah's Story

As women increase their presence in the workforce, the personal and professional expectations upon them mount. Accordingly, "demands at home have increased, fueled by greater numbers of employed mothers, dual-earner families, and employed individuals with elder care responsibilities" (Higgins, Duxbury, & Lyons, 2010, p.847). This burden weighed heavily on me as I tried to navigate my partnership and education. As a full-time doctoral student who was married, worked outside of the home, and was involved in research, service, and clinical work, I was very familiar with the mounting demands, seeking to balance the responsibilities of career and family. This concept was not new to me, as I had been working to attain this elusive *life balance* during my master's (while working full-time and going to class at night). The demands of a doctoral program were different, and I found myself, once again, reexamining my many roles. My partner (at the time) worked as well, and we struggled to make time for one another as dual-income families often do.

Partnership and the Role of Support

Women in dual-income households who work the same or more hours a week than their male partners are less likely to have spousal support and are still pressured to excel at homemaking (Cha, 2010). Research examining dual-earner families further supported the notion that women report higher levels of stress and work overload than men (Higgins, Duxbury, & Lyons, 2010). Accordingly, "for women, the executive career/family combination is problematic, because women generally do not have access to full-time help from husbands comparable to what stay-at-home wives provide to men" (Ezzedeen & Ritchey, 2009, p. 271). This was certainly true in my case. While the work hours and demands of my doctoral program increased, my responsibilities at home were not diminishing. In addition his expectations—and those of others and of the general culture—that I keep up with everything became an additional stressor in the relationship. Added to that stress was an increase of misunderstandings on both sides in what used to be a mutually supportive relationship.

I was frequently reminded that my studies were optional, "my choice," with the unspoken message that duties to my partnership/family were *not* optional. This was the theme of a constant struggle. Previous research supports the notion that intimate partnerships influence individual health and well-being (Amatea & Fong, 1991). However, recent research also outlined adverse symptoms of health and the role of support in a partnership. Kostiainen, Martelin, Kestila, Martikainen, and Koskinen (2009) reported that

> support from a partner appeared to be very strongly associated with both self-rated health (SRH) and psychological distress, even when adjusting for education and household income. Those who receive good support from their partner were far less likely to show adverse symptoms of health than those who had poor support. (p.1143)

This research also indicated that individuals in poor relationships are more likely to show symptoms of psychological distress than those who are not in a relationship at all.

As a counselor and a researcher, I struggled to find meaning in the information regarding supportive partnerships as I felt my relationship was lacking the nurturance I needed. It felt like a lose-lose situation. As for women, being in an unsupportive relationship has negative effects on psychological health; however, the alternative (separation/divorce) also comes with similarly negative consequences. Nonetheless, the alternative seemed to be the best choice for both of us. While this decision was nothing less than a leap of faith, I learned to once again rebalance my life and deal with the negative implications and life changes that would accompany separation and then divorce as I worked toward my doctorate and a later position in academia.

Divorce is said to be "one of the most pervasive personal disruptions in Western culture" (Lorenz, Wickrama, Conger, & Elder, 2006, p.111). Professional women are three times more likely to get divorced as stay-at-home women (Wilson, 2008). Research examining the short and long-term effects of divorce on women's psychological and physical health found that in the years immediately following divorce, women reported significantly higher levels of psychological distress than their married counterparts (Lorenz, et al., 2006). A decade later, the women who were divorced reported significantly higher levels of illness (while controlling for prior health, remarriage, education, age, and income). Further, in comparison to married women, the higher levels of stressful events reported by divorced women led to higher levels of depressive symptoms perhaps due to cultural messages and expectations about divorce.

Partnership and Work Hours

In evaluating my feelings leading up to divorce, I wondered about my work and the contribution made to our separation. Wilson (2008) stated "workplace departures by women underscore that women experience the tensions between work and family in a way that men largely do not" (p.98). Research suggests that the working hours of women are more highly correlated with divorce than are men's working hours (Johnson, 2004). Time spent at a job means less time spent on other things such as caring for others in the family, promoting wellness, time spent with spouse, and promoting time spent together with other family members and relatives (Stolzenberg, 2001), all socially constructed and perpetuated responsibilities of women. All of these factors were considered as I made decisions about my future. This information suggests that if women are not taking care of household responsibilities and looking after the health of their husbands, then his health will soon suffer. Much of these social constructions leave men as powerless to deal with such circumstances as it does women.

Perhaps the previous factors mentioned increase the likelihood of divorce. It certainly seems that these factors contribute to women's feelings of failure, grief, and loss related to divorce and failed partnerships, since traditional views of marriage place more responsibility for the success of that marriage on women than men. I found this to be true in my case. Coming to understand socially constructed aspects of gender role expectations and their impact on my life assisted in my healing process. It was also a very powerful week when the court date for my divorce and my dissertation defense date were only two days apart. The chapters that closed, and the doors that opened that week were also very powerful in my life as I had previously accepted a tenure-track faculty position and felt that I could finally look forward.

Conclusion

Focusing forward, through all of the struggles, we have found that even a modicum of stability helped us recognize and celebrate our achievements and to traverse difficult times with courage. We feel it is our responsibility as counselor educators to talk about these issues within our field so we can all work with and assist each other in making useful changes. By being advocates we can help to alter the perceptions among graduate professionals and foster the concept that work and family can coexist without the destruction of one or the other (Wilson, 2008).

Questions for Reflection

1. What expectations have you encountered at work that did not fit with your personal value system? What did you do to address this conflict?
2. Who are the people in your life that support you professionally? How is their support beneficial to you on a personal level?
3. When you began a new relationship, what were some of the biggest challenges you faced?
4. How did career aspirations fit into your decision-making process when starting, or staying, in a relationship?
5. What implications does a partnership have for your career and familial goals?

References

Acker, S., & Armenti, C. (2004). Sleepless in academia. *Gender and Education, 16*(1), 3-24. doi:10.1080/0954025032000170309

Allan, G., & Crow, G. (2001). *Families and households in society*. New York, NY: Palrave.

Amatea, E. S., & Fong, M. L. (1991). The impact of role stressors and personal resources on the stress experience of professional women.

Psychology of Women Quarterly, 15(3), 419-430. doi:10.1111/j.1471-6402.1991.tb00418.x

Aron, A., & Aron, E. N. (1986). *Love and the expansion of self: Understanding attraction and satisfaction.* New York, NY: Harper & Row.

Aron, A., & Fraley, B. (1999). Relationship closeness as including other in the self: Cognitive underpinnings and measures. *Social Cognition, 17,*140-160. doi:10.1521/soco.1999.17.2.140

Briggs, C. A., & Pehrsson, D. E. (2008). Research mentorship in counselor education. *Counselor Education & Supervision, 48*(2), 101-113. doi:10.1002/j.1556-6978.2008.tb00066.x

Cha, Y. (2010). Reinforcing separate spheres: The effects of spousal overwork on men's and women's employment in dual earner households. *American Sociological Review, 75,* 309-329. doi:10.1177/0003122410365307

Cobble, D. (2003). Halving the "Double Day." *New Labor Forum, 12*(3), 62-72. doi:10.1080/10957960390237487

Ezzedeen, S. R., & Ritchey, K. G. (2009). Career and family strategies of executive women: Revisiting the quest to "have it all". *Organizational Dynamics, 38*(4), 270-280. doi: Forster, N. (2001). A case study of women academics' views on equal opportunities, career prospects and work-family conflicts in a UK university. *Career Development International, 6*(1), 28-38. doi:10.1108/1362043011 0381016

Guldner, G. T. (1996). Long-distance romantic relationships: Prevalence and separation related symptoms in college students. *Journal of College Student Development, 37,* 289–296.

Harris, R. J., & Firestone, J. (1998). Changes in predictors of gender role ideologies among women: A multivariate analysis. *Sex Roles, 38*(3/4), 239-252. doi:10.1023/A:1018785100469

Healey, A. C., & Hays, D. G. (2012). Evaluation of gender differences associated with professional identity development. *Journal of Counseling & Development, 90*(1), 55-62.

Healey, A. C. (2009). Female perspectives of professional identity and success in the counseling field. Old Dominion University. ProQuest. Retrieved from https://ezproxy.shsu.edu/login?url=http://search.proquest.com/docview/89181807?accountid=7065

Higgins, C. A., Duxbury, L. E., Lyons, S. T. (2010). Coping with overload and stress: Men and women in dual earner families. *Jour-*

nal of Marriage and Family, 72, 847-859, doi:10.1111/j.1741-3737. 2010.00734.x.

Hill, N. R., Leinbaugh, T., Bradley, C., & Hazler, R. (2005). Female counselor educators: Encouraging and discouraging factors in academia. *Journal of Counseling & Development, 83*(3), 374-380. doi:10.1002/j.1556-6678.2005.tb00358.x

Johnson, John H., IV (2004). "Do long work hours contribute to divorce?" *Topics in Economic Analysis & Policy, 4*(1), 1-23. doi:10. 2202/1538-0653.1118

Kjeldal, S., Rindfleish, J., & Sheridan, A. (2005). Deal-making and rule-breaking: Behind the façade of equity in academia. *Gender & Education, 17*(4), 431-447. doi:10.1080/09540250500145130

Kostiainen, E., Martelin, T., Kestila, L., Martikainen, P., & Koskinen, S. (2009). Employee, partner, and mother: Woman's three roles and their implications for health. *Journal of Family Issues, 30*, 1122-1150. doi:10.1177/0192513X08329597

Kurtz-Costes, B., Helmke, L. A., & Ulku-Steiner, B. (2006). Gender and doctoral studies: The perceptions of Ph.D. students in an American university. *Gender and Education, 18*(2), 137-155. doi: 10.1080/ 09540250500380513

Lorenz, F. O., Wickrama, K. A. S., Conger, R. D., & Elder, G. H., Jr. (2006). The short-term and decade-long effects of divorce on women's midlife health. *Journal of Health and Social Behavior, 47*, 111-125. doi:10.1177/002214650604700202

Lydon, J., Pierce, T., & O'Regan, S. (1997). Coping with moral commitment to long-distance dating relationships. *Journal of Personality and Social Psychology, 73*, 104-113. doi:10.1037//0022-3514.73. 1.104

Mason, M. A., & Ekman, E. M. (2007). *Mothers on the fast track: How a new generation can balance family and careers*. Oxford, England: Oxford University Press.

Mason, M. A., & Goulden, M. (2004). Marriage and baby blues: Redefining gender equity in the academy. *Annals of the American Academy of Political and Social Sciences, 596*, 86-103. doi:10.1177/ 0002716204268744

Medina, S. (2008). The impact of motherhood on the professional lives of counselor education faculty: A phenomenological study. 68, ProQuest. Retrieved from http://search.ebscohost.com/login.aspx? direct=true&db=psyh&AN=2008-99010-550&site=ehost-live

National Center for Education Statistics (2007/2009). Employees in postsecondary institutions and salaries of full-time instructional faculty. U.S. Department of Education.

National Center for Education Statistics (2008). Descriptive summary of 2003-04 beginning postsecondary students: Three years later. U.S. Department of Education.

On Campus with Women. (2008). Early-career equity in social sciences "subsidized" with sacrifices at home. *Association of American Colleges & Universities, 37*(2), 11.

Philipsen, M., & Bostic, T. (Col). (2008). *Challenges of the faculty career for women: Success and sacrifice.* San Francisco, CA: Jossey-Bass.

Pistole, M., Roberts, A., & Chapman, M. L. (2010). Attachment, relationship maintenance, and stress in long distance and geographically close romantic relationships. *Journal of Social & Personal Relationships, 27*(4), 535-552. doi:10.1177/0265407510363427

Pruitt, N. T., Johnson, A. J., Catlin, L., & Knox, S. (2010). Influences on women counseling psychology associate professors' decisions regarding pursuit of full professorship. *The Counseling Psychologist, 38*(8), 1139-1173. doi:10.1177/0011000010377666

Scott Carter, J. J., Corra, M., & Carter, S. K. (2009). Interaction of race and gender: Changing gender-role attitudes, 1974–2006. *Social Science Quarterly, 90*(1), 196-211. doi:10.1111/j.1540-6237.2009.00611.x

Shelton, B. A., & Firestone, J. (1989). Household labor time and gender gap in earnings. *Gender and Society, 3*(1), 105-112. doi:10.1177/089124389003001007

Simon, R. W. (1995). Gender, multiple roles, role meaning, and mental health. *Journal of Health and Social Behavior, 36*(2), 182-194. doi:10.2307/2137224

Slotter, E. B., & Gardner, W. L. (2009). Where do you end and I begin? Evidence for anticipatory, motivated self-other integration between relationship partners. *Journal of Personality and Social Psychology, 96*(6), 1137-1151. doi:10.1037/a0013882

Stafford, L. (2005). *Maintaining long-distance and cross residential relationships.* Mahwah, NJ: Erlbaum.

Stafford, L., & Merolla, A. J. (2007). Idealization, reunions, and stability in long-distance dating relationships. *Journal of Social & Personal Relationships, 24*(1), 37-54. doi:10.1177/0265407507072578

Stolzenberg, R. M. (2001). It's about time and gender: Spousal employment and health. *American Journal of Sociology, 107*(1), 61-100. doi:10.1086/323151

U.S. Department of Labor. (2009). Women's Bureau: Quick stats on women workers, 2009. Retrieved from http://www.dol.gov/wb/stats/main.htm

Van Horn, K. R., Arnone, A., Nesbitt, K., Desilets, L., Sears, T., Griffin, M., et al. (1997). Physical distance and interpersonal characteristics in college students' romantic relationships. *Personal Relationships, 4*, 25–34. doi:10.1111/j.1475-6811.1997.tb00128.x

Wilson, R. F. (2008). Keeping women in business (and family). In Gregg, S., & Stoner, J. R., Jr. (Eds.), *Rethinking business management: Examining the foundations of business.* (95-117). Wilmington, DE: ISI Distributed Titles.

Chapter 7

Can You Have It All? The Competing Worlds of Women Balancing Motherhood With an Academic Career in Counselor Education

ELLEN S. AMATEA AND
SONDRA SMITH-ADCOCK

Over the past five decades, women have been encouraged to "have it all"—pursuing a demanding professional career as well as starting a family and raising children. In the seventies, the response to the frequent question of "Can I combine a professional career with having a family?" was typically the optimistic retort, "Of course you can!" with little amplification as to how these often conflicting, multiple roles might be combined. By the 1980s and 90s, what had seemed like blind optimism began to give way to harsh reality as many professional women described the stresses and pressures they faced in attempting to fulfill these multiple roles (Clark & Corcoran, 1986; Menges & Exum, 1983; Elliott, 2008). Moreover, several research studies (Mason & Golden, 2004; Olsen, Maple, & Stage, 1995; Sax, Hagedorn, Arredondo & DiCrisi, in press; Winkler, 2000), when examining the career progression of women in academia who were rearing children, painted a gloomy picture of the costs paid by academic women who were trying to have it all. These costs included but were not limited to slower advancement up the academic ladder relative to men and to their single, or non-mothering peers. Yet, at the same time, a growing body of research has depicted many women occupying multiple roles as often feeling more satisfied with their lives than women who exclusively pursue either the career or family role (Barnett & Hyde, 2001; Noor, 1995; Halpern, 2008). How could there be such contradictory news—that working mothers experience more stress and more satisfaction? What happens in the lives of mothers in academia to help bridge the stress and the satisfaction? As more and more women seek to combine family responsibilities with academia, they need to be prepared to deal with the unique issues which they will, in all likelihood, experience.

In this chapter, two women counselor educators—one who has successfully raised children while in academia, and the other raising young children now—combine literature on motherhood in academia with their collective experience and describe a "helping" model for present and future counselor educators who are mothers. This discussion grows out of research literature, their own personal experiences, and those of other women attempting to balance these different roles. By examining these dilemmas, and the unevenly successful coping strategies employed, they hope to share ideas with women who either are currently in, or are planning to blend, these two roles.

Competing Worlds, Competing Standards

The woman engaged in the roles of academician and spouse and mother seems to be struggling with combining two different worlds where the criteria for success are discrete and, to a large extent, mutually exclusive (Allison, 2007). The challenges of combining these two different worlds of work and family are not merely those of dealing with competing responsibilities that demand time and attention. The problems exist at a deeper level as women attempt to deal also with competing standards and expectations as to how these responsibilities should be carried out. Sources of these competing standards and expectations are: (a) a woman's own internal expectations for herself as both mother, mate, and career professional; (b) her perceptions of the expectations of significant others (e.g., spouse/partner, children, employer, colleagues) regarding performance of these roles; and (c) the external demands of these roles in terms of task performance, skills, motivations, products, and time and energy resources. Obviously there is both an internal and external core to these two sets of standards. What are these? What constraints and supports operate for the woman striving for success in both worlds?

The Family World

Although marriage and childrearing continue to be sought and chosen by most professional women, studies repeatedly identify the stresses and additive nature of these roles (Coltrane & Adams, 2008; Elliott, 2008). The social role expectations of wife and mother are clearly different from those of husband and father in the U.S. culture. Despite the substantial increase in the number of families in which both partners work and aspire to an eqalitarian division of labor, the research has demonstrated that women in these families continue to shoulder the executive burden for domestic operation of the home and for childcare (Bianchi, Milkie, Sayer & Robinson, 2000; Meier, McNaughton-Cassill, & Lynch, 2006).

Home Management Role Expectations

While the incidence in which husbands performed chores in the home was greater in families in which the wife was employed than in families in which the wife was not working outside the home, husbands still participated to a much lesser extent in home care and child care than their working wives (O'Laughlin & Bischoff, 2005). Moreover, although working women tended to use outside help and resources—like paid childcare and housekeeping services—with greater frequency than did families with non-working wives, and fathers often contribute significantly to household tasks, the actual organization, division and delegation of home and childcare tasks remained firmly entrenched as the wife's responsibility (Meier et al., 2006; Spalter-Roth & Erskine, 2005).

Thus, while many women may be opting to pursue an academic career, it is typically pursued in addition to their family roles rather than with a substantial reduction of her family responsibilities. In Sondra's family (with two young sons), her husband contributes his time to cooking, laundry, and paying bills. However, when it comes to keeping track of activities, finding a babysitter, and getting children to appointments, these duties fall to her, unless she asks for his help. Her husband's role is more co-worker (and he works hard) than executive. Adding to this role confusion is the expectation that academic jobs are flexible, meaning (to him) that her time is more expendable and less rigidly controlled by her workplace than is his.

Motherhood Role Expectations

By far the most painful area in which the success criteria of an academic career and home seem to compete is in the area of child rearing. Studies repeatedly support findings that professional spouses and mothers (especially those with young children) experience difficulty in meeting the role demands of both rearing children and advancing in their careers (Elliott, 2008; Halpern, 2008; Winkler, 2000). The question of how much a mother needs to be present to meet a child's emotional needs is paired with deciding how much mothering is enough. Such questions clearly reflect a concern with standards for success in this role. Regrettably the academy not only has no clear answer, but current childrearing philosophies have tended to complicate and idealize the demands of the mother's role (Dillaway & Pare, 2008).

One day in a class on feminist theory, Sondra explained her mothering role expectations to a group of students. A young woman exclaimed: "But Dr. Smith, don't you *want* to take care of your children?" Taken aback, Sondra said, "Well, of course I do. I think you missed the point about the *expectations* and how they are socially constructed." While there exists a "motherhood mandate" for women, there is no such mandate for men. It is now fashionable for men to be good fathers. When a woman occupies a dual role, it is often assumed that she is negligent in meeting the needs of her children. When another student went on to say, "I think if you have children, you should be home with them," Sondra burned a little behind her ears and replied, "Then I wouldn't be here to teach you." It is important for academic women to nurture their multiple selves and savor their multiple roles. Furthermore, who will advocate for mothers in academia if the mothers themselves are not confident about being there?

The World of Academia

A professional career in academia typically provides opportunities for autonomy, creativity, challenge and leadership—extras beyond simple performance of tasks that most professional women are both trained to do and to which they are encouraged to aspire. Such increased opportunities, however, inevitably require increased productivity—reading, research, writing, leadership, and service in professional organizations or in the community—and a flexible availability that the professional woman and spouse/mother does not always have. The "extras" that separate the successful academician from the merely competent, require time and energy that cannot be spent with family and a time flexibility that a working mother cannot always accommodate.

Yet such a professional commitment is frequently equated with productivity, with the pressure for productivity an increasing expectation. Even when choices in favor of family that limit career activity are met with verbal support from colleagues, many academic women may find that both the tangible and intangible rewards in the work world are based solely on traditional expectations for their productivity. A work setting typically awards promotion, tenure, salary increases and even continuing job placement solely on scholarly productivity. Women with multiple roles rarely can keep pace in the "extras" (O'Laughlin & Bischoff, 2005). Thus mothers begin to see themselves as "unproductive," with this perception becoming an incongruent part of their own identity. For Sondra, post-tenure, it was a matter of redefining her own ideas about herself. A few "slow" academic years had been among the most productive "family" years. Then when both children were in school, just last year, she recommitted herself to her research and began to see herself as a scholar again. With one paper published—two, three, and then four—it felt good. "I'm back," she often thought. But, back from what? She was the same mother, and the same professional, all along. The ebb and flow of mothering in academia is something that can be understood and defined only in terms that are self-empathic.

Over a period of time, the accrual of credentials that serve as a demonstrable track record becomes vital to career maintenance and advancement, as well as to employment mobility. Moreover, continuous contact with involved, achieving colleagues sparks interests that may be frustrated by the inability to pursue them, guilt at not being a full "member of the team," and resentment at possessing equal abilities but self-imposed unequal opportunities to demonstrate them. The question becomes one of: "Can you be only partially in the race?" Especially since the race appears to go to the swiftest runner. Thus, how can the woman with such multiple role commitments win a place, given the nature of this race? Not being the swiftest runner will seemingly continue to be a disappointing part of their experience as mothers in academia. Little has changed in most university settings about how faculty are evaluated. At the same time, the sacrifices that successful competition often requires are not worth it to some of those who are mothers. Sondra's children sometimes ask her why she has a job. The question challenges her. "Some mommies like to work," Sondra replies. Retaining the pleasure you find with your job, when you often feel like you're at the back of the pack, takes perseverance.

Another internal conflict revolves around women's own confusion about what is fair—a combination of the need to stand on one's own merits in the work place and pull one's equal weight in dealing with work tasks, versus sensing some real differences and vaguely desiring to somehow have those needs accommodated by "the system." For example, during the early years of her career, Ellen was the only woman in an all-male department at a research-intensive university and the only faculty member with young children. She often found herself in a "Don't treat me differently, but do" emotional bind in which she alternatively blamed her university's lack of sensitivity to the multiple demands she was trying to juggle in raising two children and pursuing career tasks, or blamed herself for "needing exceptions." This often resulted in a sense of frustrated resentment at not being able to reconcile the source of confusion. Moreover her work environment seemed unsupportive to her advancement. She wrote:

> I got no assistance or mentoring in learning how to balance service and teaching responsibilities and develop my research and scholarship. It was a very Darwinian climate of 'survival of the fittest' in which both my colleagues and my department chair seemed to believe that a necessary part of becoming tenured was to figure it out without any guidance.

Unfortunately, many of the academic institutions in which women are employed still provide limited information and guidance about tenure and promotion criteria or about options that might assist women in coordinating their work and family responsibilities (Halpern, 2008; Marcus, 2007).

Less Effective Coping Strategies

The authors began to notice that their responses to these conflicts and competing standards were often reactive. They seemed to operate in a demand hierarchy that fluctuated among job, marriage and children, depending on a number of factors that included which wheel was squeaking loudest, one's own emotionally reactive state, changing perceptions and standards in these various roles, and the coping mechanisms which they might currently be using. The overall effect often seemed to be one of an uncomfortable and unseemly lack of control. Though they frequently used them, the authors found the following mechanisms or strategies to be less than maximally productive: (a) denial and rationalization; (b) compensation; (c) displacement and resentment; and (d) talking without doing.

Denial and Rationalization

These strategies are used frequently to diminish the pull of one or the other of life's arenas. Child rearing concerns are frequently appeased with the rationalization that quality of time spent is more valid than the quantity. The realities of the job world may be ignored and/or distorted by pursuing one's own interests within a limited time frame rather than pursuing those activities producing the greater reward value. There may exist the pretense that one's very involvement in both work and family will be evaluated positively in the academic realm since personal conversations with colleagues clearly indicate an awareness, and usually approval, of these dual commitments. A colleague recently introduced Sondra in front of a large group of students. She stated, ". . . and Dr. Smith has a dual commitment so you might be lucky enough to see her little boys around here sometime." Dr. Smith's colleague continued, "Not everyone agrees about this, but I think having children around reminds us why we are here and what is really important." It was heartwarming that her colleague validated her mothering in such a kind way, yet Sondra was left with the words ringing in her ears, "Not everyone agrees about this . . ." Our colleague spoke from her heart that day. She also spoke the truth about mothering in academia.

Compensation

Many women spend inconsistent and sometimes disproportionate amounts of time and energy alternately on family and on job in an effort to compensate for time and energy lost in the recent past. Such expense of time and energy in either arena seems to always carry with it the consequence of getting behind in the other. The resulting distress and possible realignment of an original commitment always seems to result in a new level of guilt and frustration. The constant struggle to play catch-up in both domains creates an on-going cycle of avoidance, rationalization and blame (and obvious and growing piles of work to do both at home and the office that, at the same time, both mock and beckon). The "tipping" point in Sondra's office and home seemed to be the birth of her second child. That's when the piles and the list of things to do became unmanageable. So she stopped making lists and went into a less stable, less organized, and more process-driven state. "Forgetting appointments is something I would not do two years ago, she often lamented. Now, I just cannot seem to keep up. Some days, stepping over the piles is an opportunity to laugh at myself and reflect on a life well lived. Other days, well, those are the days that I bitterly contemplate the seeming unmanageable state that my life is in right now. These moments are hard."

Displacement and Resentment

Frequently, Ellen and Sondra have found themselves blaming either the work world or family world for the stresses encountered in the other and resenting the people in each world who do not have to operate, seemingly with one foot in each. For example, as academics and mothers, they have an absurd fantasy that their male colleagues have a quiet study where they spend any evening or weekend time they choose working steadily while a support system operates around them, and their mind is not interrupted with thoughts bubbling up like "Does Chris need to practice his spelling words?" or "What groceries need to be bought for tomorrow night's dinner party?" Another part of them realizes both the absurdity of the fantasy (Certainly their own husbands do not have that conventional support) and the self-elected nature of their own situation. Combined with the resentment and jealousy, therefore, is some element of dislike at their own pettiness and frustration at not being able to juggle their lives without railing against the world.

Talking Without Doing

Like many other women, they have found support and some reduction of discomfort in sharing concerns with other women in both formal and informal conversations and friendships. Seeking social and emotional support from other women is, in fact, one of the most common experiences of modern women encountering role strain and changing role expectations (Hill, Leinbaugh, Bradley, & Hazler, 2005). However, while social support may feel good and reduce some of the negative emotions they are experiencing, women may find themselves wallowing in the emotional catharsis of sharing common concerns rather than looking inward, examining the "dynamics" of the situation they find themselves in, and using more conscious, problem-focused coping strategies. Ellen and another female colleague would often talk about how difficult it was to find time and space to write (either at home or at work) along with rearing young children, but after several sessions of "Ain't it awful?" they realized that they could spend all day blaming others for their situation (husbands were not helpful enough, colleagues were not supportive enough, etc.) or they could exploit the value of the experiences they were garnering. Thus, they began a new line of research, investigating coping strategies of multiple-role women and of dual-career couples, research that they were able to translate into several research grants and articles.

More Effective Coping Strategies

If these frequently used coping strategies seem less than effective, how then *does* one deal with the stress of competing demands and standards experienced by the professional woman and mother? The authors have found that suggestions for handling these multiple role demands have all too frequently focused on women's efficient use of time and optimization of resources. However, these types of strategies overlook two very important dimensions of these dilemmas: the emotional component of personal choice in these conflicting role criteria, and the variability of situations in which women find themselves. As they have observed the ineffectiveness of the more reactive strategies described previously, they have found themselves moving toward a balance of emotion-focused and problem-focused coping strategies. In the following section they discuss how both types of coping strategies can be helpful to academic women engaged in multiple roles.

Emotion-Focused Coping

As the name implies, emotion-focused coping entails active strategies designed to manage a person's emotional reactions to a challenging situation and to regain emotional balance, such as physically discharging emotions, catharting, seeking social support, or reframing the situation (Smith & Kirby, 2009a; Wong, Wong, & Lonner, 2006). Reframing one's experience by thinking of the benefits of this dual lifestyle—for instance, considering the enrichment provided to one's research and work by living in these different roles—can be a productive emotion-focused strategy. For example, Sondra's tenure decision came the same month as the birth of her second child. While this timing could be seen as precarious and overwhelming, which it was at times, the anticipation of tenure and another birth really challenged her to focus on the excitement and successes she enjoyed at both work and home. Obviously there are some stressful situations which cannot be resolved—situations such as coping with loss of a loved one, loss of a job, or the onset of a serious health challenge. Hence, in some situations, emotion-focused coping strategies may be most appropriate. However, this strategy, while momentarily effective for reducing the pressures of these competing roles, often does not ease the strain of competing worlds. In contrast, problem-focused coping uses strategies that deal with the source of the emotion by changing the situation.

Problem-Focused Coping

This style of coping attempts to address the source of emotional stress by either changing the nature of the role demand or changing how one responds to the demand or stressor (Smith & Kirby, 2009b). The authors have found themselves using three general types of problem-focused coping to balance their multiple roles: (a) redefining role demands, (b) role restructuring and (c) role efficiencies. They believe that the work/family stresses that they have experienced are not fully resolved by trying to do all that needs to be done. Whatever personal and management decisions there are to be made, need to be made within a context of greater self-acceptance and personal control as well as a recognition of contextual factors.

In their opinion, specific strategies such as altering timeframes, utilizing more resources at home, purchasing more resources, or learning to be assertive in negotiating to change others' expectations vis-à-vis their roles, are too often used prematurely, based on the assumption that the woman's role strain is the result only of social or situational demands. However, what seems needed prior to utilizing these strategies is a more fundamental, individualized process of self-examination. Hence they have routinely engaged in a process of personal redefinition of role demands and expectations. This process of self-examination demands concerted effort. One of Sondra's colleagues, a mother of two young children, once said to her, "I just know my path is not the same." It took some time for what she meant to sink in. The idea that the role strain of mothering on the tenure track could be of my own design was not novel and not wholly realistic. However, as it sank in, Sondra saw that it was at least partly true. As mothers, academics can focus less on the ideology of the institution and more on the quality of the experience of having both worlds.

Redefining role demands through a process, either of personal/internal, or contextual/external role redefinition, requires a woman and members of her social contexts of work or family to redefine the nature of their specific role expectations by assessing the standards and relative benefits associated with those expectations. The *personal internal role redefinition* process requires a woman to examine her own overt and covert set of valued role expectations at a given time in order to build a set of priorities that would serve as a frame of reference for selecting coping strategies. For example, as is typical in many academic institutions which value scholarly productivity as measured by publications and scholarly presentations, Ellen—who was married and rearing two preschool children—was expected to publish peer-reviewed papers, present at conferences, and write fundable grants. She reports:

> Knowing that I had limited time and flexibility when my children were young and that tenure depended on a record of publications and adequate teaching evaluations, I concentrated on writing and publishing papers (which I wrote in the wee hours of the morning when my family was asleep), only presented at two conferences per year (thus forgoing the benefits of professional visibility and networking), and was minimally involved in service or community activities or in homecare. Later after tenure was awarded, I was able to commit time both to consulting in the schools and to serving as a den mother with my son's Cub Scout troop.

A process of *external/contextual role redefinition* requires that members of the work context rethink their role expectations and standards. For example, only recently did the authors' university develop a maternal leave policy which would allow women/men to take a semester off from work and also stop the tenure clock. When the program coordinator role was open and Sondra was approached (in fact, pressured) to take the job, her first thought was, "Well, yes, it is time—moving into more leadership is important at this stage of my career." However after thinking it through, she decided not to take the position in order to focus on her scholarship (and because her little boy was still in preschool) and withdrew her name. At this point in her career, she also learned how to say *no* with more ease. The security of being tenured certainly played a role in her newfound confidence and freedom to choose. However, she also decided that, having tenure behind her, it was time to nurture her well-being and her family, without apologizing for it.

Role restructuring involves rethinking how role demands might be met so that one might do a certain task differently or negotiate with others so that they take on responsibility for carrying out the demands/tasks. For example, the authors have both found themselves modifying their ideas about how certain family responsibilities should be implemented. When Ellen's children were young, rather than cook a full meal for the family every night, ". . . we ate sandwiches two out of the three nights I got home late from work. Then, when my sons became adolescents, they took on the responsibility of cooking on those nights I would get home late." In Sondra's family with young children, her husband has the responsibility for cooking family meals every night. Ellen can remember times when she caught herself thinking about how lopsided her expectations were about how she and her husband would care for their home. Whether it was in washing clothes, loading and unloading the dishwasher, making dinner or buying groceries, she assumed that she needed to be in charge and that her husband—raised in an era when men did not do these things—seemed ill-equipped to carry out these responsibilities. Then she broke her leg and could not get around. Her husband took over all these responsibilities and carried them out quite adequately much to Ellen's amazement. "Our roles have never been the same since. My husband routinely washes clothes, makes coffee, shops for groceries and loads and unloads the dishwasher. Both he and I joke around about his new-found competence!"

Role efficiencies involve efforts to work more productively by multitasking in such ways as folding the laundry while quizzing one's children on their spelling words, or learning how to make one product count in two places by conducting research on what one teaches. As an example of the latter, rather than have three separate domains—research, teaching and service—that need to be addressed each year, Ellen formulated a research agenda examining how school staff interact with students' families; that agenda grew out of teaching family counseling and consulting with school staff. Her teaching was enhanced by her experiences of counseling with students and their families and interacting with school staff, and she was able to generate a line of scholarship about how families and schools might relate differently to solve student problems. Sondra is following her lead.

Can We Have it All?

Much of the discussion of women in academia has focused on describing the problem. It is not the aim of the authors of this paper to minimize the importance of the problem or of the discrimination that many mothers face in the academy. Overall, there is a lack of institutional attention to how women cope with the demands of competing worlds—a situation that is unlikely to change in the near future. Although several institutions are taking constructive steps to alleviate the stressors on academic women who have young children—including options to "stop the tenure clock" or to allow part time employment for those women who want or need to reduce work demands for a period of time—such changes come slowly (Marcus, 2007). Meanwhile, it is time to consider how women might better manage the competing demands of their life roles without undue cost, either to their well-being, or to their career advancement.

Sondra and Ellen, both tenured academicians, were talking one day about Sondra's plans for advancement to full professor. Ellen said, "I took longer to get promoted to full professor because it was important for me to also care for my children." Having taken a more measured, albeit productive, pace in their scholarship than some other faculty members in their programs, and having acknowledged this dilemma to each other throughout their chat, Ellen was modeling a healthy self-examination and self-empathy that Sondra needed to hear that day. Since then, fewer of their chats have been about "talking without doing" or "overcompensating." That evening, when Sondra plopped her children into their beds and settled in at her computer, she decided that women can indeed have it all—depending on the definition of *it*.

Questions for Reflection

1. Have you ever felt that you had your feet firmly planted in two worlds: family and work?
2. Have you observed yourself using one of the coping strategies that we have considered to be ineffective? If so, which one, and what was its impact, short and long term?
3. Are you aware of some of your overt and covert value priorities? How have your values and personal expectations influenced your choice of coping strategy?
4. Are there particular role demands/tasks that you have restructured to make them more manageable? How did you do this? How satisfied were you with the result?

References

Allison, J. (2007). Composing a life in twenty-first century academe: Reflections on a mother's challenge. *NWSA Journal, 19*(3),23-46.

Barnett, R. C., & Hyde, J. S. (1992) Women, men, work and family: An expansionist theory. *American Psychologist, 56*, 781-796.

Bianchi, S., Milkie, M., Sayer, L. & Robinson, J. (2000). Is anyone doing the housework? Trends in the gender division of household labor. *Social Forces, 79,*191-228.

Clark, S. M., & Corcoran, M. (1986). Perspectives on the professional socialization of women faculty: A case of accumulative disadvantage? *The Journal of Higher Education, 57*(1), 20-43.

Coltrane, S., & Adams, M. (2008).Gender and families (2nd ed.). Lanham, MD: Rowman and Littlefield.

Dillaway, H., & Paré, E. (2008). Locating mothers: How cultural debates about stay-at-home versus working mothers define women and home. *Journal of Family Issues, 29*, 437-464.

Elliott, M. (2008). Gender differences in the causes of work and family strain among academic faculty. *Journal of Human Behavior in the Social Environment, 17*(1/2),157-173.

Halpern, D. (2008). Nurturing careers in psychology: Combining work and family. *Educational Psychology Review, 20,* 57-64.

Hill, N. R., Leinbaugh, T. Bradley, C., & Hazler, R. (2005). Female counselor educators: Encouraging and discouraging factors in academia. *Journal of Counseling & Development, 83,* 374-380.

O'Laughlin, E., & Bischoff, L. (2005). Balancing parenthood and academia: Work/family stress as influenced by gender and tenure status. *Journal of Family Issues, 26,* 79-106.

Marcus, J. (2007). Helping academics have families and tenure too: Universities discover their self-interest. *Change: The Magazine of Higher Learning, 39*(2).

Mason, M., & Goulden, M. (2004). Do babies matter (Part II)? Closing the baby gap. *Academe* (November-December). *90*(6) 10-15.

Meier Meier, J. A., McNaughton-Cassill, M. & Lynch, M. (2006). The management of household and childcare tasks and relationship satisfaction in dual-earner families. *Marriage & Family Review, 40(2-3),* 61-88. Doi: 10.1300/J002v40n02_04

Menges, R. J., & Exum, W. H. (1983). Barriers to the progress of women and minority faculty. *The Journal of Higher Education, 54*(2), 123-144.

Milkie, M. A., & Peltola, P. (1999). Playing all the roles: Gender and the work-family balancing act. *Journal of Marriage and the Family, 61,* 476-490.

Noor, N. M. (1995). Work and family roles in relation to women's well-being: A longitudinal study. *British Journal of Social Psychology, 34,* 87-106.

Olsen, D., Maple, S. A., & Stage, F. K. (1995). Women and minority faculty job satisfaction: Professional role interests, professional satisfactions and institutional fit. *The Journal of Higher Education, 66*(3), 267-293.

Sax, L., Hagedorn, L., Arredondo, M. & DiCrisi, F. (In press). Faculty research productivity: Exploring the role of gender and family-related factors. *Research in Higher Education.*

Smith, C. A., & Kirby, L. D. (2009a). Putting appraisal in context: Toward a relational model of appraisal and emotion. *Cognition & Emotion, 23*(7), 1352-1372.

Smith, C. A., & Kirby, L. D. (2009b). Relational antecedents of appraised problem-focused coping potential and its associated emotions. *Cognition & Emotion, 23*(3), 481-503.

Spalter-Roth, R., & Erskine, W. (2005). Beyond the fear factor. *Change, 37*(6), 18-25.

Wong, T. P., Wong, C. J., & Lonner, W. (2006). *Handbook of multicultural perspectives on stress and coping.* NY: Springer.

Chapter 8

Balancing Personal Life and Career

LeAnne Steen and Christine Ebrahim

We're sure that we aren't the only professional women who have contemplated or wondered whether balancing personal and professional life is possible. And, although sometimes it may *seem* like an impossible feat, we believe that it *is* possible and, that if done effectively, all aspects of our life flourish. As counselor educators, modeling clear boundaries and balance within and between our personal and professional lives is imperative for us and our students.

Over 55% of female faculty members in Gerdes' (2003) study cited their major sources of stress as being their volume of work, time pressure and the challenges of balancing work. For female counselor educators, being able to comfortably balance professional and personal life serves two purposes: it can reduce or even alleviate feelings of stress and anxiety, and can ultimately decrease the chances of burn out. Conveying the importance of recognizing and honoring the many aspects of our lives (professor, researcher, writer, private practitioner, mother, sister, wife and friend) helps our students realize that, first and foremost, it is possible to find a comfortable balance, and that they too must find a balance that is comfortable for them.

What is Balance?

Oxford Dictionaries (n.d.) defines "balance" as "an even distribution of weight enabling someone or something to remain upright and steady; a stability of one's mind and feeling." According to Bird (2003), work-life balance is defined as the ability to have *achievement* and *enjoyment* in day-to-day living. In addition, the idea of balance is unique to each individual according to life priorities, relationships, and career goals. In this chapter, we outline our thoughts on some meaningful priorities female counselor educators may struggle with and how we've successfully managed to achieve balance in our lives.

Schedules

Many of us struggle with the simple concept of time management. Although the schedule of a university faculty member can be fairly flexible, the schedule can be very demanding because of the expectation for teaching, research, and service to the university and community. This may be a difficult adjustment for a junior faculty with an entire lifetime of scholastic student-oriented experience. Autonomy is beneficial and detrimental at the same time!

Women with children and extended family obligations have another important piece of this puzzle to incorporate. Female parents have notably felt an added pressure to develop their tenure portfolio while raising children with very little university policy in place to recognize the circumstances for motherhood in academia (Rieman, 2005; Stockdell-Giesler & Ingalls, 2007; Wolf-Wendel & Ward, 2003). Many universities allow family accommodations to the tenure clock (stopping, or delaying tenure); however, very few advertise this benefit, leaving faculty mothers to discover it on their own (Stockdell-Giesler & Ingalls, 2007; Wolf-Wendel & Ward, 2003).

We find that scheduling oneself "in" for 50% of the time is essential. Scheduling time for self-care, exercise, research and writing facilitates a balanced lifestyle. Research should be done without distractions such as email, phone messages, and student interruptions. This time should be safe-guarded; otherwise, it will be lost. We recommend closing the office door, when possible, or reserving a private space in the library for research without interruptions. Other obligations schedule themselves. Classes have to be taught; students have to be met, and emails and phone messages have to be returned. When we create a base schedule of priorities—exercise, research & writing—our other obligations fall into place.

In creating a schedule, we both use the shared calendar function so our colleagues and the department assistant can see our schedules. We color code off-campus meetings, or days we plan to work from home so that no one drops an appointment into our calendar when we are off campus. We also block out times for research and writing, clients we see in our private practices, and *exercise*. Most departments and colleges are moving to the format when others can see your calendar in order to plan meetings, and so on. If we do not block out times that are designated for certain work and personal priorities, they will be snatched up by meetings, student appointments, and administrative time.

We are also fortunate enough to have created a culture of approachability and diversity among our teaching faculty; we all have different teaching strengths, areas of expertise and preferences. We are very lucky to have a faculty who respect each other and recognize and value each other's strengths. Although our classes have traditionally been taught in the evenings, occasionally a second section of a class is offered normally in the morning to give students an option. Some of us with children prefer teaching in the mornings because it allows us to teach while our children are at school and therefore frees up evenings for us to be with family. As a faculty, discussing our preferences to teach certain classes at certain times has proven quite successful. In situations where there are no options regarding teaching schedules, it is even more important to block times in the calendar to ensure that our "extra" time is guarded for a variety of professional *and* personal needs.

Personal Relationships

Regardless of culture, the importance of personal relationships and quality time is essential to balanced, healthy, human living (Letherby, Marchbank, Ramsey, & Shiels, 2005). As discussed in the above section, sometimes we have to schedule our leisure time! Otherwise, it will be sacrificed. So, how do we connect with friends when life feels too busy? We love to combine our leisure time with friends and the other things that we already do such as having lunch or lunch coffee, exercising, and riding to work.

Making friends can sometimes be complicated. Being a new female faculty member in a new town is quite intimidating. We offer some suggestions for women interested in finding new friends.

- **Joining alumni associations**
  Reconnecting with individuals who share your alumnae affiliation is a simple way to find friends with whom you can easily connect. Most towns have a club that facilitates connections, and these are usually reconciled through the primary university. If you were a member of a sorority or other social service organization, it is likely that you can find connections to other members of those organizations as well.

- **Getting involved with the Junior League or some other non-profit group**
  Joining a service organization such as the Junior League, or volunteering with a non-profit organization will help a new faculty member to find persons with whom she can connect who share similar passions.

- **Getting involved in hobby groups**
  Most towns have networks of individuals interested in certain hobbies and sporting activities. It is important for you to connect with people of similar interests and to use your research prowess to find where people are meeting and when you can join them.

- **Joining faculty interest groups**
  Most universities have faculty interest networks. If you are interested in collaborative research, find out who is organizing these opportunities. If you are interested in community service, student activities, lectures, or the arts, find opportunities, offered through the university, to connect with other faculty members with similar interests. Many universities have women's resource centers, which offer discussion groups, brown bags, and research opportunities.

- **Engaging in faculty development/ mentoring**
  Faculty development and mentoring are emerging through quality enhancement planning in most universities. Faculty development committees and centers are resources that foster teaching and research as well as a healthy life balance. It is important to discover what resources may be in place at any university through the faculty development committee, or center. Similarly, it is important to have a mentor. If the university did not provide one, we suggest finding

someone you trust and asking that person to be your mentor, discussing expectations and opening a transparent connection.

Quality vs. Quantity

Because we have family and career obligations, we sometimes don't have as much of an opportunity to spend time with friends as we once had. However, spending time with friends is an important part of how we "balance" our lives; therefore, we find it important to spend our free time with quality friends doing what we enjoy. The bottom line is to remember that with all the other obligations and responsibilities in our lives, it's important to make the time that we do spend with our friends quality time and certainly don't waste time being around people who we do not feel good being around.

Integrating Family & Motherhood

The question is, "Can you be a good, effective, full-time counselor educator while being a good, effective, full-time mother?" We believe that the answer is, without a doubt, *yes*. Full-time motherhood can be stressful and anxiety provoking in its own right but adding the pressures of being a full-time faculty member and trying to accomplish what needs to be done in order to achieve tenure, can be somewhat challenging (Rieman, 2005; Stockdale-Giesler & Ingalls, 2007; Wolf-Wendel & Ward, 2003). In this section we discuss several areas which we found to be potentially stressful or challenging, and methods we used for diminishing stress and attaining "balance."

Christine's Perspective

Intimate Relationships

In my opinion, communicating to my husband the expectations that my department chair, dean and even other faculty members have of me as a faculty member, is of utmost importance. First, it helps him understand the time commitments and the pressures I am experiencing. It also gives him the opportunity to act as a support and help me deal with the pressures of the role of faculty member; it allows him to understand that he is a part of my academic life.

Additionally, by knowing in advance what is expected of me, he is not surprised when I say that I have to have some quiet alone time to work on writing or that I'll be working on Saturday or arriving home later than usual because of the President's Convocation, a Chi Sigma Iota board meeting, new student orientation or graduation. Although my husband is also in academia and understands some of the pressure of this part of my life, it helps him understand *my* role in my department and university community and the pressure that accompanies it.

Finding Quality Childcare

An important aspect that makes it easier for me to balance motherhood and career life is being confident that my children are being educated and cared for by qualified, reputable people. I was fortunate enough to have parents and in-laws who were available to watch my children from the time they were infants until they were about 18 months old and ready to go to school at least part time. For me, there was great comfort in knowing that my children were being loved, nurtured and well cared for, even in my absence. Since I was not constantly worried about my children, I was better able to concentrate at work; it was easier for me to be able to devote more physical and emotional time to whatever other task I was doing while at work.

In preparation for my children's starting school, I took the time to research schools by visiting them, reading about them and talking to parents with children in those schools. In order for me to be able to dedicate my day to teaching, researching, writing, advising students, mentoring students, sitting on department and university committees, sitting on various boards and participating in community service work, I had to be comfortable with the school facility where my children were spending their day.

Many universities offer on-campus child care facilities. These centers tend to have a child development focus and are also helpful in training education, nursing, and child development university students in normal childhood behavior patterns. These centers are well run, close by, and often offer discounts to faculty, staff, and student parents. Our university childcare center allows parents to visit during the day, which is very nice and convenient for mothers who breastfeed or who simply want to check in on their children.

Unfortunately, our child care facility it is also very popular, which leads to a very long waiting list. If you are a university faculty mother who is interested in using the onsite child development center, be sure to find out the waiting list protocols as early as you can (before pregnancy if possible) in order to maximize your ability to ensure your child will have a spot when you are ready to return to work after maternity leave. Even if you are not privy to an on campus center, most competitive child development centers have waiting lists, and your research skills will come in very handy in determining the different procedures needed to enroll your infant or young child for day care or pre-school.

Spending Quality Time with Children

Creativity is important in developing strategies for quality time with children (Jacobowitz, 2005). Many primary schools are expanding their populations to include students from other neighborhoods. LeAnne and I both chose schools for our children, beyond daycare, that are close to our university, rather than close to home. We find comfort in knowing we are close by if they need us. Having our children either at school with us (LeAnne has one who is still attending the university day care center) or attending a school close by, allows us to spend the majority, if not the entire, drive to work/school with our children. Although it was very tempting for us to return phone calls (especially when our children were too young to talk to us) these times in the car proved to be wonderful opportunities for us to interact with our children. We talk to them about school (ours and theirs), sing songs, practice counting, practice speaking Spanish and French or simply talking about whatever come to mind. The point is that we are interacting with our children, trying to reinforce what they are learning in school, and building relationships.

LeAnne and I are fortunate enough to also be able to share our academic lives with our children. Our department is very family, dog, and child friendly. Faculty members with children often bring them to campus for "visits" to our offices, the play therapy room, and even the swimming pool. Not only do we get to spend quality time with our children, but we expose them to our world of academia.

Twice a year we as a department sponsor family-friendly functions (a BBQ in the fall and a crawfish boil in the spring) to which students, as well as faculty, are encouraged to bring children, parents, friends, roommates and even pets. We eat, sing, dance, and have volleyball tournaments! Just as we as a faculty have had numerous conversations about what kind of culture we want to create for our students, we also discuss the culture that we want to create in our department. We all agree that we want to create a "family-oriented" culture, even if our "family" includes dogs. We have had very open conversations about how we want to relate to each other and that has proven to be very helpful. We strive to be a healthy, well-functioning faculty system.

Being Creative with Our Available Time

As difficult as it is for me, I have made it a habit to do "school work" after my children are asleep and after I've had a good long conversation with my husband about the day. I also talk to him throughout the day about "random" things, so we really don't have to focus on those things when we get home. This started while I was writing my dissertation. During my PhD program I gave birth to two children; when I was writing my dissertation I had two children under the age of 2. My writing time started at 11 PM and ended about 3 AM. Of course this is not ideal, and I am happy to say that I no longer need to stay up *that* late to complete writing, research, and class preparation projects. However, if I need to stay up late now, I can.

I also take advantage of any available time to be with family—especially my children. I have made the decision that attending my children's baseball games, taking them to swim lessons, dropping them off at school and camp, taking them to the park to play after school, taking them to the zoo and friends' birthday parties on the weekend, and even being a *room mother* is far more important than sleep. So I have made the decision to do all those things with my children while I still can (and they still want me to!). Now that they are older and at school all day, I take advantage of the extra time I have between classes, supervision sessions, and private practice clients to attend to all the activities that are required of me by my college and department. For me, prioritizing what's important has been very helpful. Sometimes work *has* to be a priority, but other times I have to focus on my young children, and I acknowledge that I can't always be supermom . . . and that's okay.

I also try to keep in mind that my hard work and my ability to balance the many aspects of my own life will not only keep me on track for attaining tenure. They will also give me a better chance to enjoy my family, allowing me to be a positive role model for my children and my students. During a recent graduation party, I had the opportunity to stand in front of the new graduates and their families, present a new student, and welcome her into the counseling profession. She was a nontraditional student who had two teenage children at home. She had gone to school part time to ensure that she was home every night to help them with homework and attend their school functions. She also worked part time. Although she often joked about taking so long to go through graduate school, I reminded her that by returning at this stage of her life, she was providing a valuable role model for her children, especially her daughter: she showed that it was possible to balance home and family life with work and school life without causing either one to suffer.

Connecting with Other Moms

Most large cities and a lot of smaller communities have "mommy groups." Sometimes these groups are stay-at-home mothers who want social contact and interaction with other women. Others are professional women whose children are not yet of school age and who want their children (and themselves) to benefit from social interaction. I joined my first mommy group when my oldest was in nursery school and my youngest was less than eight months old. Because I hadn't become friends yet with women who had children around the same age (or who were around my age), I found these weekly get-togethers at girlfriends' homes invaluable.

Since our children weren't in school yet, this group provided our children an opportunity to learn how to interact with other children. Just as important though, was that the group allowed me to have the social interaction that I craved, and gave us the opportunity to share stories about raising children and to process frustrations we had about lack of sleep and feeling like we had to be super-mom/-wife/-woman/-daughter/ -sister. Activities that we did together included going to the zoo, aquarium, children's play centers, parks or just hanging out at each other's homes. We also took advantage of nice weather and planned walks in the neighborhood or areas parks. These walks combined social interaction with exercising.

Additionally, once a month we had a "Mommy's Night Out" during which time we let our husbands or parents watch the children while we enjoyed margaritas and Mexican food. Although everyone in the group I joined had some kind of connection to someone else in the group (some were high school friends; others were neighbors during the Katrina evacuation), my suggestion would be to ask around about mommy groups either at the neighborhood playground, health club, or your children's school. Even though our children are a little older, and we certainly don't see each other as often as we once did (once a week), we still manage to make getting together a priority, and it always feels good to reconnect.

LeAnne's Perspective

Creating Social Experiences at Home

I am a very social person. When I began having children, I often felt isolated because of my inability to socialize outside of work. I discovered that integrating my social life with my home family life was affordable and helped meet my personal need for interaction. Opportunities to invite friends over for grilling, sporting events, pot-luck dinners, and game nights, have been abundant and fruitful. This helped me meet the needs of my children and connect with my partner while also keeping the expenses of outside social events to a minimum.

Being Prepared to Travel

On another note though, being tied down to the house all of the time after children is not healthy! As a new mother, it was intimidating at first to leave the house. It is difficult and takes a lot of planning (snacks, diapers, changes of clothes, and the like), but it is important for us to bring ourselves out to the community, with our children in tow. This helps our children adapt to being outside of the house while our attention is diverted, as well as feel more confident when traveling (Jacobowitz, 2005).

I have found that my children love attending music festivals with me. I bring a blanket, sunscreen and lots of snacks. We sit near the back so the children can crawl and play, and I can still enjoy the music. The interaction the children have with others is fun and creative. Often, someone sets up a "kid's area" at the festival with fun art activities, or drum circles. This allows me to get several of my creative and social needs met, while also meeting the developmental needs of the children.

On occasion, Christine's husband and children have met her at conference cities. They go either a few days early or stay a few days after. It gives their family an opportunity to enjoy a little time away from home and, although she still attends the conference during the day and the social events in the evening, she can still enjoy being with them, while they all get to enjoy exploring the conference city together.

Creating Time

Unlike Christine, I cannot stay up late in order to grade or develop course plans. I will literally fall asleep sitting up! I have to find other ways to be creative with my time for these activities. As discussed earlier, I schedule myself a full day for research activities during the week. I also will sometimes schedule out times for grading (when papers or tests are due) in order to anticipate the extra workload and not overload myself with other meetings on those weeks.

Most of the classes I teach are in the evening with students beginning to show up at my door with questions and requests for help around 3 PM. On this note, I find it is better to grade in the mornings when there are fewer people milling around the department, and I may have an uninterrupted hour or two. I also find this works well with research for the same reasons.

On another note, I enjoy being around others who will not interrupt me. Sometimes I find it difficult to focus at home or in my office because I am distracted by emails and unclean floors. If I move myself to a coffee shop and set up to grade or write, I often find I am much more productive. I enjoy taking short breaks to people watch, but others generally do not interrupt me. Some would find this very distracting, but for me this strategy is facilitative to my production.

Wellness and Self-Care

We are both moms who are academics, but self-care is important for everyone. Just as we teach our students the importance of self-care, we ourselves must practice it. We have decided to be cognizant of these factors in developing a lifestyle. Of course, on occasion, our work consumes us! However, we also find time (even if that means scheduling that time on the calendar) to step back and enjoy life and engage in our own wellness. Wellness is a buzz word lately that we enjoy bringing to the attention of our students. As counselor educators though, we have an obligation to practice wellness in order to create a healthy program and develop healthy students. According to Myers, Sweeney, and Witmer (2000), wellness is:

> A way of life oriented toward optimal health and well being, in which body, mind, and spirit are integrated by the individual to live life more

fully within the human and natural community. Ideally, it is the optimum state of health and well-being that each individual is capable of achieving. (p. 252)

According to this definition, wellness is a lifestyle. Sweeney and Myers (2004) developed the Indivisible Self Model (IS-Wel) in order to better understand wellness as counselor educators (Foster, n.d.). The model has been empirically validated through extensive factor analysis. According to the IS-Wel model, there are several factors of wellness that are each unique and must be acknowledged in order to have a lifestyle of wellness. The factors include, but are not limited to, *control, work, positive humor, leisure, stress management, self-worth, realistic beliefs, friendship, love, spirituality, cultural identity, gender identity, SELF-CARE, exercise, and nutrition.*

It is clear, in looking at the definition in conjunction with the factors, that it is impossible to have a healthy life, and to model mental health to students, without attending to self. The strategies that we have discovered and share here with you are part of our own evolution of growth.

Mental Health

In thinking about mental health specifically, it is imperative that we ensure our engagement in our own mental well-being. Counseling is an important part of life adjustments. Most of us encourage our students to participate in counseling while they are attending the program. We both engage in counseling as counselors educators. If we are not modeling well-being and a commitment to our own personal mental health, then our students won't either, and their clients will possibly be impacted!

Conclusions

Balance is attainable, but it is not simple. Much like the work required in maintaining a healthy relationship with another, the work required for creating balance in life, and hence, facilitating a more positive relationship with self, is imperative for success. It isn't something that just happens to some people! Being mindful and working towards wellness and balance in all aspects of life will help create a space that is comfortable for us and our loved ones.

Questions for Reflection

1. When you have had a meeting scheduled off campus and someone tried to schedule a meeting with you on campus, do you generally cancel your off-campus meeting, or find another time? How is exercise or research different (do you tend to cancel the scheduled exercise time)?

2. For the mommies: Think of something that you loved to do before you became a mom that you could re-integrate into your life and into your child's (or children's) life. How easy or difficult would that be for you to do? What would make it possible?

3. How might you advocate for yourself if you felt you were not being supported by your faculty to balance home life and work life?

References

Bird, J. (2003). *Work-life balance defined—What it really means!* Retrieved from http://www.worklifebalance.com

Foster, T. (n.d).*Wellness defined.* Retrieved from http://css.loyno.edu/counseling/wcm-wellness-defined

Gerdes, E. P. (2003). Do it your way: Advice from senior academic women. *Innovative Higher Education, 27*, 253–275.

Jacobwitz, S. (2005). Chuck E. Cheese at noon: Adventures in parenting and higher education. In Bassett, R. (Ed.), *Parenting and professing: Balancing family work with an academic career* (pp. 133-140). Nashville, TN: Vanderbilt Press.

Letherby, G., Marchbank, J., Ramsay, K., & Shiels, J. (2005). Mothers and "others" providing care within and outside of the academy. In Bassett, R. (Ed.), *Parenting and professing: Balancing family work with an academic career* (pp. 204-216). Nashville, TN: Vanderbilt Press.

Myers, J. E., Sweeney, T. J., & Witmer, J. M. (2000). The wheel of wellness counseling for wellness: A holistic model for treatment planning. *Journal of Counseling and Development, 78,* 251-266.

Oxford Dictionaries Online (n.d.). Balance. Retrieved from http://
www.oxforddictionaries.com/definition/balance?region=us

Rieman, J. (2005). Tenure-track to mommy-track: In search of my scholarly self. In Bassett, R. (Ed.), *Parenting and professing: Balancing
family work with an academic career* (pp. 56-70). Nashville, TN:
Vanderbuilt Press.

Stockdell-Giesler, A., & Ingalls, R. (2007). Faculty Mothers. *Academe.*
93(4), 38-40. Retrieved from http://www.aaup.org/AAUP/pubsres/
academe/2007/JA/Feat/stoc.htm

Myers, J. E., & Sweeney, T. J. (2004). The Indivisible Self: An Evi-
dence-Based Model of Wellness. *Journal of Individual Psychology,*
60(3), 234-245.

Wolf-Wendel, L., & Ward, K. (2003). Future prospects for women faculty: Negotiating work and family. In Ropers-Huilman, B. (Ed.),
Gendered futures in higher education: Critical perspectives for change
(pp. 111-134). Albany, NY: State University of New York Press.

Chapter 9

Living in Two Worlds: Personal Perspectives in the Long-Distance Commuter Relationship

CAROL KLOSE SMITH AND ANNA VIVIANI

As non-traditional family lifestyles proliferate, the dual-career commuter couple has become more common, especially within higher education (Schliebinger, Henderson, & Gilmartin, 2008). The dual-career commuter couple has been defined as "a couple that has chosen to live apart and maintain homes in separate cities in separate geographic locations, with periodic visitation, for the purpose of equal career advancement for both members" (Rhodes, 2002, p. 398). Historically, a relationship is considered a dual-career commuter couple if only one member lives in the commuter home (versus the family home) at least 3 days per week (Anderson & Spruill, 1993). Interestingly, very little up-to-date research exists on this phenomenon, despite its growing prevalence.

Recent estimates indicated that approximately 3.6 million couples are currently in a commuter relationship (Conlin, 2009). Wolf-Wendel, Twombly, and Rice (2004) reported the average commuter couple as well educated and having a professional/executive career or being graduate students. In a now-classic study, Anderson and Spruill (1993) found that approximately half of all dual-career commuter couples have children and more than half have been married at least nine years. This demographic reflects relationships in various stages of family life: the younger couples trying to get started in their careers, couples with children, and more mature couples with adult children who are out of the home. In addition, this information reflects that women as well as men are pursuing professional and executive positions within their fields. As universities strive for increasing diversity, more dual-career commuter couples may develop to meet this need (Schliebinger, Henderson, & Gilmartin, 2008). Unlike other couples who may choose to live apart due to war, immigration, travel for work, or military service (Rhodes, 2002), individual members in dual-career commuter couples are pursuing career aspirations that require significant commitment, specific training, and considerable responsibility.

One type of commuting relationship that has received some research interest has been that of the dual-academic commuter relationship (van der Klis & Mulder, 2008; Wolf-Wendel, Twonbly, & Rice, 2004). Academic positions are competitive; therefore dual-career academic couples are frequently challenged when finding faculty positions within the same university or location. Historically, one individual within the couple (typically the female) chooses to take a less desirable job or opts not to work at all in order to support the career aspirations of the other person (Bergen, 2010a). Some authors have called this phenomenon the "captive spouse syndrome" describing the lot of those individuals who are unable to advance their careers, being geographically tied to one person's employment (Deitch & Sanderson, 1987).

Therefore, significantly, these dual-academic commuter couples have chosen to sustain independent homes in separate geographic regions in order to pursue their career goals (Rhodes, 2002; Schliebinger, Henderson, & Gilmartin, 2008). This choice signifies not only a change in the importance of satisfying careers for both partners in a parental/committed relationship, but also the advent and proliferation of internet use. Couples are now afforded the advantages of weathering periods of family separation with the use of technology. Software which offers face-to-face video conferencing using personal computers provides opportunities for consistent meaningful connections.

The Personal Side of Commuter Relationships

However, the story of the commuter couples is a personal story, involving everyday couples making the best of difficult situations. This chapter explores two stories of women who have chosen to pursue their career and educational goals while maintaining distance relationships. Both authors of this chapter have lived as the commuter in their relationships, so it is the aim of this chapter to infuse the somewhat limited literature on this topic with our own personal experiences in order to deepen our understanding of this type of relationship—and perhaps catch a glimpse of changing definitions of relationships and family in these non-traditional partnerships. Coauthor Carol Smith found herself wanting to become a counselor educator after 10 years as a licensed professional counselor. She writes:

> I was working as a counselor in the same town where my husband had a tenure-track position at the local university in a small, rural Midwestern town. There were not many opportunities for advancement in my workplace or in the area. I began to long for a more satisfying career, which, in my case, meant first obtaining a PhD in counselor education. The closest university that offered a competitive program was three hours away.

The term "trailing spouse" has been used in some academic circles to describe this phenomenon, while the platitude "bloom where you are planted" is used to encourage trailing spouses to do the best they can with their career within a given locale. However, at some point, for some couples, having one person not work, having them work at lower-paying jobs, or less satisfactory jobs, may no longer be economically or practically viable. The researchers, van der Klis and Karsten (2009), pointed out that the economic need for two-earner families, along with poor employment security, fluctuating housing markets, and regionalized employment opportunities, affect the prevalence of dual-career commuter couples. Even higher education faculty positions, once thought to be relatively stable, have been subject to job insecurity in recent times. Budget cuts, layoffs, and hiring freezes force faculty to seek new positions. A two-educator couple with one member facing unemployment may be forced to make difficult lifestyle choices in order to provide for themselves and their families. Specifically, one member may have to move to a different locale in order to continue as a professor thus creating a dual-career commuter couple, or to find a position outside of higher education. This circumstance has been the case for Carol, who now has academic appointment three hours from her family home, in another state. She writes:

Initially, my husband and I saw the decision to live apart while I worked toward the Ph.D. in counselor education as a temporary fix. I would take classes three-to-four days per week and return home every weekend. Upon my graduation, my husband and I would engage in a dual-academic search and "Poof" we would both be gainfully employed at institutions of higher education in close proximity. Unfortunately, this scenario did not play out. The dual-academic search ended with the decision that we either both live apart again and have career fulfillment or both live in the same community in which one of us would need to adapt to a less-than-satisfactory job outlook—which is part of what initially prompted me to get my Ph.D.

The decisions are not simple. For individuals who have invested a great deal of time and energy in their academic careers, settling for less, moving to another location, or changing careers are agonizing alternatives. The dual-career commuter couple lifestyle is qualitatively different from that of other dual-career couples, in part based upon characteristics such as the decision-making process, commute distance, work schedule, and the needs of the family members. Studies show that few couples thoroughly discussed the commuter lifestyle prior to engaging in it, and most did very little research regarding what would be involved (van der Klis & Mulder, 2008). Making a quick decision when a job offer was presented often accounted for this lack of careful consideration (Miller, 2009). This was not the case for coauthor Anna Viviani. She reports:

A great deal of conversation went into the decision for me to return to academia to pursue my doctoral degree; however, my husband and I were not prepared for the realities of academic life as a commuter couple. We had originally believed that a daily drive would allow completion of the program in a timely fashion. However, we quickly discovered this was not feasible and then needed to adapt quickly to the situation, thus engaging in a commuting relationship.

Furthermore, Bergen (2010a) reported that couples spent little time re-evaluating their choice. They also did not typically consult with other commuter couples prior to making the decision. Anna reports:

I had never known anyone who had tried to live a commuter lifestyle, so I had no idea how hard it would be.

Carol had a slightly different experience:

> Fortunately, I have known many other academic couples experience
> this same choice during their careers. It was not uncommon among my
> partner's colleagues that many academic couples chose to live apart to
> pursue their career, at least at some points within their academic lives.

For most, the decision to engage in a commuter lifestyle was simply
arrived at because it made sense if both partners were going to pursue
their professional goals. Carol says,

> Our decision to become a dual-career commuter couple went hand in
> glove with my decision to attend graduate school. I seriously consid-
> ered all choices, but I knew I wanted the learning dynamic of a resi-
> dential counselor education program. I lived in a rural location and
> decided it was necessary to move to a university community. The de-
> cision to pursue a Ph.D. was a challenge. Not only would I be under-
> taking a rigorous curriculum, but my husband would not be able to
> relocate due to his position in which he had the security of tenure. I
> had to decide if my goal was important enough to risk upheaval in our
> lives.

Even though travel is much easier than 50 years ago, distance still
plays into the quality of life for the dual-career commuter couple. Bergen
(2010a) found that the greater the distance involved and the longer the
time apart, the greater the stress on a dual-career commuter couple.
Greater distances also typically increase travel costs. In addition, increased distances tend to make it more difficult for commuting parents to
attend children's activities and to be actively engaged with the children
on a frequent basis. Long separations often lead to feelings of losing
touch with one another thus impacting relationships with other family
members such as children still living at home. For Carol, this was the
single hardest concern.

> While I was in the planning stages for selecting a Ph.D. program in
> counselor education, I knew I needed to be close to home. Distance
> played a large role in the decision. I was very fortunate that I had the
> choice of a solid variety of programs all within weekly commuting
> distance. In the end, I chose to commute home almost every weekend.
> As tiring as the constant driving can be, being together as a family is
> precious.

Literature has suggested that the length of marriage and the effectiveness of domestic arrangements already established within their home appear to be factors in the couples' satisfaction undertaking the commuting lifestyle. Rhodes (2002) reported that couples who had been married longer seemed to struggle less with such commuting. Rhodes attributed this decrease in interpersonal struggle in part to the couple's shared history and the fact that their chldren were most likely no longer in the home. However, younger couples (those under age 38 and married less than 13 years) experienced dual-career commuting differently. These couples were, in some ways, still creating their life together and building their relationships and roles as a couple and as parents. Hence individual members of these younger couples were more likely to experience resentment regarding perceived unfair burdens of childcare, increased responsibilities, and lack of respect for the time given to the family while the other spouse was away (Rhodes, 2002). With a fairly long marriage but with young children, Carol straddled the groups.

> Before I began commuting, I had been married for over 10 years. Our routines were pretty set as a couple. However, we did have young children. So I would come home on weekends and take care of everything I could to help with the daily parenting responsibilities my partner was encountering. I did all the shopping, laundry, cooking—basically anything that would help prepare for the next week. When the children were little this was exhausting for both of us.

The family dynamics of the dual-career-commuter relationship include: the division of labor within the relationship, the family life cycle, the distance traveled, and the presence of children. The division of labor in many of the commuter couples was found to be traditional with regard to gender. Women typically continue to have more household chores than men that are done on at least a daily or weekly basis (Bergen, Kirby, & McBride, 2007). In Anna's case:

> My husband took on the lion's share of the daily home tasks, with me supplementing on the weekends and breaks. I had to accept that I could not manage the traditional role of housewife.

Commuter couples are less likely to be concerned about societal norms and are more likely to be interested in occupational mobility (van der Klis & Mulder, 2008). Decreased role stress was also related to job commitment and satisfaction and the ability to compartmentalize home and work environments.

Research indicates that commuting-career couples enjoy increased professional opportunities, professional autonomy, and personal independence (Schliebinger, Henderson, & Gilmartin, 2008). Anna says:

> While we both felt the commuter lifestyle served a purpose, I found that spending time alone came naturally for me and freed my mind to focus on the goal at hand.

Commuter couples find that living apart provides them the needed time for meetings, classes, and the concentrated effort necessary to excel in their fields without the obligation of time dedicated to family. The level of focus and concentration gained while away from home enables academic productivity and decreased distractions during the work week. In addition, employment in an academic setting with a 9-month contract allows the couple to enjoy predetermined breaks for holidays as well as summers spent reconnecting with friends and family. They are then able to spend quality time with their spouse or family during the times they are in the family home. Anna says:

> As commuting continued, the "home" world took on greater meaning for me. It wasn't just the physical comfort of home, but mainly my connection to my husband and family. I took photos and other things from home to give the illusion of home away from home while commuting. My husband and I had specific times each day when we would phone each other, and there were sporadic text messages when something special would occur during the day. I found that while I am typically a social person, I wanted weekends spent quietly with my husband. The last thing I wanted to do was jump back in the car and drive anywhere. This proved difficult for my friends and family to deal with, as there were birthdays, holidays, and other family events and celebrations that I chose not to attend. There were many such sacrifices along the way.

It is a flexible academic schedule that allows the commuting situation to be a livable solution and may be a reason why this lifestyle is chosen more and more frequently among couples in higher education (Schliebinger, Henderson, & Gilmartin, 2008). Hence, the time couples spend apart is devoted to their career responsibilities and the time spent together is dedicated to each other and the relationship. Commuter couples who have this dedicated time may experience an increased appreciation of time together, of each other, and a decreased focus on interpersonal conflicts or arguments (Glotzer & Federlein, 2007). Commuting couples are then able to spend time together planning or engaging in leisure activities and completing communal household tasks such as shopping and general cleaning (Bergen, Kirby, & McBride, 2007). Those couples without children are also more likely to engage in social activities with friends and other family members.

Disadvantages of Commuting

While literature suggests many advantages of the dual-career commuting couple as discussed above, there are some obvious disadvantages: loneliness, financial problems, negative attitudes, increased family tension, decreased sexual satisfaction, missed family moments, and lack of a social life are several suggested in the literature. Bergen, Kirby and McBride (2007) point out that marriages in which the female partner in a marriage commutes are often more strongly criticized by their social networks for their choice due to societal expectations of women as caretakers. We both have things to say about our friends' reactions to our decisions. Anna says:

> Then there were the friends . . . both for and against this lifestyle, however temporary it would be. Many of the people I knew stated that pursuing the doctoral degree and a commuter lifestyle was not a reasonable goal. There were questions about our marriage and whether we were "having problems" because a reasonable person would not choose to live away from her spouse. There was a definite gender bias in many of the conversations I had with friends. Fortunately, I had the support of a few girlfriends who were willing to talk on the phone late when I was driving home, to help pass the time, or would send a funny email to remind me that they were cheering for my success.

Carol had a similar experience:

> One unanticipated aspect of being a commuter couple has been the reaction of my friends, family, and others within our lives, to the news of my living away from home. Those individuals who knew me well, as well as other academic couples in our circles, had very little diffi-

culty understanding the choice. However, I could see disapproval on the faces of some individuals within our social circles, although most did not address it openly.

Winfield (1985) noted that women who commute experienced greater criticism from their social contacts. Groves and Horm-Wingerd (1991) in their research on commuter couples found that many people incorrectly believe that when a couple decides to commute, it indicates a lack of commitment to the family and is likely the first step toward a divorce. Interestingly this expectation, noted nearly 25 years ago, still exists. In a culture which traditionally expects a woman in a marriage to subjugate personal goals for the sake of the family, women in commuting marriages are less socially acceptable and receive greater criticism than a commuting male member of the family (Bergen 2010a). For Carol this aspect was very true.

> In fact, many of my closest friends did wonder if this was just the first step toward dissolution of my marriage. Of course, only my very closest friends asked if my marriage was having difficulties. Those who did not know me as well personally would react with silence or a grimace. My partner also encountered many awkward comments. Individuals really did not know what to say. Actually, after the first few months of a solid case of homesickness, a new homeostasis was established. New routines, new patterns, and new roles were adopted and became more commonplace. While it is not my wish always to live a commuting lifestyle, I have come to an acceptance of the challenges and benefits this non-traditional family process has brought.

Perhaps the biggest disadvantage suggested in the literature was a lack of a professional support system in the academic environment (Rhodes, 2002). Since professional relationships are frequently built around informal bonding situations such as cocktails, dinners, or other social venues that typically occur on weekends, the dual-career commuting couple must often sacrifice the time needed to build these professional relationships (and, therefore, the relationships themselves) in favor of their families. Anna says:

> Relationships developed slowly in the academic world for me. This was in part due to my reserved nature, but also due to the knowledge that the living arrangement was temporary. Having moved many times

in my life, I was initially hesitant to develop deep relationships that might not be portable when the commuting stopped.

Carol found:

> As a commuting student I did not feel much pressure to build professional relationships with other students. It came naturally since we were all taking classes together and working on projects. However, once I became a faculty member the expectations did change for professional involvement. The culture of the department and how much informal collegiality it expected did change. This became a new balancing act between time with colleagues and time spent away from the office. I am pretty cognizant of the time I spend at work and away from the office. I want to have a presence in the office, yet I find myself needing time with family as well. Having understanding colleagues has been a wonderful support and extremely helpful in my personal situation.

Commuter couples with children experience more stress related to loss of time with family and trying to find that balance between work and family (Duncan & Phillips, 2010). Carol says:

> There is a certain level of disconnection that occurs. Involvement in my children's academic and extracurricular lives is sharply reduced to activities that happen during the weekend. And while various avenues of communication do exist to keep us in touch, we both feel, at times, a lack of support and companionship as a result of the distance during the week. There is just less time to be with family, to engage in leisure activities, and complete household tasks.

Since the division of responsibilities for the children changes dramatically for a dual-career commuter couple, one individual within the relationship may find he or she is "essentially taking on the role of a single parent" (Rhodes, 2002, p. 399). Limited research has shown the commuting parent may struggle with a variety of feelings including guilt, isolation, stress, and role frustration. Carol says:

> All said, my biggest personal challenge has been the guilt of choosing to work away from my family in order to pursue professional goals. The feeling of constantly balancing family and work obligations is always a challenge. It is the feeling of constantly not living up to the

expectations of either work or family that leaves me feeling inadequate. Each commitment made is not as simple as a drive across town to attend that quick little meeting or that mid-week basketball game. Planning and negotiating simple daily events is the norm for my commuting relationship. While the academic life has its own set of demands, though, it does give me some flexibility on how and when to meet the challenges of the position. However, it is always a balancing act to meet departmental responsibilities, fulfill obligations to students, and to flourish as a family with a commuting parent.

While these commuter parents may be excellent role models and offer their children quality time, many struggle with missing the little daily moments (Rhodes, 2002). For Carol:

> I know this may sound incredibly silly, but I remember clearly missing Halloween. For our family, this is a big event. After much consultation with my children, I sew the costumes they and I dream up. Missing this was, and is, still very hard. While I still make the costumes I have missed the big day. Sometimes pictures and Skype are just not the same thing. It is those moments when, as committed as I am to my career, I challenge myself on the choice I made to commute.

The stress of parenting among commuting couples appears to be relieved, at least in part, by the fact that the commuting couples have clear expectations of child care responsibilities based on who is living in the family home with the children. In Anna's case, her responsibilities for caring for her mother presented greater challenges than parenting her daughter.

> My mother struggled with my decision to live a commuter lifestyle. My mother was accustomed to being able to spend a week or two with me whenever she wanted. However, with the commuter lifestyle and my work on the doctoral degree, my mother was no longer able to spend extended amounts of time with me in either location. My mother commented many times that she felt cut off from me and couldn't understand why I had made this choice. Additionally, during the four years I commuted, my mother had four heart attacks. Since I was my mother's only support, I had to balance home, commuter life, academic demands, with my responsibility to assist her.

In a study examining commuter relationship from a strength-based perspective, Rispens, Jehn, and Rexwinkel, (2010) found that although some commuting couples experience a certain level of frustration in their marriage relationship, many report much higher levels of career satisfaction. Intuitively, this makes sense, given the choices they made to pursue careers and the sacrifices inherent in the commuting lifestyle. Rethinking the traditional caretaking roles is one way that commuter couples have been able to find greater satisfaction with their commuter lifestyle (Rhodes, 2002).

Given the lack of research into the commuter lifestyle, it is interesting that the negative opinions of family and friends related to the dual-career commuter lifestyle can have profound effects. Societal expectations that a married couple live together can complicate dual-career commuter couples' lives (Bergen 2010a). Often, when women are the commuting partners within relationships, they have to endure extensive questions from family and friends about the quality of the marriage and the couples' dedication to it, as well as their commitment to parenting. Bergen (2010b) pointed out that many see the female commuting in the dual-career commuter lifestyle as incongruent with a family. However, commuter relationships require commitment and trust from both partners. Both must value their own and the other's careers as well as their marriage.

Conclusion

Dual-career commuting couples seem to experience many challenges within their personal lives. Deciding to become a commuting family or couple may be a short-term solution or even a permanent lifestyle choice for some. Regardless, it is not easy living in the two worlds of home and career. While the challenges are well-documented, the benefits of enjoying fulfilling career lives have not been given much consideration in the literature. More research is needed to assist in the understanding of the unique dynamics of commuting families in the current economic and political climate especially since some societal values have changed dramatically.

Questions for Reflection

1. Achieving balance between work and personal life is always a challenge. In what ways do you find balance in your life?

2. How would others in your life react to the decision to engage in a commuter relationship? How would you handle these reactions?

References

Anderson, E. A., & Spruill, J. W. (1993). The dual-career commuter family: A lifestyle on the move. *Marriage and Family Review, 19,* 131-147.

Bergen, K. M. (2010a). Accounting for difference: Commuter wives and the master narrative of marriage. *Journal of Applied Communication Research, 38*(1), 47-64. doi: 10.1080/00909880903483565

Bergen, K. M. (2010b). Negotiating a "questionable" identity: Commuter wives and social networks. *Southern Communication Journal, 75*(1), 35-56. doi: 10.1080/10417940902951816

Bergen, K. M., Kirby, E., & McBride, M. C. (2007). "How do you get two houses cleaned?": Accomplishing family caregiving in commuter marriages. *Journal of Family Communication, 7*(4), 287-307. doi: 10.1080/15267430701392131

Conlin, J. (2009, January 4). Living apart for the paycheck. Retrieved online August 29, 2011, from http://www.nytimes.com/2009/01/04/fshion/04commuter.html

Deitch, C. H., & Sanderson, S. W. (1987). Geographic constraints on married women's careers. *Work and Occupations, 14,* 616-634.

Duncan, S., & Phillips, M. (2010).People who live apart together (LATs)–how different are they? *The Sociological Review, 58* (1), 112-134.

Glotzer, R., & Federlein, A. C. (2007). Miles that bind: Commuter marriage and family strengths. *Michigan Family Review, 12,* 7-31.

Groves, M. M., & Horm-Wingerd, D. M. (1991). Commuter marriages: Personal, family, and career issues. *Sociology & Social Research, 75*(4), 212-217.

Miller, R. G. (2009). Wither thou goest: The trailing spouse or commuter marriage dilemma. In K. C. Wieseman & M. H. Weinburgh (Eds.), *Women's Experiences in Leadership in K-16 Science Education Communities, Becoming and Being.* Springer Science. doi: 10.1007/987-90-481-2239-4_8

Rhodes, A. (2002). Long-distance relationship in dual-career commuter couples: A review of counseling issues. *The Family Journal: Counseling for Couples and Family, 10*(4), 398-404. doi: 10.1177/106648002236758

Rispens, S., Jehn, K., & Rexwinkel, R. (2010). *Asymmetry in dual career and commuting couples.* Paper presented at the 23rd Annual International Association of Management Conference, Boston, MA.

Schiebinger, L., Henderson, A. D., & Gilmartin, S. K. (2008). Dual-career academic couples: What universities need to know. Michelle R. Cayman Institute for Gender Research, Stanford University. www.stanford.edu/group/gender/ResearchPrograms/DualCareer/DualCareerFinal.pdf

van der Klis, M., & Karsten, L. (2009). The commuter family as a geographical adaptive strategy for the family-work balance. *Community, Work & Family, 12*(3), 339-354.

van der Klis, M., & Mulder, C. H. (2008). Beyond the trailing spouse: The commuter partnership as an alternative to family migration. *Journal of Housing and the Built Environment, 23,* 1-9. doi: 10.1007s/10901-007-9096-3

Winfield, F.E. (1985). *Commuter marriage: Living together, apart.* New York: Columbia University Press.

Wolf-Wendel, L., Twonbly, S. B., & Rice, S. (2004). *The two-body problem: Dual-career couples hiring practices in higher education.* Baltimore: Johns Hopkins University Press.

Section Three

Cultural and Individual Identity

Chapter 10

Transitions: A Woman on the Move!

CHRISTINA M. ROSEN

My career has included several transitions and in each one I have never been alone. Many people have inspired, supported, guided, challenged, mentored, loved, and stood by me as I struggled, faced doubts and fears, and found success. While other people were negative and discouraging, my fears nearly stopped me. My usual outlook, however, is that of an optimist, and as such I learned to trust, to stay the course, and to remain open so I could grow and become the person I am today.

The first phase of my journey that focuses on my mid-adulthood and the decision to make a career transition from counselor to counselor educator, includes overcoming obstacles, taking chances, letting go of fear, and listening to my dreams. This transition has an important prelude and without this background, the decision seems like an isolated event when, in reality, it was about overcoming a lifetime of negative messages. My friends and family would say I have strong determination and can persevere in spite of obstacles. I am a hard worker and a spiritual person, who always searches for the solutions or answers, and enjoys giving back. These qualities came from my parents, who often instilled in us kids to give 110% and to be of service to our whole community. Of course, my experience is not unique. Everyone's decisions regarding coupling and career paths are influenced by generational family messages, patterns, and themes, as well as community experiences and interaction with friends (Bowen, 1985; Conyne, & Cook, 2004; Holland, 1992; Mitchell & Krumboltz, 1996; Medved, & Graham, 2006).

Prelude to Deciding to Return to Graduate School

At age 37 and in middle adulthood, my developmental task was to become either generative or stagnant (Erikson, 1959; Hill & Yeung, 1999). Accordingly, my choices were to continue to grow and contribute to the next generation or to become content (Erikson, 1959; Hill & Yeung, 1999). I was restless since I had achieved career success and because my developmental task and dream of being married and having children had not been achieved. I wondered if this was all there was to do (Erikson, 1959; Hill & Yeung, 1999). I was living in the so-called middle class and was seen as successful.Therefore, friends and family were initially confused when I decided to make a transition from my long and successful career as a Licensed Professional Clinical Counselor (LPCC) and become a counselor educator. Frankly, I was also confused, which is why the decision came slowly, as I considered the possibility of going against logic and giving up my sense of security. As I faced the naysayers, I remembered the old, haunting messages from my elementary school teachers and at times from my parents because of their fears. However, I also had many supporters including my parents and brothers, once their fears abated. In addition, I learned to listen to both my spiritual and intuitive side, and I took a leap of faith.

The following stories give the reader a fuller appreciation of how this decision was a leap of faith and a major accomplishment for me. They illustrate the beginning of my journey and the potential obstacles that could have permanently derailed me at any time if not for my resilience. Furthermore, after each significant turning point there is a segment discussing my attempts to integrate my experiences and lessons as a counselor educator.

Overcoming Obstacles

Hearing negative messages, feeling discouraged, but being self-determined, began in elementary school and continued through high school, and into college. In K-12, nearly every report card or teacher-parent conference stated that I was lazy and not working up to my potential even though I studied for hours every night, completed all my homework, and rewrote many assignments several times. Later, college professors often commented on my lack of writing skills. Complicating matters was the fact that my parents did not experience me as lazy, yet they also believed that the teachers would not lie, which led to arguments between my mom and me as she tried to help me reach my potential. In school I was a polite and shy kid who made sure everyone liked me. In class, I would answer the teachers' questions correctly and, since I had a full understanding of the material presented, they saw me as smart. However, in class if I had to do something aloud or quickly, my performance was poor, especially in reading, writing and spelling skills. During elementary school, I went to speech therapy because I had a speech impediment. I also received hearing tests often because of my frequent earaches. However, I never required tubes in my ears. Since I performed orally so well in class, the teachers often thought I was not working up to my potential; they thought I was lazy and not pushing myself in reading and writing.

During grades K-12, and then throughout my undergraduate education and on into my master's degree, I did not fit the image of a student with a disability, yet I had an undiagnosed problem. I was resilient and succeeded without its being detected for several reasons. First, I was able to perform within reasonable standards. Second, I had the ability to compensate: my high verbal intelligence and strong comprehension skills enabled me to master the material. Third, my agreeable personality allowed me to cooperate with my teachers and adapt. Finally, my struggles were mostly with the mechanics of written expression, and oral mastery of certain words and sounds. Therefore, my disability remained unidentified until my two graduate internship site supervisors confronted me. Until that point, teachers tended to focus more on my low writing ability versus my high comprehension, and therefore perceived me as not working hard enough—except for my graduate professors who understood my comprehension ability. My final grades were consistently high.

As a result of my childhood school experience, I now emphasize to my counseling students the importance of staying curious and exploring any such discrepancy they notice in their clients. It is vital to avoid labels such as *lazy*, but instead to explore clients' circumstances and strengths from every aspect of their life if possible. I challenge my students to see their clients from developmental, holistic, and ecological points of view and to explore every potential influence on those clients' lives. I do this by using case scenarios and posing questions such as: "What else could be going on for the client?" and, "What does this mean for the client and the family considering their circumstance, ability, culture and environment?" In addition, I ask students to consider clients' strengths in each situation and to evaluate their own strengths in working with them. I remind students that each of us has resources or strengths that we can use to face challenges and demonstrate resilience.

My Strengths

Success came from compensating throughout my education and work life. I have compensated through perseverance, hard work, loyalty, dedication, and the ability to collaborate with others. Through my parents and my life experiences, I have learned to take risks and advocate for myself. I am devoted to people, organizations, and my own dreams. I have a strong sense of curiosity and determination. I have come to understand the value of learning lessons and facing challenges in spite of naysayers, fears, and discouragements. I have found my voice, gratitude, and my intuition. I have come to trust my spirituality, to trust people to support me, to face feelings of shame, and to be humble. I found mentors that have challenged and guided me. I learned the value of not hiding my disability but also not wearing it on my sleeve. Instead, I now own the impact it has on me, and continue to learn to manage and accommodate it. I have learned: *I* am not my disability; I *have* a disability. That is, I am not flawed, but I need accommodation. I have learned to embrace my imperfections.

In high school, I had my first lesson in the value of self-advocacy and finding my voice by not giving people in authority automatic power over my future; instead, I learned to negotiate and speak for myself. Of course, at the time, I did not know or understand that that was to be a lesson. My high school counselor told me I could not attend college, and that I would never survive two weeks there. Therefore she scheduled all my junior and senior courses in the vocational school curriculum. This was supposed to deny me entry to any academic college-bound courses. Even though I felt deeply discouraged and confused, I decided to take matters into my own hands and talk to a teacher of the college-bound courses. This courage came from my parents who were leaders of several community organizations. They taught me that I could do anything if I worked hard enough and put my mind to it. Without the knowledge of my parents or the school counselor, and with much trepidation, I asked the teacher for permission to take her college-bound class. I spoke about my love of the subject and made a deal with her. I promised that after the first 4 weeks, if I could not keep up, I would drop the class. To my counselor's surprise, I earned a high grade in that class. What the counselor did not count on, but my parents knew about, was my strong work ethic and self-determination that helped me to succeed. From this I learned not to let others decide my success; this was not the last time I would face this challenge and overcome it.

This experience and future experiences taught me the importance of taking chances as well as having a voice, being courageous, developing assertiveness skills, and being resilient. I discovered through this and subsequent experiences the power of advocating for self and others in a professional manner through being assertive and collaborative. As a counselor educator approaching promotion and tenure, I continue to learn this lesson. I have faced new experiences that require new levels of advocacy; I have learned to take risks and to ask for help as an assistant professor. As a mentor, supervisor and professor, I have modeled and taught students, supervisees and new faculty the importance of professional advocacy and assertiveness instead of complaining, whining or using hostile communication. My students are challenged to think about the following: (a) What are their needs? (b) How are they communicating their needs to me and others? (c) What are their expectations of others? (d) What are they willing to do for themselves? and (e) If they were "wearing the other person's shoes," how would their communication be perceived by the other person?

Finding Support

After receiving a successful grade in the college-bound course, my thoughts were, *I could go to college, I will show my high-school counselor!* In hindsight I was challenging myself to see what I was made of, to imagine what I was capable of, and to prevent anyone from foreclosing my future. Therefore, without my parents' knowledge, one day I mustered up the strength to ignore those doubting messages from teachers and the school counselor and asked to be in the college-bound course. This strength came from a nagging sensation (my spirit) and a realization that no harm would come from my asking. I think I intuitively understood on some level the importance of not letting others determine my future. Furthermore, I knew I could trust my parents to support me. After all, they advocated for us three kids and for children in the community, particularly in the arena of sports and leadership opportunities. In addition, I had learned to listen to my spirit, which said, *Yes, you can! Yes, you can at least ask.* Therefore, I went to my vocational school counselor and asked about colleges. She was extremely supportive! She showed me the several colleges that I was eligible for and explained the process of applying. She recognized my positive attitude, my determination, and my passion. She also listened well to my dreams and desires and did not focus on my fear or my "lack of aptitude." Without her vision and support, I would not have applied to or received admission to my local university. I learned to keep searching for support and not let one person's negative opinion determine my future.

As I expected, my parents did support my college aspirations but not without some worry. Because our nation was at the tail end of the deep recession of the '80s, my family like many others had financial struggles. Therefore, the idea of my having enough skills to support myself in a professional job was especially important to my dad. My grandparents were happy that I was going to college to meet a man and get married! Early in my college life, I transferred from my local university to a college out of state, also changed my major. Intuitively, I knew it was necessary to make these changes if I wanted to survive three more years of college. This knowledge came as my body was telling me what I did not really know or understand until much later. I was under so much stress that I was developing an ulcer at age 18. I was simultaneously studying psychology and accounting when I discovered that while I was indifferent to accounting, I felt drawn to psychology. I asked my friends what I did well and naturally everyone said, "You are great at listening and helping us solve our problems." It would be seven more years before I intellectually *and* logically understood what my intuitive self had already grasped: that with my disability, accounting was the wrong degree program. From that experience, I learned to listen to the signals that my body sends me and to heed my intuitive voice.

This transfer meant that at 18—for the first time in my life—I was leaving my home. According to Erikson's (1959) developmental model, I was in the transition from late adolescence to young adulthood. I was striving to be independent and find my identity separate from my family by challenging their values, beliefs, and traditions. I was scared and full of doubt, yet I listened to my spirit that said, *Yes, you can leave home and develop new friendships*. Although leaving home may not seem like a big deal in today's society, back then our country was not so mobile, and it was not very common in my family.

Transferring to an out-of-state college was a positive step since my stomach problems stopped, and I eventually earned my BA with more credits than necessary. Learning many life lessons and overcoming many challenges, I demonstrated my resilience. I was victorious in spite of my high school counselor's initial lack of faith in me. No one could tell me that I could not follow my dreams and succeed! Amazingly, I graduated with my disability still undetected because I was able to continue to compensate without requesting accommodation, aided by a comprehension rate of 98%. It took another 3 years before someone in graduate school would suspect my disability.

Although I paid a price for my resilience in college, it was worth it. I was exhausted; therefore, I took a year off between undergraduate and graduate school—a great decision. I was then able to begin working as a senior child care worker with emotionally abused adolescents. Both my clients and my two supervisors were very influential. They taught me the value of courageous self-discovery. They believed in my compassion, leadership, and relationship skills before I did. They challenged me to accept my mistakes and to listen to my own ideas. They assisted me by understanding my fears and my need to be perfect, which stemmed from past messages regarding being lazy.

After my year of rest, I applied for a program leading to the master of arts in rehabilitation counseling. Once again I graduated early with more credits than I needed, while working and attending school full time. Also, I developed relationships with people (who continue to be in my life today) who could challenge me to see my weakness and whom I could trust to be honest and genuine. I continue to count on their support. They understood my drive and my intelligence long before I did. They inspired and motivated me to find courage.

As a counselor educator, I impress on students the importance of remembering that counselors are not the experts on their clients; their clients are experts on themselves. Counselors cannot tell a client what the client is able or not able to do or achieve. Instead, counselors support, guide, and challenge clients, supporting them in facing their challenges and beginning to understand themselves. I teach students to step back, listen to the internal strengths of each client, and then inquire about external resources while being supportive. I challenge students through experiential activities to understand their own resources as they face their own challenges as students. I encourage them to find mentors, to learn how to listen to their intuitive self and dreams. Further, I urge them to recognize they have control of their future. I empower students to slow down the counseling or supervision process and discern for themselves what is in their best interest by understanding their own resources, needs, and challenges. After reaching out to others and listening to their input, they should then reflect on the next step in their decision-making process.

Being Challenged and Almost Losing My Dream

The last semester of my master's degree was the first time I ever confronted a professor about a grade. I remember being angry with him, thinking he gave me B on a paper, and this was my final grade. There were other B's in my history, but this B really felt personal. I thought he was being unfair; I had performed well in class! So I decided to advocate for myself and speak to him about the grade. In a matter-of-fact voice he said, "Tina, I hope no one ever meets you just through writing. I hope they are able to meet you in person; you have a lot to offer." I walked away not understanding that remark until many years later. Moreover, both of my internship site supervisors had just challenged me about having a disability because of the discrepancy they saw between my writing and my speaking abilities.

I sat there listening with fears, doubts and uncertainty about my future. I saw all my dreams disappear—at least that was my fear. In that meeting, every negative past message came flooding in. I felt unable to think or understand. Yet I needed to maintain a professional posture; therefore, I decided to have courage, to stay and to listen, instead of being reactive and leaving to protect myself. To my surprise, I heard compassion, acceptance, understanding, and a term I had never heard before. As I started to breathe and support myself, I heard that I had a learning disability. I asked if I could be tested, but at that time I was told testing was not available for adults. I was relieved that I couldn't be tested because now I could graduate without my professors' knowing that I was stupid. Can you believe? I thought having a learning disability meant being stupid. To my surprise, when I shared this event with my closest friend she was not surprised. Her response was, "Yeah, I knew you were like Einstein and probably had dyslexia." I felt lost, vulnerable, and scared. How did people know that I had a disability and I not know? How was I still graduating? I graduated with the realization that good counseling skills are not always accompanied by great writing skills. I graduated with a mixture of feelings: lucky, accepted, empowered, but a little discouraged. I thought I had hit my career ceiling in education.

In my many roles as a counselor educator, when students appear to be reactive or impulsive, I try to wear their shoes, thinking about their situations and circumstances to see if I can understand their reaction. Then I challenge them to look at their response, to think through how they would like me to respond in return. For example, students often think they should reply quickly to e-mail, instead of taking a moment to think about the best way to respond. Therefore, when they write an e-mail that could be easily misunderstood, I challenge them think about how a potential employer might read their message. Then I have them imagine how the potential employer might respond to the e-mail, thereby helping the students begin to "wear the employer's shoes."

Transitioning from Student to Professional Counselor

After graduating from my master's program, I felt alive and passionate. I was still single and dating then. I wanted to put my skills to work, have fun, and be a bit more adventurous. The job market was still tight, and my spirit suggested I should obtain a doctorate. I discounted that idea believing I was not smart enough, needed a break from college life, did not have enough money, and that the sacrifice would be overwhelming. Nevertheless, I enjoyed research and writing even though I struggled with both and, because of that, obtaining a doctorate did not make sense. So I buried that idea. In addition, I was feeling pressure from my family to get married. According to Erikson (1959) and my culture, I was in disharmony by being in my late 20s, single, and on a career path instead of being focused on getting married or on both. My dream was to be a successful counselor, financially stable, traveling around the world, and married with kids—in that order.

As a counselor educator, I help students envision their dreams by having them focus on their future as counselors. When faced by challenges that have the potential to interrupt or interfere with their studies, I am supportive, but realistic about the impact such difficulties have on them. As necessary, I recommend that they obtain support. One such way is self-support, to guide them in exploring their priorities and being realistic when balancing their needs and time. Moreover, while teaching a course, I attempt to keep in mind the many stressors that our students have to manage. I attempt to bridge students' reading with applications, giving them an immediate awareness of the value of the material or skills. Furthermore, while discussing the importance of self-care, I model self-care. I check in with students to see how they are progressing. I remind them to manage their time so as to include fun and laughter.

I was thrilled to get my first counseling job. I was on fire, ready to take on the world as a novice counselor! In doing so, I met another very dear and close friend who taught me a lot about self-care. However, after 9 months at this job, I became disillusioned. My dreams were challenged, and I doubted my career choice. Uncertain that this was the right organization or career, I quit my job because of perceived ethical and value-related conflicts that I could not resolve. In addition, my caseload was mainly children from alcoholic homes with active addiction, which meant the children were powerless over effecting any change, and so I felt the need to work directly with the parents. Quitting was a leap of faith because I did not have another job waiting for me, and the economy was still in recession. My mind focused on many "What ifs." However, I meditated, networked, and stayed open by focusing on the solution and not the problem. Later in life, I understood my first counseling job was not a good person-environment fit (Bronfenbrenner, 1979; Dawis, 2002; Tang & Russ, 2007; Savickas, 2002; Super 1972). Upon reflecting, I realized my need both to advocate in the work place for professional and personal values, and to work for an agency that embraces those values.

After several months of working on my disillusionment, fears, and blues, I was able to obtain another counseling position. I took my time and asked myself hard questions. This position was working in a community mental health agency specializing in substance abuse clients and their family members. Subsequently, the state upgraded its licensure laws for professional counselors. This required additional college credit, which meant I had to return to college for an Advanced Counseling Certificate. I was in the process of finishing those courses, and had just completed the exam for the highest certification as a chemical dependency counselor in that state, when a week later, my father suddenly died. I remember being in the funeral procession wondering how I would finish my course work. Who would help my mom? These worries quickly faded because of the support of my dear friends and understanding professors.

As a result of receiving such compassion, I attempt to give the same type of compassion to my students and co-workers. I try to balance this compassion with accountability in that I listen, support, and challenge them to grow. Further, I encourage students to evaluate their personal demands with their school demands and, as necessary, communicate their needs to their professors. This allows the student to make an informed decision concerning a course versus feeling isolated or misunderstood. I believe this is an important professional skill for the students to develop because as counselors they need to navigate between professional and personal life.

Staying the Course

Interestingly, I almost did not learn this lesson. At the onset of my application process for the certificate program, I became fearful and assumed that I would be denied admission to a program because of my low Graduate Record Examination (GRE) scores, even though my grade point average (GPA) was nearly 4.0. As I started the process of applying, I began remembering every past negative message and experience. Therefore, I nearly convinced myself that I would be rejected. I pushed past those messages and fears with the support of my friends, my spiritual beliefs, and my self-determination. I began to challenge myself and face my fears. I moved past them by journaling and art work as well as having many conversations with friends. After I applied and before receiving official notification, I anxiously called the chair of the program and asked to be accepted on probationary basis. I explained why. The chair granted my request on one big condition: I had to be tested for my disability so that in the future I could receive appropriate accommodation. And, even though I felt fear and heard all the negative messages again, I managed that fear through self-talk, meditation, and conversations with friends and decided to trust the process. Finally, I was tested and diagnosed with *written expressive learning disability*, which was later changed to *dysphonic dyslexia*. Suddenly my self-image changed. Instead, of being lazy and stupid, I was a creative, hard worker who had become successful by compensating.

This pattern would repeat itself, about five years later, with slight differences, when I applied for a doctoral program. The difference was that I already knew about my disability. But I did not know the process of using or obtaining accommodation. So when I applied for my doctoral program, I wrote a letter and called the department chair. I wanted to make sure the faculty knew that my GRE scores were not a reflection of my ability. Because of my late diagnosis, I had not used accommodation in my master's program; therefore, I wanted to be accepted on a probationary basis. In hindsight, I realized that I probably did not need to take this extra step, especially since I was applying to the same department where I had earned my master's degree. I had a solid GPA and reference letters; however, I also felt the need to advocate for myself. Because of this I still wonder if my acceptance was because of my ability or my disability.

As a counselor educator, my experience in applying for admission to both the certificate and doctoral program has influenced my course structure, advising, and admission decisions. My syllabi include various assignments geared towards different learning styles and abilities. Nearly all my courses include quizzes, experiential activities, a skill-related activity, and a written assignment. Students are able to choose where and when to take the quizzes, and then take them online. They are typically given a 12-hour window to take a quiz with two minutes given to deal with each question. Experiential activities include group work and a presentation. The skill portion includes role-plays or group leadership activities, and the written assignment includes blogging, and/or a paper. In addition, I tend to recognize any potential discrepancy between in-class and out-of-class performance, as well as between comprehension and writing ability. If I find a discrepancy, I discuss it with the student and speak about possible testing and/or tutoring. As part of the admission process, I try to recognize any potential discrepancy with the application, or listen for colleagues' awareness of a discrepancy. I then advocate for students who need accommodation.

Mid-life Transition and Following the Dream

My mid-life transition actually started when I was in my mid-30s and left a job that I enjoyed to pursue professional growth and more challenges. In doing so I learned that I place a high value on growing and achieving my professional dreams. By 1995 I was living my dream! I was a successful counselor and a supervisor. I felt empowered and great! Then my agency started a transition; as a result I was not promoted and became discouraged and confused. I tried to advocate for myself. However, I did not understand that my professional goals were no longer in alignment with the agency in transition. That is to say, there was no longer a good person-environment fit. After much deliberation, I moved to another agency with a heavy heart; I had felt supported, cared for, and had been working with a great group of people. However, I needed to grow and be challenged. My goals were to be a supervisor, integrate spirituality into my counseling sessions, and develop more programs. This was a difficult, scary time and I felt self-resistant, but I achieved resiliency and overcame this resistance. This was ultimately a good decision for me.

My new job was at a semi-private practice where I initially set up a counseling office— something I had never done before. Eventually a director was hired leaving me to focus on providing counseling, consultation, retreats, prevention, and student supervision. I was challenged and loved it! After 2 years or so, I became an instructor, which I found exciting. I felt passionate and energized when teaching. According to Erikson's (1959) developmental stages, I was on track even though I was still single. I had settled into life and was achieving my developmental tasks as I transitioned into middle adulthood. I felt very content again. And then a new challenge arose after my supervisee (a student) invited me to talk on a panel for the local chapter of Chi Sigma Iota. I felt both thrilled and nervous since I was returning to campus after nearly 8 years.

As soon as I stepped onto campus again, I felt a strong pull to stay. My spirit jumped for joy, and I remembered my desire and past conversations about obtaining my doctorate. I also began remembering those old negative messages and felt internal resistance to change. Nevertheless, I saw the excited faces of the students! I appreciated their eagerness to understand the world as a professional counselor. The urge to be in academia filled every cell of my body, and yet I felt fear, doubt, and confusion as I asked myself, *Why change*? I was developmentally where I was supposed to be in middle-adulthood. Even more important, I felt great, both emotionally and cognitively. I had faced many of my fears, except this big one: dealing with my disability in an academic setting. I was not even sure I needed to! I felt at ease and at rest, *Why take on more*? I thought. Over time, the discernment process (dreams, meditations, retreats, journaling, and conversations) clarified my desire to research the body, mind, and spiritual connection in counseling, especially related to substance abuse disorders. Therefore, six months later, I overcame my self-resistance and applied to a counselor education program. I knew I had the resiliency to succeed.

I overcome this self-doubt (resistance) by keeping an open mind and by exploring my resistance. I did this through listening to my desires. My desires and decisions culminated while working with clay during a spiritual retreat, followed by a writing activity and meditation exercises. After this I clearly understood that I would be okay in the doctoral program, and there was nothing to fear. I would not be alone and it was time for me to study the role of spirituality in counseling. Of course, the doubter in me was activated again once I received a mixture of support and concerns from family and friends. However, as I answered their questions with calmness and clarity, I knew it was time to move forward and face those negative messages! In addition, they heard my clarity, trusted my decision, and supported me throughout my program.

During my doctoral program, I discovered some excellent accommodation strategies for my disability—speech recognition software, reading software, and a special editor. I also met some wonderful people who provided support, guidance and acceptance. My acceptance of my disability was still in its initial stages so their support and challenges taught me to advocate for myself and come to terms with my disability. Even now, they continue to support me when I hit an obstacle. My family is relieved that I have graduated and have a career that supports my endless desire to learn. Furthermore, they were excited that a year after completing my dissertation I was married. They and I thought, *Wow, all my dreams are fulfilled*! At that time, he seemed to be a good match since we had many things in common and our values seemed in alignment. I felt happy and centered. I thought I was living my dream. However, as often happens, situations and people change. The marriage has ended—presenting yet another test for my resiliency.

In theory, I was in step with Erikson's (1959) developmental stages for mid-life transition. I evaluated my needs and life-style. I assessed my dreams left unfilled—and I filled them. I faced my fears and overcame obstacles. I grew and changed as a result. Now I attempt to give back through service, publications, teaching, mentoring, and sharing when appropriate.

As a professor, I teach my students that resistance to change is a normal part of the process of healing and growth (Marlatt & Donovan, 2007; Miller & Rose, 2009, Prochaska & DiClemente, 1992). After introducing this concept, I use an experiential activity with my students. One such activity is a role-play with me as the counselor and them as the clients. Another activity is having them recall the last time they attempted to change, and then discuss in small groups the feelings they experienced. Another activity is to have each student attempt to change something. They are allowed 11 weeks for this and are assigned to a small group to gain support while they are attempting to make the change. I make necessary connections to their readings with what they probably are experiencing. I do not use all of these activities in one course. However, in every course I highlight the importance of recognizing and supporting clients as they cope with resistance, change, and the discernment process. They learn to accept the fact that it is normal to have mixed emotions when facing major decisions and making changes—even positive ones.

As a counselor educator, I also share my professional and personal experiences with my students to teach them the importance of compassion, to help them clarify their belief systems and to encourage them to find trusted mentors and supervisors. Moreover, I teach the value of genuine, honest support of clients and the value of advocating for them, for themselves, and for the profession. In addition, I teach the importance of integrating developmental theories with career theories and counseling theories, while developing a good counselor-client relationship. For honest growth and healing to occur, a client needs to feel safe and understood. Therefore, those studying to be counselors need to understand their clients as deeply as possible in order to empower them to accept resistance, expect changes and practice advocacy. I remind counselors-in-training that when the going gets difficult, they have the resiliency to keep going and get through it.

Questions for Reflection

1. What quality relationships have you built to assist in your success?
2. How do you assess your person-environmental fit?
3. How do you identify when to use self-care and to advocate for yourself and your profession?

References

Bowen, M. (1985). *Family therapy in clinical practice.* Northvale, NJ: J. Aronson.

Bronfenbrenner, U. (1979). *The ecology of human development.* Cambridge: Harvard University Press.

Conyne, R., & Cook, E. (Eds.) (2004). *Ecological counseling: An innovative approach to conceptualizing person-environment interaction.* Alexandria, VA: American Counseling Association.

Dawis, R. V. (2002). Person-environment-correspondence theory. In D. Brown & Associates (Ed.), *Career choice development*(4th ed.) (pp. 427-465). San Francisco: Jossey-Bass.

Erikson, E. H. (1959). Identity and the life cycle: Selected papers [Monograph]. *Psychological Issue, 1(1, Pt. 1).*

Hill, M. S., & Yeung, W. J. (1999). How has the changing structure of opportunities affected transitions to adulthood? In A. Booth, A. C. Crouter, & M. J. Shanahan (Eds.), *Transitions to adulthood in a changing economy: No work, no family, no future?* (pp. 3-39). Westport, CT: Praeger.

Holland, J. L. (1992). *Making vocational choices* (2nd ed). Odessa, FL: Psychological Assessment Resources.

Marlatt, A., & Donovan, D. M. (2007). *Relapse prevention: Maintenance strategies in the treatment of addictive behaviors* (2nd ed.). New York: Guildford Press.

Medved, C. E., & Graham, E. E. (2006). Communication contradictions: (Re)Producing dialectical tensions through work, family, and balance socialization. In L. H. Turner & R. West, (Eds.), *The family communication sourcebook* (pp. 353-372). Thousand Oaks, CA: Sage.

Miller, W. R., & Rose, G. S. (2009). Towards a theory of motivational interviewing. *American Psychologist, 64*, 527-537.

Mitchell, L. K., & Krumboltz, J. D. (1996). Krumboltz's learning theory of career choice and counseling. In D. Brown, I., Brooks, & Associates (Eds.), *Career choice and development* (3rd ed.) (pp. 233-276). San Francisco: Jossey-Bass.

Prochaska, J. O., & DiClemente, C. C. (1992). Stages of change in the modification of problem behavior. In M. Hersen, R. M. Eisler, & P. M. Miller (Eds.), *Progress in behavior modification* (pp. 183-218). Sycamore, IL: Sycamore Publishing.

Savickas, M. L. (2002). Career construction: A development theory. In D. Brown & Associates (Ed.), *Career choice development* (4th ed.) (pp. 427-465). San Francisco: Jossey-Bass.

Super, D. E. (1972). Vocational development theory: Person, positions, and processes. In J. M. Whiteley & A. Resnikoff (Eds.), *Perspectives on vocational development* (pp. 17-31). Washington, DC: American Personnel and Guidance Association.

Tang, M., & Russ, K. (2007). Understanding and facilitating career development of people of Appalachian culture: An integrated approach. *Career development quarterly, 56*(1), 34-46.

Chapter 11

Fostering Inclusivity in Counselor Education for Culturally Diverse Women

CIRECIE WEST-OLATUNJI

Once I put pen to paper to write about the experiences of women of color in counselor education, I immediately had a visceral reaction to just thinking about my own reality as an African American woman. My heart began to pound as my heart rate increased, and my palms felt sweaty. Just thinking about the pervasiveness of microaggressions that I experience on a daily basis from colleagues and students caused me to pause and wonder, *Does anyone really want to hear this*? I hope that this chapter reaches out to women and men who strive to, not only better understand what it means to be a woman of color in counselor education, but who also want to take action to pave a smoother path toward including and involving women of color in the profession.

Over 150 years ago, Sojourner Truth gave her powerful *Ain't I a Woman?* speech at the Women's Rights Convention in Akron, Ohio, to raise issues of complex identities and cultural hegemony within the context of the women's movement. The concerns she raised then are still evident today for female faculty of color in counselor education. Issues, such as differential treatment from peers and lack of sufficient support, advocacy, and mentoring, are prevalent challenges for the profession. While more research is needed, the existing literature suggests that female faculty of color in counselor education receive few or no opportunities for collaborative research with their peers, are often alienated and isolated within their programs/departments, and experience low expectations from their colleagues (Allen, Epps, Guillory, Suh & Bonous-Hammarth, 2000; Arredondo, 2003; Bonner, 2004; Constantine, Smith, Redington, & Owens, 2008; Marbley, Wong, Santos-Hatchett, Pratt & Jaddo, 2011). Additionally, accounts from women of color report inadequate support mechanisms, insufficient advocacy, and poor or non-existent mentoring relationships with experienced faculty (Bradley, 2005; Kelly, 2008; Marbley et al., 2011; Turner, 2003). The purpose of this chapter is to provide a brief overview of the literature on the experiences of women of color in academia and more specifically, in counselor education. This information, along with anecdotal cases, is presented in order to raise awareness, spark discourse, and promote change within the profession.

Unique Concerns of Culturally Diverse Women

For culturally diverse women in counselor education, challenges to a successful career are often due to how others perceive them (Patitu & Hinton, 2003). While racial/cultural theories can explain some of their experiences, other factors, such as gender and social class, can influence how women of color navigate through academia (Bradley, 2005; Constantine et al., 2008; Marbley et al., 2011). The intersected identities of female faculty of color in counselor education make for complex interactions with their peers and students alike. This concept of *intersectionality* has its roots in Black feminist (or womanist) theory (Shields, 2008; West-Olatunji & Conwill, 2010). Womanist theorists assert that the dichotomous, oppositional labeling of identities stems from the Western/Eurocentric paradigm that is pervasive among scholars (Collins, 2000; Delgado Bernal, 1998; Dillard, 2006; Phillips & Stewart, 2008; Shields, 2008). Critical theorist, Patricia Collins (2000), has suggested that the interaction of multiple identities and oppressions has been a core element in the lived experiences of culturally marginalized individuals. Moreover, the complexity of intersected identities reflects multiple subordinate-group identities that result in dehumanizing experiences, causing both intrapersonal and interpersonal conflicts (Hairston, 2008; Purdie-Vaughns & Eibach, 2008).

Culturally diverse scholars comprise approximately 3% of faculty employed in research institutions (Bradley & Holcomb-McCoy, 2003) and female faculty account for only 24.4% of all full professors (American Association of University Professors, 2006). Issues of inequality are evident in the professoriate wherein many culturally diverse faculty are recipients of differential treatment from their peers, particularly in matters concerning tenure and promotion (Allen et al., 2000; Arredondo, 2003; Bonner, 2004; West-Olatunji & Behar-Horenstein, in press). Inadequate support systems and mentoring relationships have been cited as the main reasons given why faculty of color face inordinate challenges in the tenure and promotion process (Turner, 2003; West-Olatunji, 2005). Researchers have noted that African American female faculty, for example, are given fewer opportunities for collaborative research than their White female counterparts (Bradley, 2005; Bradley & Holcomb-McCoy, 2003).

In contrast, Asian/Asian American female faculty members are often perceived as being well represented in the academy and, thus, successful (Loo & Ho, 2006). However, little attention is paid to the context of their representation. Asian female faculty members are often overrepresented in entry level positions. Further, issues faced by Asian/Asian American female faculty are often invisible to their White peers thereby further contributing to the marginalization of this group of faculty (Marbley et al., 2011; Turner, 2002). This inadequate discourse about Asian/Asian American female faculty, in general, and, more specifically, counselor educators, has been attributed to White faculty members' perceptions of these female scholars as "model minority," showing that ethnic minorities can overcome discrimination and bias in the academy (Loo & Ho, 2006). Moreover, lack of adequate scholarship in this area has also been attributed to issues of racial/cultural identity in which many Asian/Asian American scholars become aware of their racial/cultural identity as they undergo marginalizing experiences on the road toward tenure (Shrake, 2006).

Traumatic Stress and Resilience in the Academy

Several scholars have suggested that there is a relationship between traumatic stress and systemic oppression (e.g., racism, classism, and other forms of institutionalized bias) (Carter, 2007; Paradies, 2006; Utsey, 1998). Pervasive acts of microaggression have been shown to correlate with psychological distress, such as depression, anxiety, interpersonal conflicts, high blood pressure, and hypertension (Din-Dzietham, Nembhard, Collins & Davis, 2004; Fang & Myers, 2001). For example, among African Americans, discrimination has been linked to lower levels of life satisfaction (Schultz et al., 2000), lower levels of mastery (Forman, 2003), and lower emotional wellbeing (Deitch et al., 2003). For women of color, systemic oppression can be experienced in a multidimensional manner. The concept of intersectionality of identity has been offered to articulate how women of color view and experience their multiplicity of identities as a whole (culture, class, gender, sexual orientation, etc.) rather than dichotomized "either-ors" (Brah & Phoenix, 2004; West-Olatunji & Conwill, 2010; Yuval-Davis, 2005). Thus, while their White female peers often encounter sexism, many women of color have additional layers of oppression to combat and resolve (Shields, 2008). Yet, women of color in counselor education can not only endure but also thrive.

While little has been written about resilience and coping in culturally diverse female faculty of color in counselor education, related scholarship in higher education provides a framework for discussion. For instance, the *Superwoman,* or Strong Black Woman, role has been suggested as a form of coping for female faculty of African descent whereby women demonstrate their ability to achieve as scholars and overcome the stereotyping and low expectations from peers (Woods-Giscombe, 2010). However, while the Superwoman role may serve as a form of self-preservation, this form of coping can cause relationship strain, stress-related health behaviors, and stress embodiment (Beauboeuf-Lafontant, (2007).

Other scholars have suggested that culturally marginalized individuals often choose not to disclose their stress symptoms as a sign of independence and control, particularly in the workplace setting (Hunn & Craig, 2009; Woods-Giscombe, 2010). Consequently, African American and other faculty of color can suffer from what has been labeled as *John Henryism*, reflecting on the Black folk hero who worked himself to death (Bennett et al., 2004). Moreover, it has been suggested that, for female faculty of color, disconnection can result from living in a society that devalues both their gender and their culture (Constantine et al., 2008; Marbley et al., 2010; Patitu & Hinton, 2003). Concerning Native American female faculty, issues of isolation, being treated as token members of their units, believing that their peers undervalue their scholarship, the lack of mentorship, and cultural hegemony have been cited (Tippeconnic Fox, 2008).

Several ways in which women of color cope in the academy have been proposed, such as (a) acts of resistance to challenge bias and inequity, (b) use of testifying and *testimonios*, and (c) the creation of strong support systems within the personal and professional realms (Burke, Cropper & Harrison, 2000; Flores & Garcia, 2009; Sulé, 2011). Active resistance to cultural and engendered dominance, the suppression of voice, and social positioning outside of circles of power and influence is a key element in coping for women of color in the academy (Flores & Garcia, 2009; Marbley et al., 2011; Shields, 2008; Sulé, 2011). That is to say, if no one will speak on behalf of women of color and advocate for opportunities toward success, then these women are left to advocate for themselves. Given their systematic marginalization within the academy, not speaking out will almost assuredly lead toward unsuccessful academic careers. Alternatively, speaking out often further marginalizes them among their peers but at least affords them an opportunity for their concerns to be heard (West-Olatunji & Behar-Horenstein, in press).

Another coping mechanism often used by women of color in higher education is to engage in expressive acts of resistance through testifying and testimonios (Sulé, 2011). Testifying has been defined as asserting, affirming, and reclaiming one's sense of humanity while resisting oppression (Burke et al., 2000). This powerful form of coping allows individuals to name the oppressive forces, thus making them explicit, and bear witness to pervasive acts of inequality (Heath, 2006). Many Latina faculty cope by creating space for *testimonios* that allow *mujeres* (women) to name themselves, record their history, and demonstrate the power to create their own destinies (Flores & Garcia, 2009). Testimonials can also help women to contextualize their experiences within their own sociohistorical realities (Williams, 2005).

Lastly, support networks have been useful tools for many women of color in the academy to overcome isolation and marginalization (West-Olatunji & Behar-Horenstein, in press). It is likely that emergent forms of depression, anxiety, and other manifestations of psychological distress are countered by creating buffers between the oppressive environment and one's sense of self (Williams, 2005).

Personal Narrative

During my first three of years as a junior faculty member, I experienced much of the marginalization that is reflected in the literature. Specifically, the students in my classes challenged my authority and complained about my teaching abilities, often giving me below par evaluations. The response from some senior faculty was to collude with the students in critiquing my teaching skills, creating an overall perception that I was underperforming. Conversely, another female faculty in the department had been experiencing less than stellar student evaluations but the discourse surrounding her scholarship was that she had extenuating circumstances in her personal life. Despite the fact that I had gotten divorced within the first eighteen months of taking this position—making me the parent of two adolescents who had been uprooted from their friends and family—and had become the sole breadwinner in my family, my colleagues rarely mentioned my circumstances, took steps to lighten my load, demonstrated empathy, or mediated students' perceptions of me as a scholar. Even more egregious, I was told by a counselor educator who had interviewed for a senior faculty position at my university that one of the senior faculty in my department had confidentially shared the opinion that I would never get tenure. During these first three years, I was not invited to co-author manuscripts with my colleagues (as was the tradition in the department with other junior faculty), and I was rarely invited to informal social events, such as group lunches, dinners at each other's homes, and sports/leisure activities, that periodically occurred among my colleagues. It was only after a female senior scholar in another department noticed that I was showing signs of despair, that she notified the dean of my plight to ensure that I had a fair chance at becoming tenured. Thanks to her interest, intervention, and informal mentorship, I began receiving more equitable mentoring from the senior faculty in my unit.

Like many women of color in the academy, I received very discouraging feedback in the mid-tenure review and also sought outside scholars for mentoring. Several critical incidents define my pre-tenure journey. One is the less-than-enthusiastic response received from a senior faculty member when I (along with two teacher education colleagues) received a grant of half a million dollars from the National Science Foundation (NSF) to conduct a longitudinal research study. The second narrative is how I was discouraged from pursuing scholarship in the area of disaster counseling (an emergent issue nationally). The third is how marginalization is not only perpetuated but exported to other programs and departments exemplified in the narrative about a *selective referral*.

The first narrative occurred during lean economic times when outside funding became imperative for survival. So it was that while I was solidifying my research agenda by disseminating my work in peer-reviewed journals, I was also attempting to develop ties with other educators in the college and across the university to maximize my chances of securing funding. In my fourth pre-tenure year, I was fortunate enough to become a co-principal investigator on a half million-dollar grant from NSF. While previous grant activity involved college of education faculty in the role of consultant, this was the first time that any of the faculty in the college had become leaders on a funded grant from NSF. Even more precedential, all three principal investigators were African American educators. The response from the college was lukewarm; the response from my colleagues in counselor education was minimal. This was exemplified in a statement made by one of the senior male faculty in my unit. In responding to an inquiry about his thoughts on my having been awarded the grant, he responded, "It was a fluke." Thus, even when my scholarly achievements are outstanding, senior faculty members are often unsupportive and unwilling to view me as a legitimate scholar.

The second incident occurred soon after Hurricane Katrina hit the Gulf Coast area. Having lived in New Orleans for fourteen years, raised my children there, and earned two graduate degrees from the University of New Orleans, I was personally affected by the disaster impacting that region. At the time, I had recently become a single parent and was experiencing less than supportive feedback from my department chair about my productivity. Thus, I was hesitant to request deployment to the Gulf Coast area. However, about six weeks after Hurricane Katrina hit New Orleans, I began receiving messages from friends and colleagues with pleas for my return in hopes that I would provide disaster counseling. Since I had maintained a limited private practice during my time in New Orleans, I was well known in the local counseling community as well as among neighborhood residents. People thought that I could bring a much-needed perspective to mental health service provision. Yet, I resisted until I began asking myself the question, *Why not?* When I approached my supervisor, he empathized but strongly discouraged me from going and cited my publication record to date. He believed that my time would be better spent working on manuscripts. In the end, we decided on a compromise in that I would request deployment over the winter break. During my deployment, I realized that my clinical expertise and research knowledge blended very well in disaster counseling. My peers found my contributions to be quite valuable. I kept notes on how I would alter my teaching to better prepare students for possible deployment following future disasters. Nine months later, when the Substance Abuse Mental Health Services Administration (SAMHSA) administration was planning its final deployment to New Orleans, they picked the crème de la crème of all mental health professionals who had been deployed, and I was on that list.

When I approached my chair with this news, I was told that I went at my own peril and that my job was at stake. As a single mother of two adolescents, I did not believe that I had a choice and declined the invitation to participate in the final deployment. Since then, I have been able to demonstrate that disaster counseling is a legitimate area of inquiry, that it is not solely service but also a form of engaged scholarship in which the researcher is engaged in investigations that matter and have real outcomes for community stakeholders. Even more exciting, the 2009 standards for the Council for the Accreditation of Counseling and Related Educational Programs (CACREP) (2009) now consider disaster/crisis counseling so important that this content area is to be infused throughout the counselor curriculum. No matter how fulfilling my professional experiences are now and despite the fact that I have resolved my feelings toward my former chair, I will always remember how discouraged, unsupported, and marginalized I felt when I sought support to pursue this new area of scholarship.

My final personal narrative highlights the phenomenon of selective referral. I had been working with a national database for over a decade to explore issues of educational hegemony and the associated psychological and affective outcomes for culturally marginalized children. One day, while attending an education research training event sponsored by the college, during the question and answer period I mentioned that I worked with this database. At the conclusion of the training, one of the research methods program faculty member approached me with a puzzled look and stated that he had asked the department chair for the name of a counselor education faculty member with whom he could collaborate using the very same database in which I had training. He was more excited when I told him that I had received approval for a restricted data user license to access files that contained confidential information on the participants. Only three faculty in the entire college were working with that dataset, two of whom were faculty in the research methods program area. I was the only other faculty member in the college with knowledge and skills to work with the dataset. Yet, the department chair, who is required to sign restricted data application forms, referred the research methods faculty member to someone else, despite clear knowledge that I would be the most likely person. Again, I felt discouraged, marginalized, and unsupported. However, I was happy that the chance meeting afforded me the opportunity for collaboration.

Recommendations

Although mentoring is important in the professional development of all junior faculty, scholars have suggested that it is especially important for women and faculty of color (Butner, Burley & Marbley, 2000; Tillman, 2001). Mentoring allows the opportunity for those being mentored to see those who have traveled a similar road and survived. It also enables a relationship that provides moral support, guidance, feedback, and encouragement throughout the journey. Additionally, the use of planned mentoring events that link early career faculty to the surrounding community and other scholars of color can foster mentoring opportunities and relationships (Quezada & Louque, 2004). Programmatically, predominately White universities can partner with Historically Black Colleges/Universities (HBCUs), Hispanic-Serving Institutions (HSIs), and tribal colleges to provide experiences for culturally diverse graduate students and junior faculty to be mentored by successful tenured faculty of color. Moreover, such a partnership would allow White faculty (male and female) to learn from their counterparts at minority-serving institutions how to effectively mentor culturally diverse scholars.

My own mentoring experiences are reflective of my relationships with senior scholars within my academic unit, within the university, and beyond the walls of the university. During the two years just prior to my earning tenure, a senior faculty member (female) took me under her wing and offered me the opportunity to collaborate with her on several writing projects. With her support, I was able to experience a sense of belonging and to learn more about the writing process. Although the experience seemed to be more ritualistic than altruistic, I remember the day that she really began listening to me and valuing the knowledge I was contributing to our work. Outside of my unit, I have been able to develop informal mentoring relationships with other women who have given me advice, provided opportunities for collaborative writing, and invited me to participate in research projects, such as the NSF-funded study. Of value, through my leadership activities in the American Counseling Association (ACA), I have been taken under the wing of several outstanding female counselor educators who have given me support, and authentic, caring feedback about my work and my personal concerns. In this way, they helped me see, beyond marginalization, broader visions of the profession and of myself.

In sum, women of color in counselor education continue to have educational experiences vastly different from their White counterparts. While education is often regarded as a great equalizer to reduce educational and institutional disparities, culturally diverse women in academia face struggles—simultaneously intra-psychic and interpersonal—such as alienation from, and epistemological conflicts with, colleagues. Nevertheless, a beacon of light that buffers these negative experiences is the resilient attitudes of many of these women. The intra-psychic conflicts refer to expectations of both the Eurocentric reality of the tenure and promotion processes and the internal drive to pursue scholarship steeped in their own often-conflicting realities. Interpersonal conflicts exist as both an epistemological struggle as well as in the day-to-day interactions between female faculty of color and their White counterparts.

Counselor educators need to become advocates for female faculty of color who continue to make scholarly contributions in what they perceive as culturally hostile and unsupportive environments. Early in their career, women of color in counselor education need to strategize creatively for success in academia by: (a) seeking the knowledge of seasoned scholars (b) maintaining a dialogue with other faculty of color (c) building networks within and across disciplinary boundaries, and (d) maintaining a belief in themselves to promote resilience.

Questions for Reflection

1. What is the history of hiring and promoting female faculty of color in your counselor education program/department?
2. How does your counselor education program/department faculty reflect inclusivity with their female faculty of color?
3. If you could increase your level of advocacy for female faculty of color in your counselor education program/depart-

ment by 5%, what would you do differently over the next 12 months?

References

Allen, W. R., Epps, E. G., Guillory, E. A., Suh, S. A., & Bonous-Hammarth, M. (2000). The Black academic: Faculty status among African Americans in U.S. higher education. *The Journal of Negro Education, 69*(1/2), 112-127.

American Association of University Professors. (2006). *AAUP faculty gender equity indicators.* Washington, DC: Author.

Arredondo, P. (2003). Latinas and the professoriate: An interview with Patricia Arredondo. In J. Castellanos, & L. Jones (Eds.), *The majority in the minority: Expanding the representation of Latina/o faculty, administrators and students in higher education* (pp. 220–39). Sterling, VA: Stylus.

Beauboeuf-Lafontant, T. (2007). You have to show strength: An exploration of gender, race, and depression. *Gender & Society, 21*(1), 28-51.

Bennett, G. G., Merritt, M. M., Sollers J. J., Edwards III, C. L., Whitfield, K. E., Brandon, D. T., & Tucker, R. D. (2004). Stress, coping, and health outcomes among African-Americans: a review of the John Henryism hypothesis. *Psychology & Health, 19*(3), 369-383. doi:10.1080/0887044042000193505

Bernal, D. D. (1998). Using a Chicana feminist epistemology in educational research. *Harvard Educational Review 68*(4), 555-582.

Bonner, F. (2004). Black professors: On the track but out of the loop. *Chronicle of Higher Education, 50,* B11.

Bradley, C. (2005). *The career experiences of African American women faculty: Implications for counselor education programs. College Student Journal, 39,* 518-527.

Bradley, C., & Holcomb-McCoy, C. (2003). Current status of ethnic minority counselor educators in the United States. *International Journal for the Advancement of Counselling, 24,* 183-192.

Brah, A., & Phoenix, A. (2004). Ain't I a woman? Revisiting intersectionality. *Journal of International Women's Studies*, 5, No.3 (2004): 75-86.

Burke, B., Cropper, A. & Harrison, P. (2000). Real or imagined: Black women's experiences in the Academy. *Community, Work, & Family, 3*(3), 297-310.

Butner, B. K., Burley, H., & Marbley, A. F. (2000). Coping with the unexpected: Black faculty at predominately white institutions. *Journal of Black Studies, 30*(3), 453-462.

Carter, R. T. (2007). Racism and psychological and emotional injury: Recognizing and assessing race-based traumatic stress. *The Counseling Psychologist, 35*, 13-105.

Collins, P. H. (2000). *Black feminist thought: Knowledge, consciousness, and the politics of empowerment* (2nd ed.). New York: Routledge.

Constantine, M. G., Smith, L., Redington, R. M., & Owens, D. (2008). Racial microaggressions against black counseling and counseling psychology faculty: A central challenge in the multicultural counseling movement. *Journal of Counseling & Development, 86*(3), 348-355.

Council for Accreditation of Counseling and Related Educational Programs [CACREP]. (2009). *2009 CACREP Standards*. Alexandria, VA: Author. Retrieved from http://www.cacrep.org/2009standards.html

Deitch, E. A., Barsky, A., Butz, R. M., Brief, A. P., Chan, S. S. Y., & Bradley, J. C. (2003). Subtle yet significant: The existence and impact of everyday racial discrimination in the workplace. *Human Relations, 56*, 1299-1324.

Delgado Bernal, D. (1998). Using a Chicana feminist epistemology in educational research. *Harvard Educational Review 68*, 555-582.

Dillard, C. B. (2006). When the music changes, so should the dance: Cultural and spiritual considerations in paradigm 'proliferation.' *International Journal of Qualitative Studies in Education 19*, 59-76.

Din-Dzietham, R., Nembhard, W. N., Collins, R., & Davis, S. K. (2004). Perceived stress following race-based discrimination at work is associated with hypertension in African–Americans: The Metro Atlanta Heart Disease Study, 1999-2001. *Social Science and Medicine, 58*, 449-461.

Fang, C. Y., & Myers, H. F. (2001). The effects of racial stressors and hostility on cardiovascular reactivity in African American and Caucasian men. *Health Psychology, 20*, 64-70.

Flores, J., & Garcia, S. (2009). Latina testimonios: A reflexive, critical analysis of a 'Latina space' at a predominantly White campus. *Race, Ethnicity & Education, 12*(2), 155-172. doi:10.1080/1361332090 2995434

Forman, T. A. (2003). The social psychological costs of racial segmentation in the workplace: A study of African Americans' well-being. *Journal of Health and Social Behavior, 44*, 332-352.

Hairston, K. R. (2008). Dehumanization of the Black American female: An American/Hawaiian experience. *Spaces for Difference: An Interdisciplinary Journal, 1*(1), Article 6. http://repositories.cdlib.org/ ucsb ed/spaces/vol1/iss1/art6

Heath, C. D. (2006). A womanist approach to understanding and assessing the relationship between spirituality and mental health. *Mental Health, Religion & Culture, 9*, 155-170.

Hunn, V. L., & Craig, C. D. (2009). Depression, sociocultural factors, and African American women. *Journal of Multicultural Counseling and Development, 37*(2), 83-93.

Kelly, B. L. (2008). Conceptualizations of leadership among five female counselor educators (doctoral dissertation). Retrieved from OhioLINK ETD. (Document No. kent1221584359).

Loo, C. M., & Ho, H. (2006). Asian American women in the academy: Overcoming stress and overturning denials of advancement. In G. Li, & G. H. Beckett (Eds.), *"Strangers" in the academy: Asian women scholars in higher education* (134-160). Sterling, VA: Stylus.

Marbley, A. F., Wong, A., Pratt, C., & Jaddo, L. (2011). Women faculty of color: Voices, gender, and the expression of our multiple identities within academia. *Advancing Women in Leadership, 31*, 166-174.

Paradies, Y. (2006). A systematic review of empirical research on self-reported racism and health. *International Journal of Epidemiology, 35*, 888-901.

Patitu, C. L., & Hinton, K. G. (2003). The experiences of African American women faculty and administrators in higher education: Has anything changed? *New Directions for Student Services, 4*, 79-93.

Phillips, L., & Stewart, M. R. (2008). I am just so glad you are alive: New perspectives on non-traditional, non-conforming, and transgressive expressions of gender, sexuality, and race among African Americans. *Journal of African American Studies, 12*, 378-400.

Purdie-Vaughns, V., & Eibach, R. P. (2008). Intersectional invisibility: The distinctive advantages and disadvantages of multiple subordinate-group identities. *Sex Roles, 59,* 377-391.

Quezada, R., & Louque, A. (2004). The absence of diversity in the academy: Faculty of color in educational administration programs. *Education, 125,* 213-222.

Schultz, A., Williams, D., Israel, B., Becker, A., Parker, E., James, S. A., et al. (2000). Unfair treatment, neighborhood effects, and mental health in Detroit metropolitan area. *Journal of Health and Social Behavior, 41,* 314-331.

Shields, S. A. (2008). Gender: An intersectionality perspective. *Sex Roles, 59,* 301-311.

Shrake, E. K. (2006). Unmasking the self: Struggling with the model minority stereotype and lotus blossom image. In G. Li, & G. H. Beckett (Eds.), *"Strangers" in the academy: Asian women scholars in higher education* (178-194). Sterling, VA: Stylus Publishing.

Sulé, V. T. (2011). Restructuring the master's tools: Black female and Latina faculty navigating and contributing in classrooms through oppositional positions. *Equity & Excellence in Education, 44*(2), 169-187.

Tillman, L. C. (2001). Mentoring African American faculty in predominantly White institutions. *Research in Higher Education, 42,* 295-325.

Tippeconnic Fox, M. J. (2008). American Indian women in academia: The joys and challenges. *NASPA Journal About Women in Academia, 1*(1), 202-221.

Turner, C. S. (2002). Women of color in academe: Living with multiple marginality. *The Journal of Higher Education, 73*(1), 74-93.

Turner, C. S. (2003). Incorporation and marginalization in the academy: From border toward center for faculty of color? *Journal of Black Studies, 34,* 112-125.

Utsey, S. O. (1998). Assessing the stressful effects of racism: A review of instrumentation. *Journal of Black Psychology, 24,* 269-288.

West-Olatunji, C. (2005). Incidents in the lives of Harriet Jacobs' children—a readers theatre: Disseminating the outcomes of research on the Black experience in the academy. In J. King (Ed.). *Black education: A transformative research and action agenda for the new century* (329-340). Mahwah, NJ: Lawrence Erlbaum Associates Publishers.

West-Olatunji, C., & Behar-Horenstein, L. (*in press*). Mentoring African American women in the academy: A conversation across intersections of identity. In D. S. Sandhu, J. B. Hudson, & M. Taylor-Archer (Eds.), *Handbook of diversity in higher education*. New York: Nova Science Publishers.

West-Olatunji, C., & Conwill, W. (2010). *Counseling African Americans,* a book in the Supplementary Monograph Series to accompany D. Choudhuri, A. L. Santiago-Rivera, & M. Garrett, *Multicultural Counseling Competency*. Boston: Houghton Mifflin.

Williams, C. B. (2005). Counseling African American women: Multiple identities—multiple constraints. *Journal of Counseling & Development, 83*, 278-283.

Woods-Giscombé, C. L. (2010). Superwoman schema: African American women's views on stress, strength, and health. *Qualitative Health Research, 20*(5), 668-683. doi:10.1177/1049732310361892

Yuval-Davis, N. (2005). Intersectionality and feminist politics. *European Journal of Women's Studies, 13*, 193-209.

Chapter 12

Leaving Home: Relationships and Experiences of a Lifetime

ATSUKO SETO

Looking back on the past 20 years of living in America, I can identify several relationships and events that have significantly shaped the way I approach life. Facing a myriad of challenges associated with learning new cultures and the English language has proven to be invaluable to both my personal and professional growth. I have learned that true friendships span through years even from a distance and offer much-needed support in times of difficulty. I have come to believe that having a positive outlook on life and finding the kindness in people helps cope with hardships and puts things in perspective. These ideas are nothing earth-shattering but have increased meaning in my life now because my personal experiences confirm them.

The decision to study abroad initially strained my relationship with my father, a single parent who raised two daughters. While growing up, I seldom saw my father cry, but I still remember the tears on his face when he dropped me off at Narita Airport in Tokyo for my first departure to America. On one hand, my heart was filled with excitement and the hope of new possibilities. On the other, I felt sadness and guilt about going to the United States against my father's wishes. Over the years, he gradually became more accepting of my decision and has been able to see positive changes in me. I came to have greater empathy towards my father because I better understood the pain he had to endure for being far away from his daughter. It took us several years to establish the emotional bond we enjoy today, and I feel peace, knowing that he is sure I love him and am grateful for his support.

My initial reason to study in the United States was rather vague: to experience new cultures and learn a new language. I eventually moved onto earning advanced degrees in some American institutions, but I had no knowledge of the counseling profession until my sophomore year in college. I cannot recall hearing about the profession in Japan, and this may be because the development of counseling there began much later than in the United States. For example, one of the earliest major counseling movements took place in 1995 when Japanese Ministry of Education placed part-time school counselors at elementary and middle schools (Inoue, 2005; Tanami, 2001).

I first heard about counseling as a profession in one of the psychology courses I took as an undergraduate student. I was not aware of the power and meaning of self-exploration and reflection. Taking the course gave me the opportunity to think about my life from a new angle. I was inspired by the course instructor who happened to be a counselor educator, especially the way he connected with students and encouraged them to be genuine with themselves and others in class. Without knowing where this journey would take me, I applied for a master's level counseling program. I am glad that I made this decision, but it took me some time to feel this way because the first several years in America were filled with many unknowns and challenges.

Challenges of Living and Studying in America

Stressors commonly experienced by international students can be divided into three categories including (a) problems with adjusting to new cultural and social contexts, (b) academic struggles, and (c) difficulty making one's career decision (Wang, Lin, Pang, & Shen, 2007). I can identify most with the first category (a), but struggles in all three areas are often intertwined (Wang et al., 2007) and certainly made the acculturation process complicated and emotionally difficult. Coping with varying degrees of acculturative stressors has taught me some important life lessons that I carry into my teaching. My deepest appreciation goes out to people who have helped me along the way.

Adjustments to New Social and Cultural Contexts

Becoming a Minority

I don't think I realized the significance of race and ethnicity until I came to this country the first time. Japan has become more diverse but continues to be quite a racially and ethnically homogeneous country. While roughly 13% of foreign nationals make up Japan's total population (Ministry of Internal Affairs and Communication, 2011), 99% of the population claim Japanese as their ethnic group (U.S. Department of State, n.d.). Growing up in a small rural community in Japan rarely afforded me with the opportunity to interact with people from different racial and ethnic backgrounds; therefore, while growing up, I had developed limited awareness of the impact of race and ethnicity on human relations. Becoming a racial minority as a result of moving to America opened my eyes to both overt and covert forms of discrimination against non-dominant groups. Experiencing prejudice and discrimination firsthand made the issues of "isms" much more personal. I remember the fear I felt in my bones by being the target of derogatory words. A little boy spit on me once and said I took his dad's job. I later learned that his father worked for an American car company.

The above story is one of the most extreme examples of mistreatment I ever encountered. However, it is hard to deny that many forms of prejudice and discrimination continue to occur frequently in today's society (Utsey, Ponterotto, & Porter, 2008). It was during this time that I also became more aware of the privileges that contribute to social inequity. When I became a racial minority in America it made me realize some of the privileges I was entitled to as a member of the mainstream group in Japan. In the last few years, my focus has shifted from my own experience to nurturing my daughter's development as a biracial and multiethnic person. My hope for her is that she will be humble and have a gentle soul but be able to hold her own with strong conviction and confidence when she faces varying degrees of "isms"—something I need to do better in my life so that she sees examples either to follow or to deviate from.

Connecting with Ethnic Roots

I desperately tried to fit into the mainstream culture during the first few years of living in America. For example, I gave myself an English nickname a few months after being in the country. I thought my Japanese name was a constant reminder of my outsider status and felt embarrassed when people could not pronounce my name. I struggled to embrace my identity of being Japanese, did not want to be different, and was eager to fit in. While assimilating into the host culture helped me feel more comfortable with its lifestyle, culture, and customs, it created superficial, rather than authentic, connectedness. The more I focused on "fitting in" to the new culture, the more out of touch I became with my own culture of origin and felt a greater degree of marginalization.

To develop a better understanding of my roots, I began learning American history in relation to Japanese and Japanese American populations. These included a large wave of immigrants to Hawaii, the attack on Pearl Harbor and Japanese internment camps during World War II. Learning the history from this angle shed some light on the collective experiences of Japanese in the United States and how this particular group came to exist within the overall social composition. I had a chance to visit Pearl Harbor several years ago. This event brought forth a great amount of pain in me but reminded me of the importance of reflecting on the past in order to create a more peaceful future. On the boat that carried tourists to the USS Arizona Memorial in Pearl Harbor, I gazed at the ocean trying to hold back my tears. I was not even born when the attack happened, but visiting the memorial brought overwhelming feelings of anger, sorrow, and shame to my heart. This experience left me with sadness of knowing that I am a member of an ethnic group that has been discriminated against but has also inflicted tremendous trauma on other groups that will linger for generations.

Although the visit to Pearl Harbor was emotionally difficult, it was healing to me on some level to face a painful past rather than turn away from it. One's ethnic identity is positively associated with some of the core elements of a person's well-being, including self-acceptance, authenticity, meaningful relationships (Iwamoto & Liu, 2010) and satisfaction in life (Yoon, Jung, Lee, & Felix-Mora, 2012). Understanding successes, adversities, and the dark side of the previous generations helps me feel more connected with my ethnic roots and renews my commitment to promote humanity in today's ever-changing, diverse world. I have a deeper appreciation and respect for my ancestors and feel more whole as a person because of that.

Acculturative Stressors

Individuals with a higher level of acculturation are likely to feel part of the mainstream society and experience optimal cultural adjustment (Yoon et al., 2012). I was on the other end of the spectrum for the first few years and struggled to find a place in my new surroundings. My first destination in America was Alabama where I spent a few months in an ESL program before enrolling in some courses at a local community college. In retrospect, every day was an adjustment to some extent. I wanted to call my father to let him know that I arrived in America safely but did not know how to use a phone! Shopping for shoes or clothes was confusing since I was not familiar with the US customary units of measurement and clothing sizes. Opening a bank account, driving a car, using postal services, ordering meals at a restaurant all required some adjustment and learning. While learning daily functions was exciting, it felt like a never ending process: exhausting and at times overwhelming.

My lack of English language proficiency made me feel like a very young child who cannot yet articulate her needs. I felt inadequate and frustrated when I clearly knew what I wanted to say in my own language but could only communicate with others by gestures and fragmented sentences in English. Additionally, isolation coupled with homesickness created self-doubt about whether or not coming to the United States was a right decision for me. Individuals who establish friendships with people from the host country are less likely to feel homesick and more likely to feel satisfied in a new environment (Blake, Devan, & Kelly, 2011). This statement is true in my experience, and the feeling of loneliness has been diminished significantly over the years because of incredibly caring friends. I also recognize the fact that I will always have a place for my family in my heart that cannot be replaced by any friendships; this acceptance makes homesickness somewhat less of an issue.

Academic Challenges

International students may struggle to do well academically due to limited language acquisition and deficient understanding of the American education systems (Wang et al., 2007). I personally did okay in terms of course work because I would spend endless hours catching up on readings and working on the assignments. I also took additional semesters to finish some of the degree work to compensate for limited language proficiency. Learning a new language can be complex. It is not only understanding the grammar, structures and vocabulary, but also grasping the versatility of the language and its nuances. Using idioms, expressions, and jokes requires a person to be familiar with their particular cultural, social, and historical contexts. For example, in order to avoid using derogatory words or to understand jokes I would hear in movies and on television, I needed to have a stronger background in the history of US race relations. Expressions that are embedded in daily conversations were also difficult to comprehend. How are non-English speakers supposed to know what "Fly by the seat of your pants" means unless someone explains it to them? I am sure my eyes glazed over when I heard this expression for the first time. Trying to find the meaning of this phrase in a Japanese-English dictionary was an exercise in futility.

I made up for my lack of English proficiency by working diligently. If I would need 20 hours to read a chapter, I spent as much of my extra time as needed to make that happen. One of the first classes I took at a community college was an introductory speech class. I figured learning how to give a speech would force me to speak up more. While I felt embarrassed and self-conscious about my accent, I was eager to improve my language skills. I have quickly learned that pretty much everyone who is born in the United States has an accent of some type, but I had little awareness of this until I moved from Alabama to Wyoming. Learning a new language is an ongoing process I enjoy because it has opened up many opportunities to explore the world and get to know people from different cultures. I have also learned to laugh *with* myself, and to take myself lightly when appropriate.

Making a Career Decision

Existing literature suggests some unique challenges international students face in deciding their career paths (Shen & Herr, 2004; Wang et al., 2007). Shen and Herr (2004) further explain that the deciding factors include but not be limited to loyalty and obligations to one's country and families, immigration laws, job outlook, and economic and political conditions. The quality of education I received in the United States was exemplary and prepared me to do my job well. However, the reality I had to face was that the degrees from these American institutions did not necessarily qualify me for counseling jobs in Japan. Finding a job in the United States also raised a different kind of challenge due to restrictions with the immigration laws. Perhaps many international students feel stuck in this process for many reasons. For example, they would most likely need to ask for a petition from their employers to obtain a work visa. Disclosing the need for obtaining a work visa can be a leap of faith to international students because some employers may perceive this process daunting and time-consuming, and thus, unwelcome. Even when a person finds a willing employer, the process of obtaining a work visa can be complicated. I also had to carefully think through how my career choice would not only impact my future but my extended family in Japan. Establishing a career in America meant that I would continue to be distant from my family and miss sharing both important milestones and day-to-day interactions with them. My father still cries whenever I return to the United States from a family visit in Japan, and seeing his tears is something I have difficulty getting use to despite years of being away from home and on my own.

Through the process of acculturation, individuals incorporate two or more cultural orientations into their frame of reference by adapting themselves to a new language, social norms, cultural values, and possibly even family structures (Choi & Thomas, 2008). Additionally, this progression often requires psychological and even spiritual adjustments to many (Mui & Kang, 2006). It has been a fulfilling yet challenging endeavor to make sense of cultural norms, practices, values, and beliefs of both countries and integrate them into my frame of reference. Finding my own voice in a new place away from home has been a spiritual journey to some degree. I have gotten better about letting go of control and appreciating life as a meaningful process rather than looking at it only as a time to reach certain specific goals. We often hear that life is a journey to be enjoyed lest it pass us by. I have come to realize how true that is.

Translating Life Experiences into Teaching

There are things I would have done differently or would have not done over the last 20 years had I known the outcomes in advance. I have been told I was brave for leaving home at such a young age and coming to America without speaking the language. I usually respond by saying that my lack of self-awareness made me courageous and blind-sided at the same time, and I feel fortunate that the overall experience has been remarkable. A few of the lessons I learned from my experience of living in America have been carried into my teaching and serve as a foundation for how I relate to students and approach my work as a counselor educator.

The "Glass Half Full" Perspective

Having the "glass half full" perspective—rather than half empty—has been most helpful for me in overcoming acculturative stressors and language barriers. For example, had I focused on how many mistakes I made in speaking English, I would have become too self-conscious to say a single word. Trying to reduce mistakes only increased my anxiety; therefore, I began shifting my focus from how much more I need to improve to how much I had already improved. During the first year as a counselor, or a counselor educator, I found myself struggling to trust my ability to become an effective practitioner or teacher. Whenever my fear got the better of me, I reminded myself how much progress I had made learning the new language and culture since the first day I arrived in the United States to that day. Doing so helped me put things in a more positive perspective and gave me the assurance that small steps of progress are worth taking. When I see students being overwhelmed or feeling less confident about their ability, I find myself encouraging them to move beyond the impasse and face their challenges with a "glass half full" perspective. While I am mindful about validating their struggles, I try to shift their focus from self-doubt and anxiety to their strengths, and the desires and hopes that drive them to be the best they can be at any given time.

Nurturing a Person through Genuine Sharing

Several of my mentors have been amazing role models for me in terms of their being vulnerable, competent, and genuine all at once, thus accounting for their meaningful impact on others. I have the utmost respect for them because they are exceptional educators, but more importantly, they can relate to students on a deeper, personal level and teach them valuable life lessons. While many students achieve remarkable academic accomplishments, being in a highly competitive learning environment makes it difficult for them to be in touch with the part of them that feels vulnerable or less confident. This is a part of their lives that I hope students have the courage to explore in order to feel more confident and grounded as a counselor.

Both master's and post-mater's students in the introduction course in marriage, couple and family counseling and therapy are asked to reflect on their relationships with their loved ones. I tell the students that it is up to them to decide how deeply they want to reflect on their family relationships in these assignments. My grading on these assignments has to do with the level of self-awareness as a counselor-in-training and their ability to demonstrate the knowledge of systems theories, but not the information they self-disclose. The assignments seem to allow students take ownership of their reflections rather than feeling pressured to do so. I also share with them my family genogram and talk about my struggles with acculturation as well as how my family relationships have evolved over time and influenced my approach to working with families and couples. The information I share in my genogram changes to some degree as I try to share with the students what comes to me in the moment. One year was about the birth of my daughter, another year was about my grandmother's passing, and last year was about my family's experiencing a catastrophic disaster in Japan.

I often do not know what impact my sharing and/or the assignments have on the students, but my primary purposes of self-disclosure are two-fold: creating a place for students to deeply reflect on what it means to be in their own family and fostering their ability to connect with clients from a place of genuine care and respect. This year, I received an email from a former student telling me that he had reached out to his distant father whom he had not seen in over 10 years. He said his work in the course helped him work on this important relationship and to have the courage to write to his father. I consider it a gift whenever I am in the presence of someone's genuine sharing. It seems to me that people are most impactful when they are genuine and compassionate with themselves and others. I work to create a classroom environment that fosters authenticity in each of the students.

Fostering Relationships of Trust and Compassion

Since my arrival in America, many strangers have offered me their heartfelt support simply out of their sincere care and concern for another human being. Whether these relationships are only brief in duration or last a lifetime, the people who have touched my life with their compassion made a lasting change in me. As I mentioned previously, the feelings of loneliness and isolation overshadowed the joy of living in the United States from time to time. However, these feelings were gradually softened by the kindness of the strangers who opened their hearts and became good friends. A couple in Wyoming often invited a group of international students for holiday meals. They had a one-bedroom mobile home, but it did not prevent them from hosting warm holiday celebrations or weekend dinners for those who were far away from their families. Two women in Nebraska volunteered to be my host sisters and offered me continued support throughout my college life. I doubt I would have survived college life without their friendship. I felt at home whenever I was with my host sisters and their large families because they treated me as though I were a part of the family. An elderly couple in Nebraska also helped me to make adjustments as a transfer student from Wyoming. I met them during my search for an English tutor in a new college town to which I had just transferred. As they heard about my struggle with adjusting to a new place, they invited me to stay at their home for as long as I needed. Once they took care of me over a week when I was recovering from major dental surgery and could only eat pudding or other soft foods.

What matters to me the most about these friends is that they share with me the gift of a relationship: encouragement and support that give me audacity to tackle whatever challenges I am facing. Whether I am working with clients in counseling sessions or teaching students in a classroom, I try to communicate to them that I care about them not only because I am responsible to do so as a professional but also I care about them as a person. While maintaining necessary boundaries in the climate of academia, I hope the relationships I cultivate with students are based on my genuine care for each individual and offer encouragement in times of need.

Realizing My Priorities in Life

On the morning of March 12, 2011, I was catching up on my emails like any other morning. Then, I received a call from my husband. He said, "You need to call your parents right now. Japan had a massive earthquake and tsunami yesterday." My heart sank in sheer panic. I called my parents even though it was past midnight there. The phone rang a few times, my heart was pounding, then I finally heard my father's voice on the other end of line.

Me: "Hey, dad. Are you okay?"

My dad: "Yeah. It's really dark here, and we can't really tell what's going on, but we are okay."

Me: "[Big long sigh]. Okay, good. Why don't I call you back first thing in the morning? I will call you right back tomorrow, okay?"

My dad: "Okay, that would be better."

I do not think either of us knew the extent of the damage that the catastrophic disasters had brought to Japan at that time. There was a power outage in the area where my father lived, and I had yet to see the horrifying news coverage of Japan. I hung up the phone assuming that I could call him back first thing in the morning to better assess the circumstances. After being glued to the TV and reading anything I could put my hands on about Japan for that day, being in tears and frightened, I called my parents several hours later hoping to confirm the well-being of my extended family members. No answer. Even though I could assume the phone line was impaired in the area, I kept calling them, desperately wishing that by some miracle I would be able to hear my dad's voice again. This was the beginning of a five long days with no contact with my family who lived in Miyagi Prefecture in Japan—one of the areas the 9.0-magnitude earthquake and the mega-tsunami had struck.

Before March 11, 2011, my life had a lot to do with planning things ahead of time. It is almost impossible to exist in academia without advanced planning. Courses are scheduled in advance; committees are formed and well under way before the academic year, and the "to do" list is created a few years in advance for preparations for tenure and promotion. Most things have deadlines, and I seemed to always be doing something rather than creating time to simply enjoy being with my family. The catastrophic disaster really put things in perspective for me. The status quo serves my ego and helps me feel as though I am important in some ways, but such a superficial confidence is quick to be shaken up when I focus on the *shoulds* in life. I could not have been more relieved and thankful when I finally got in touch with my parents. Some of my relatives are still rebuilding their lives one year after, but they seemed to be clear on their priorities and maintain sense of optimism in one of the most difficult times of their lives. This experience shifted my priorities in life, and I treasure my family and a small circle of incredible friends more than ever. Putting people first in my work, clients, staff, colleagues, or current and prospective students, has become my top priority. I still feel the need to check off things on my "to do" list for the day, but I keep my perspective and appreciate the time I spend with people around me.

Closing

Rogers (1961) begins one of his celebrated books titled *On Becoming a Person* by sharing personal stories that shaped his perspectives as a helping professional and revealing how his work with clients has created *personal meanings* for him. I read this book during the first year of my master's degree program—a period during which I constantly asked myself, "How can I ever be helpful to people with such limited life experience and English proficiency?" Filled with self-doubt, I often thought about whether or not the counseling profession was a right fit for me. When I read *On Becoming a Person*, I realized even one of the most influential people in the counseling profession—Carl Rogers—had also struggled to find his own voice.

The path of self-discovery in a new country, including becoming a counselor educator, has presented me with a number of challenges. Taking one day at a time was what I could do in the unfamiliar place far away from home. I wanted to have a clear future goal in mind but all I could focus on was taking one step at a time. I consider having earned a doctorate in counselor education and supervision an incredible accomplishment. However, what makes the degree most meaningful for me is the pathway to it that tested me and helped me be a better person. The experience of living in America transformed me into the person I am today, and I look forward to continuing on this journey with gratitude, optimism, and curiosity.

Questions for Reflection

1. What was your experience of leaving home or making a significant emotional departure from your family? What impact has this experience had on you?
2. What life lessons do you carry with you? How did they influence your personal growth?
3. How are these life lessons influencing your professional development?

References

Blake, H., Devan, R., & Kelly, A. R. (2011). An analysis of friendship networks, social connectedness, homesickness, and satisfaction levels of international students. *International Journal of Intercultural Relations, 35*, 281-295.

Choi, J. B., & Thomas, M. (2008). Predictive factors of acculturation attitudes and social support among Asian immigrants in the USA. *International Journal of Social Welfare, 18*, 76-84. doi: 10.1111/j.1468-2397.200.00567

Inoue, T. (2005). Multidimensional and comprehensive roles of school counselors. In S. Geshi., T. Inouel, & M. Tadokoro (Eds.), *Perspectives of counseling: Revisiting today's counselor identity* (pp. 243-259). Tokyo, Japan: Bulane Publisher.

Iwamoto, D. K., & Liu, W. M. (2010). The impact of racial identity, ethnic identity, Asian values, and race-related stress on Asian Americans and Asian international college students' psychological well-being. *Journal of Counseling Psychology, 57*, 79-91 doi: 10.1037/a0017393

Ministry of Internal Affairs and Communications, Statistics Bureau, Director-General for Policy Planning, and Statistics Research and Training Institute. (2011). *Statistics Bureau of Japan: 2010 Japan Census*. Retrieved from http://www.stat.go.jp/english/data/kokusei/pdf/20111026.pdf

Mui, A. C., & Kang, S. Y. (2006). Acculturation stress and depression among Asian immigrant elders. *Social Work, 51*, 243-255.

Rogers, C. (1961). *On becoming a person: A therapist's view of psychotherapy*. Boston, MA: Houghton Mifflin.

Shen, Y.-J., & Herr, E. L. (2004). Career placement concerns of international graduate students: A qualitative study. *Journal of Career Development, 31*, 15-29. doi: 10.1177/089484530403100102

Tanami, M. (2001). School counselor is a consultant and counselor to students and teachers. In Y. Inui, & M. Hirano (Eds.), *To become a clinical psychologist* (pp.14-26). Tokyo, Japan: Pelican Publisher.

U.S. Department of State (n.d.). *Background note: Japan*. Retrieved from http://www.state.gov/r/pa/ei/bgn/4142.htm

Utsey, S. W., Ponterotto, J. G., & Porter, J. S. (2008). Prejudice and racism, year 2008—still going strong: Research on reducing prejudice with recommended methodological advances. *Journal of Counseling and Development, 28*, 339–347.

Wang, Y, Lin, J. G., Pang, L., & Shen, F. C. (2007). International students from Asia. In F. T. L. Leong, A. G. Inman, A. Ebreo, L. H. Yang, L. Konoshita, & M. Fu, (Eds.), *Handbook of Asian American psychology* (2nd ed., pp. 245-261). Thousand Oaks, CA: Sage.

Yoon, E., Jung, K. R., Lee, R. M., & Felix-Mora, M. (2012). Validation of social connectedness in mainstream society and the ethnic community scales. *Cultural Diversity and Ethnic Minority Psychology, 18*, 64-73. doi: 10.1037a0026600

Chapter 13

An Agnostic in Full Bloom

LAURIE L. WILLIAMSON

I am turning 60 years old, and I feel I am in the prime of my life. This age suits me very well. Turns out I make a great old lady! I've got the grey hair, the elastic waistband, and the sensible shoes to prove it. I've spent much of my life not knowing if I would make it here, and it is just now that I'm feeling more comfortable and relaxed, realizing that I made it! I guess I was comfortable enough as a kid, but when adolescence kicked in, combined with a cancer diagnosis, I went on a roller coaster ride that lasted 30 years.

Menopause has since restored my sanity and truer, clearer sense of self. I really couldn't see through the hormone haze until the change that occurred 30 years ago was reversed. I have become more and more invisible, slowly but surely, since turning 40—and it somehow comforts me. But then again, I'm a good introvert. I have always felt a little invisible at times as a woman. That caused me a lot of frustration over the years, but now it is different. I am more confident in making myself known when and where there is a need. Otherwise, I sort of like being off the grid or center stage. It is with an enormous sigh of relief I move on to become an increasingly wiser and older woman. This writing, which feels awkward and a bit clumsy, is my attempt to outline a spiritual journey that is not turning out the way I had anticipated; it is becoming so much more.

Dr. Estes is well known for writing about women, women who run with the wolves (1995) and dangerous old women (2010). She tells a story about an old and twisted trumpet vine that invaded every available space in the backyard and spread along the fence line. As it intertwined in and around itself, the fence and the vine became one. The vine integrated whatever could hold it, carry it, and sustain it. But with time as the timber rots, perhaps now, it is the vine that supports the fence. This visual has become a metaphor for my life and a guided imagery that is useful with students as we counselor educators help them identify and clarify their belief systems and values. It is essential that students are challenged to understand the impact and influence of their personal journey on their effectiveness as counselors. As I share my personal journey, I provide the readers with suggested student counselor activities for concept application and integration.

Personal Journey

I learned a lot about myself and my body after being diagnosed with kidney cancer at the tender age of 21. I was given a 50-50% chance of survival. I was scared to death—literally and figuratively. It's a long story, but pathology reports revealed that the tumor had begun *in utero*. My mother was exposed to something toxic while pregnant. It took 20 years before the tumor was discovered. The infected kidney had already shut down causing the second one to enlarge and take over all kidney function. The tumor has influenced my growth and development since inception—before, during, and after the diagnosis. It has, in many ways, become the enmeshed fence upon which I have grown. I have come to refer to myself as a two-time cancer *thriver*. I have not just survived; I have in many respects thrived. I think having had cancer has propelled me to do and be more than I ever thought possible. One thing I have come to feel more strongly about is my spirituality which stems from cancer having brought me to my knees. Trying times tend to help us see more clearly. It was in the moments I was most alone that I discovered another kind of connection, not from traditional religion, but from a source within.

I discovered the power of this place in the face of pain. After numerous abdominal surgeries and being a good introvert, I withdrew into myself. I learned not to fight the pain but instead to focus on it, follow it, explore it, and eventually become *it*. When I became one with the pain,

I no longer hurt. *Heal thyself.* I confronted the age-old existential question and came away with the conclusion that I am not alone. Interestingly, in Old English, the word *alone* used to be spelled *all one* (Gove, 1986). It is so empowering to realize that it is the inner life that I had been cultivating since childhood that gave me the strength to fight for my life in adulthood. I have reinforced and deepened this connection through meditation, yoga, and dream work. It is my church and I carry it with me at all times. As counselor educators we need to challenge students to put a name to that inner life which sustains them. It is part of the developmental process of identity formation, and a timely challenge during young adulthood (Walker, 2007). We all need a touchstone to assist us in living a balanced life, and it is most helpful to know what that touchstone is. The essential ingredient to developing a safe and respectful classroom in which to discuss sensitive topics is to model authenticity. I try to have the classroom be an open democracy and I model the assignments by sharing my personal experience in an appropriate manner with the class.

Suggested Student Activity

Stephen Covey (1996) is renowned for his book, *First Things First*, regarding time management, and it all comes down to priorities. The first step is to define what your priorities are in life. How and by what standards do you want to live your life? What will you do with the precious little time you have? Some people say, "I just don't have the time!" when in reality, that's all we do have. Time. We just don't know how much or how little. So, reflect a bit. What are your personal goals?

An activity designed to demonstrate Covey's (1996) goal-setting model is to have a jar which you fill with rocks. Usually 5 or 6 rocks will fit. You then ask the question "Is the jar full?" Some will say yes, and others will say no, there are still some cracks and crevasses—exactly. So you fill in the cracks and crevasses with pebbles. Now is the jar full? Well, there are still some gaps. Fill in the remaining gaps with sand. Now is the jar full? Still some gaps? Top the jar off with water. Now is it full? Most would agree it's pretty full. What is the point of this activity you ask? The point is not, as many will suggest, that you can always squeeze more into your life. The point is that if you hadn't put the big rocks in first, you wouldn't have been able to fit so many into the jar. The big rocks represent your priorities in life. In reality, time is all we have. You are just deciding how to spend it. So, what are your big rocks? What do you want to value and honor each day? Health? Family? Faith? Nature? Nurture? Fame? Fortune? Value systems reflect our need to address the existential void, the question of why we are here. Many folks take the question and look for answers in a church, synagogue, or mosque. In this activity, you find the answers in rocks!

Religious Upbringing

My learning to become comfortable and confident in being an agnostic has taken a long time. Both my parents were science oriented—my father a pathologist and my mother a dietician. I was raised on the religion of *science*—not to be confused with Christian Science or Scientology—but the science of empirical research. While I was encouraged to visit churches and to think for myself regarding religion, it was clear my parents viewed religion as a crutch that less strong-willed people needed. The message was that religion equaled flights of fantasy and a means for people to justify the suffering in life.

Occasionally, I went to a Presbyterian church with one of my grand-mothers when she came to visit, and in high school I was ready to ro-mantically convert to Catholicism for my Italian boyfriend. But, I never felt any real connection with church itself. I never felt comfortable in the trappings of religion, all the pomp and ceremony, rules and regulations. Even as a child, I thought it was all a bit overdone and was certain there must be a simpler and more direct route to this all-knowing, ever-present deity. Over the years I've continued to be intrigued with religion and spirituality as I have attempted to explain the unexplainable.

Suggested Student Activity

Conduct a *Connected Conversation* (Public Conversations Project, 2004), a structured process designed to encourage listening skills and develop empathy. It is not a debate or an effort to change anyone's opinion. It is simply to quietly and respectfully listen to one another. The moderator participates and begins each round of comments with a question. Partici-pants have three minutes to share their thoughts or they can always pass. Timers are helpful. Round One: Have students identify their religious or spiritual beliefs. Round Two: Have them share an inspiration, a quote, or a story that illuminates their faith. Round Three: Students ask ques-tions to clarify their understanding of another member's perspective.

Round Four: Have students identify what they have learned about themselves or someone else during this process.

This is, of course, an excellent time to educate students regarding vocabulary and terms used to describe a religious or spiritual experience. Agree on a definition source such as Webster's Third New International Dictionary (Gove, 1986). During a similar exercise, I came to realize that I was an agnostic, not an atheist, as I had previously thought. The distinction is that atheists deny the existence of God and believe in only random forces. An agnostic allows that there may be an order to the world but doubts man's ability to comprehend or know "God". Participants from a diversity of religions will enrich the conversation since exposure to new perspectives encourages growth. On my journey, I experienced growth spurts with each new discussion.

Stranger in a Strange Land

When I first moved from Colorado to the South, I was in for numerous rude awakenings as to just how foreign I was here. I had moved to the Bible Belt. Through the years I have trod softly around religious folks, subdued by their sense of self-righteousness. Since I did not use their vocabulary to describe the divine, I was by their definition, a heathen and to be pitied or worse (for me) to be converted. I have learned over time to stand firmly and calmly with my beliefs and know I am a spiritual equal. I think I've gotten tired of always feeling a need to defend myself, and now I increasingly take a proactive approach, which is much more satisfying.

When I was encountered as being new to this community, within the first two minutes of meeting, the following questions were invariably asked, "You're not from around here are you? What church do you go to?" It's been a learning process but I now just smile and look up at the gorgeous sky and say, "This is my church!" If someone starts to pray, as is bound to happen, I am respectful of their beliefs, but at the same time I expect them to be respectful of mine. So now, I might ask to share one of *my* prayers. I recite a brief quote about loving-kindness and feel better for having shared something authentic of myself while positively contributing to an increased awareness and acceptance of diversity. *It's the counselor educator in me.*

Suggested Student Activity

Conduct the *Connected Conversation* process previously described to increase student self-awareness and personal reflection regarding religion and spirituality. Ask students to share samples or examples of meaningful religious or spiritual music and explain why it was selected. Adhere to the three-minute time frame and limit rounds of sharing depending on the size of the group and the allotted time available. Follow the standard series of questions; end by asking what each participant will take away from the activity.

Activism

I've always had a cautious skepticism about religion, and I am amazed by those who proclaim to have the *answers*. Sadly, their answers usually disallow the existence of any other answers. George Carlin, the comedian, does a great routine where one guy approaches another and asks, "Do you believe in God?" The man answers, "No." BAM! He shoots him. He then approaches another man and asks, "Do you believe in God?" The man says, "Yes." He then asks, "Do you believe in *my* God?" The man says, "No." BAM! He shoots him. *Is there really only one way?*

Along this line, I've decided to start standing up against "the certainty" of it all more often. Just because I'm an agnostic doesn't mean my experience with the unknown is any more or less valid than that of someone else. It's all a *mystery*. I no longer feel guilty about not celebrating Christmas. I'm not a Christian—*duh*. For a long time, I had it tangled up with cultural traditions, such as Santa Claus and the Easter Bunny. But, as we all know, it is really about retail sales, capitalism at its best. I've had to reframe my holiday mentality and now prefer to celebrate Winter Solstice, New Years, 4th of July, Martin Luther King, Jr. Day, and Harvey Milk Day. It's not just religious holidays that cause me angst; some national holidays, such as Thanksgiving are just as conflicting. A Native American friend refers to it as *ThanksTaking*. It bothers me to celebrate a holiday which is, in essence, romanticizing genocide. I want to celebrate holidays that I understand, appreciate, and can be genuinely sincere about instead of following the more popular cultural indoctrination. I have enjoyed baffling folks as, more than once, someone has commented, "You're a Christian aren't you?" And, I will reply, "No, actually I'm not." I have received incredulous looks—*how can you be a good person and not be a Christian?* I smile and say, "But thanks, I'll take that as a compliment."

One of my early experiences in moving to the South was a neighbor in her mid-30s who came over to have a serious discussion with me about the possibility of my being a witch. A witch! I wasn't from around here. I didn't go to church, and I was into yoga. I kid you not—true story. Fortunately for both of us, I have matured over the years and responded by gently reassuring her that I was not a witch. In my earlier years, I would have reacted very differently and gone on the attack. Now, I just look these dedicated folks in the eyes, smile, and explain that I think we all just have a lot of different paths and names in our pursuit to answer the existential question. I am more interested these days in increasing the middle ground between believers and *just-different* believers.

Suggested Student Activity

A powerful activity to do with students is a genogram (McGoldrick, Gerson, & Petry, 2008) in which students go back several generations and identify themes and patterns that have been handed down over generations. Students enjoy genograms as they provide a perspective on one's personal history and cultural assumptions in life. One area students can explore is the family's heritage regarding religious or spiritual practices or the lack thereof. Questions that may prompt students to consider their assumptions and grow increasingly intentional in their life include: Are there spoken or unspoken family rules about religious affiliation? Are their trends or patterns in the type of spiritual expression represented in your family? How did these influence the development of your ethical or moral compass? How will some of your morals or values impact your ability to counsel diverse clients? What bias or prejudice might you have that would make it difficult for you to stay neutral in a counseling situation?

This is an opportune time to discuss White culture and privilege with students. I will often share my experiences in recognizing my own bias and prejudice in being reared in the culture of the Anglo-Saxon Protestant work ethic, such as attitudes about time, space, organization, efficiency, and cleanliness, to name a few. Immersing myself in another culture has always proven an effective method of highlighting my cultural limitations and boundaries.

Travel as Education

Another personal experience that was insightful for me occurred when I visited with neighbors before leaving for a year on a Fulbright Scholarship to teach outside Tripoli, Lebanon. Many neighbors were horrified and certain I was going to be brainwashed and convert to Islam. One neighbor said, "Oh my, won't you feel out of place? They are all Muslims!" I just reminded him that I live here among Southern Baptists. It really doesn't matter to me; I don't follow either religion.

While living in Lebanon, I was astounded and generally delighted with a student's comment. Reflecting on my 'agnostic' status, this young man from deeply divided Lebanon where religious status must be listed on your identification card: Christian, Greek Orthodox, and Muslim: Sunni, Shiite, Alawi, or Druze. There is no Atheist or Not Applicable category; you are the same religion as your family—period. The student said to me, "You are so lucky not to have to take sides!" I have never before had someone tell me they were envious of my lack of religious identity. It felt good to be validated by someone who has seen the casualties of religious zealotry.

In an effort to promote open dialogue on sensitive topics, I once served on a panel during a multi-cultural series in our college. There were seven or so folks on the panel to discuss the various religious or spiritual paths: a Seventh-day Adventist, a Southern Baptist, a Catholic, a Muslim, a Jew, an agnostic (myself), and a Wiccan! I was a bit anxious about representing agnosticism in such a bastion of religious folks, but I took comfort in the fact that my dear colleague would follow me and divert animosity away from me with a much more volatile topic, her being a self-proclaimed Wiccan.

For my portion, I talked about my father, the pathologist, who viewed the world from the cellular and microscopic levels. My ex-husband, on the other hand, was into astronomy and viewed the world from the perspective of galaxies and light years. I was of the mindset that perhaps those two seemingly opposite aspects on the continuum actually fold back onto each other and become one. The current research described in quantum physics describes much the same (Nova, 2003). Interestingly, our panel discussion went full circle, with the Seventh-day Adventist, who went first, ending by making the historical connection between the natural cycles celebrated by Wicca and the foundations of Christianity itself. It was a great day!

Suggested Student Activity

The panel described above is the type of activity that can be implemented as course assignments. Additional activities include ethical dilemmas with many perspectives. Have groups of students prepare a presentation to the class which represents their position on the issue. The focus of the discussion is on the power of social constructivism (Gergen, 2009) where there is no *one* truth. It really is all relative, as they say.

From My Side of the Mirror

My own personal take on the great mystery is that in the vast scheme of things we are as the grasshopper. Out in a field sits a grasshopper on a blade of grass. An enormous locomotive roars by and the grass begins to sway. The grasshopper is aware that something has changed in the environment, but she can no more comprehend the locomotive than we humans can comprehend the universe. So how do I ground myself in this world?

Currently, I am an agnostic in full bloom. My spiritual path started early in life unbeknownst to me. Raised an atheist in relation to traditional religions, my "church" became my inner world and rich imagination. I had numerous invisible friends as a child, and I have always been a vivid dreamer, both in and out of wakefulness. I am a visual learner, and my day and night dreams are valued treasures, often whimsical adventures, but on occasion, profound experiences. There are many layers to the world of dreaming.

I've engaged in this inner world of 'dreaming' for as long as I can remember. Gurus, swamis, yogis from earliest history, and now quantum physicists, are attempting to explain that this state of mind is really *God* in all of us: consciousness. After much searching to define myself and my spirituality, I've come to a peaceful place somewhere in between—a place of quiet reflection where I can connect with something far greater than I. This place resides in the very core of my being and is, for me, accessed by surrendering to the breath and visualizations that occur in this reality and the dream space.

As part of my meditation practice or day dreaming, sometimes it is merely a matter of closing my eyes and waiting—waiting to see what colors explode before my eyes. It is often like a kaleidoscope of colors that vary in intensity, and I think represent the chakras (Blawyn & Jones, 1996). I can tune in visually, and then through breathing and vocal resonating (Goldman, 2005), I can nurture specific areas with vibration. Sometimes I just let the free flow of thoughts, or as Freud would call it, *free associations*, to surface. This is a particularly creative time during which I can often resolve issues or create new ideas. When finished, I often find a clear sense of direction and purpose. Then, of course, it is icing on the cake to journal or draw about the experience. It's like little drops of consciousness that seep up from the collective pool to restore and refresh my soul (Whitmont & Perea, 1999).

In regard to my night dreams, they can be even more magical. Tibetan Dream Yoga (Das, 2000) describes the *fourth time*, where past, present, and future merge into one. The Australian Aborigines refer to it as the Dreamtime, where we can tap into the river of the collective unconscious (Barnes, 2003). The Hopi Indians regard the dream world as real, even suggesting that perhaps it is more real than this waking reality (Moss, 2010). There are the busywork everyday dreams and then there are those I call *enchanted* which can have a profound impact. In my experience, enchanted dreams usually involve animals who somehow guide or transition me into another realm. Here is the synopsis of a dream that was a highlight.

> This powerful dream involved a bear which historically represented my cancer. *The bear had previously stalked me. And now, here he was, back again! He made his way into my house, and I met him in the living room. I was concerned but not frightened. I was curious about him, his fur and how it would feel and smell. I touched him. The bear asks if I need some help. I answer, yes, I could use some help. He holds me in a bear hug and then transforms into a Christ-like figure.* I woke up with the feeling of being held and comforted. It was all very nice, and it felt good to ask for help.

> In a subsequent dream, again the *Christ-like figure appears before me and there is significant sexual tension between us. It was very enjoyable. But, just as I lay back anticipating penetration, I think—Wait! I can't have sex—this is Jesus! Instead, I am overcome with a sense of pure ecstasy or rapture.* For me, these words describe a most spiritual event! Again, I woke up infused with a most amazing feeling.

If I were ever to say that I've been *born again,* I would be referring to a moment while in the dream space. The essence for me is that there is an alternative reality, a vast reserve and resource that we can become aware of, tap into, and learn from. I am a very different person in my dream world. I commune with Jesus. I can fly, walk through walls, use telepathy, and breathe underwater! It's no surprise that the dream world is one of my most spiritual places. I immerse myself and feed upon the rich and ancient symbols, metaphors, and motifs (Cirlot, 1971).

Science is demonstrating that we are composed of the same sub-molecular substance from which the universe is built. Within our cellular structure, what is known as the *body-mind*, is the genetic code distilled from all the experiences that have accompanied us as we individuate into conscious beings. We are beginning to appreciate that we might indeed be unlimited co-creators of the universe (Barnes, 2003). This, of course, is a huge responsibility!

Suggested Student Activity

As a counselor educator, I talk a lot with students about self-care. I try to model such care in an activity that evaluates how well students are meet-ing their five basic needs: physical, emotional, intellectual, social, and spiritual—as identified by Walker (2007). It is important to encourage students to achieve and maintain a healthy, balanced lifestyle as repre-sented by the five needs. I encourage students to be kind to themselves and to remember that they only get one body this go-round! Yet, I also encourage a certain amount of risk taking to encourage growth and rec-ommend that students expand their known boundaries and expose them-selves to different cultures and, consequently, different perspectives of history. I encourage students to travel internationally and to ask ques-tions whenever possible! Travel affords me the opportunity to experien-tially learn more history, geography, language, culture, current events, and so on. It is, I think, the best education money can buy! I frequently share with students my adventures and misadventures, both personally and professionally. And so, in closing—who knows? Not the grasshop-per. This brings me to a favorite story—one befitting a grasshopper. It's about an old man who lived in a small rural village (Moss, 2010). One day, his horse jumped the fence and ran off. All the neighbors said, "Oh, that's such bad luck for you! We are so sorry!" The man, shrugged his shoulders and answered, "Maybe." A few days later, his horse returned and brought some wild mustangs back with him. All the neighbors were so happy and said, "Ah, such good luck you have. You now have five horses instead of only one!" The old man shrugged and replied, "Maybe." The next day, while trying to break one of the new horses, the old man's grandson was bucked off and broke his arm. Again, the neighbors all cried at his ill fortune, but once again he replied, "Maybe." A week later, a military envoy came through the town and conscripted all the healthy young men into the army. Due to his injury, the old man's grandson remained behind and was one of the few young men in the community to survive. I now apply the "maybe" principle to my life. Life unfolds too mysteriously to take too seriously!

Conclusion

My personal life, with its many difficult challenges, has guided my professional life. I cannot really separate the two. How can I attend to others if I am not attending to myself? I cannot grow on a professional level unless I am willing to grow on a personal level. The most difficult "job" I have had is learning to live with myself; I've had to learn to be my own best friend and not my own worst enemy. I have had to learn to forgive myself and to truly enjoy the company I keep when I am alone. These are life's most difficult learnings.

I am frequently besieged by students who want to be completely prepared upon entering the field of counseling. They want to have all the answers and a recipe to fix all that ails society. It is at those times I feel most like a hypocrite. It is awkward for an educator to admit it, but most of my expertise has not come from the classroom, but rather from "on-the-job-training," or perhaps more accurately, "being-in-life training."

Overall I have learned that life is not a one-size-fits-all kind of endeavor. I have come to learn that it is developing softness, a giving-in, which makes me truly strong. I have learned to look within, to breathe, and to trust. I have cradled and soothed my fears and thus found a sanctuary in this *body-mind* of mine. My life goals are to become firmer, quieter, warmer, and simpler. I leave you with an affirmation.

> May we be filled with loving kindness
> May we be well
> May we be peaceful and at ease
> May we be happy.
> Forever oneness
> Who sings to us in silence
> Who teaches us through each other
> Please guide our steps with strength and wisdom.
> —Kornfield (1993, p. 20)

Questions for Reflection

1. Do you enjoy the company you keep when you are alone? Why or why not?
2. No matter your religion or spiritual path, how do you feel about those who do not share your beliefs?
3. How do you challenge and support yourself to be aware and remain nonjudgmental?
4. Where is your church, your holy place? Does it require bricks and mortar? What can you do to increase the amount of time you spend there?

References

Barnes, M. H. (2003). *In the presence of mystery: An introduction to the story of human religiousness*. Mystic, CT: Twenty-Third.

Blawyn, S., & Jones. S. (1996). *Chakra workout: For body, mind & spirit*. St. Paul, MN: Llewellyn.

Cirlot, J. E. (1971). *A dictionary of symbols (2nd ed.)*. New York: Philosophical Library.

Covey, S. (1996). *First things first*. London: Simon & Schuster.

Das, L. S. (2000). *Tibetan dream yoga*. Boulder, CO: Sounds True.

Estes, C P. (2010). *Dangerous old women: Myths and stories of the wild woman archetype*. New York: Ballantine.

Estes, C P. (1995). *Women who run with the wolves: Myths and stories of the wild woman archetype*. New York: Ballantine.

Gergen, K. (2009). An invitation to social constructivism. London: Sage.

Goldman, J. (2005). *Vocal toning the chakras*. Boulder, CO: Sounds True.

Gove, P. B. (1986). (Ed.). Webster's Third New International Dictionary. Springfield, Mass: Merriam-Webster.

Kornfield, J. (1993). *A path with heart: A guide through the perils and promises of spiritual life*. New York: Bantam.

McGoldrick, M., Gerson, R., & Petry, S. (2008). *Genograms: Assessment and intervention (3rd ed.)*. New York: Norton.

Moss, R. (2010). *Dreamgates: Exploring the worlds of soul, imagination, and life beyond death*. Novato, CA: New World Library.

NOVA (2003). Superstrings, hidden dimensions, and the quest for the ultimate theory. In PBS series, *The elegant universe*. Boston: WGBH.

Public Conversations Project. (2004). *Connected conversations*. Retrieved July 26, 2011, from http://www.publicconversationsproject.org

Walker, V. (2007). *Becoming aware: A text/workbook for human relations and personal adjustment*. Iowa: Kendall/Hunt.

Whitmont, E. C., & Perera, S. B. (1989). *Dreams, a portal to the source*. London: Routledge.

Section Four

Spirituality

Chapter 14

Centrality of the Relationship in Counselor Education: Our Clients, Our Students, Ourselves

STEPHANIE HALL

It is well documented that the relationship is a central agent of change in the counseling process (Gelso, 2010; Yalom, 2002). Connecting with our clients and entering their worlds to engage in a one-of-a-kind relationship is the goal for counselors; more specifically, we are charged with using that relationship to promote insight and change. Irvin Yalom (1980) has said, ". . . it's the relationship that heals" (p. 9). I agree wholeheartedly with his thoughts. Throughout my career it has been evident that relationships were at the center of my success personally and professionally. In this chapter I discuss the road that I have taken professionally and personally and how becoming a counselor has helped me to make sense of my world. The discussion that follows includes the connections and parallels between my clinical practice, my teaching, my participation in the world as a colleague, mentor/mentee, friend, and other life roles of similar import.

My Experience as a Student/Beginning Counselor

From the beginning of our first course as counseling students we are taught about the relationship and its importance in our work. In theory that idea makes perfect sense, but in practice it is a bit more difficult to grasp. How do I balance what I already know about having relationships (friends, family) with clinical work where I am asked to maintain appropriate boundaries, make diagnoses, form treatment plans, and so on. We are asked to have relationships with people, but in a way that is completely foreign to us. It is a challenge for sure. My first counseling skills course began a journey that would change me in immeasurable ways, professionally of course, but also personally. In my work as a counselor I have encountered many clients in many different settings. As a first semester internship student, I began my work with a mixture of excitement and anxiety. My training told me to focus on case conceptualization, choose a theory, and connect it to the interventions that I select to address the client's presenting problem. So that is what I set out to do.

During week two, a young woman came into my office and reported that she had attempted suicide the night before. Everything that I knew suddenly left me. I wanted to run from the office screaming, asking my supervisor to come and help. Instead, I didn't panic. I listened to the woman's story. I felt great compassion for her. By the end of that day she was being admitted to an inpatient facility. I thought that for certain she would be so angry with me that I would not see her after the experience. She came in on the day following her discharge, and I was shocked. We continued to work together for the next two semesters until she moved away. At some point I mentioned to her my thoughts about her not coming back after her stay at the inpatient facility to which she replied, "But you cared and that was what I needed, someone to listen." It was at that moment that I understood (in real life) what my professors had been talking about all along. In that moment it didn't matter if I could discuss which theory I was using and why. It mattered that I was there, was genuine, and provided support. I ended up working with that client a second time after I relocated to the city where she had moved a year prior, and she became my client again without either of us knowing until the first session. The second time we worked together for a year. That young woman taught me so much. And our relationship, one of the first of its kind that I had experienced, solidified for me that I really was meant to be doing this counseling thing!

I would later enter a doctoral program and begin training to become a counselor educator. During this time, I experienced the most changes, a real shift in worldview. I first met my mentor, Diana. I began by working alongside her in courses, participating and teaching to the degree that I was able. I admired her and watched her build relationships with students as well as demonstrate meaningful relationship building with colleagues. I noticed that she was able to negotiate her work with ease. Everyone seemed to connect to her and learn from her in a meaningful way. This is who I wanted to be! Fortunately, she invested in me and challenged me, pushing me to do what I was hesitant as well as afraid to do. We formed a strong mentoring relationship during the first year. I was beginning to feel comfortable in my role as a doctoral student, enjoying supervision, taking courses and beginning to focus on writing my dissertation. At every turn I was able to ask for suggestions, ask questions about things that I didn't understand and felt content about doing so; I couldn't believe how accessible Diana was to me. She always seemed to have time for her students.

I was studying in New Orleans and in the midst of my doctoral program under Diana's supervision. I had just begun teaching my first course when Hurricane Katrina struck. My class met one time, and then the unthinkable occurred. My entire world was upside down. I had no place to live. I wondered if I would be able to finish my doctorate. Would I be able to return to New Orleans? I was evacuated at first to Texas and then several weeks later to Kentucky. During this time I realized that the small suitcase I had with me might contain everything that I would be able to salvage. Diana kept in touch with me during those months, and because of her I stayed focused on my dissertation. During this period of unthinkable loss, my communications with Diana were what sustained me. I would write a chapter, email it to her, and we would connect by phone to discuss changes and edits. When I think back to those times, it is extraordinary that we were doing this sort of work. I was sitting in a hotel—and then temporary housing—with Diana living hundreds of miles away in a trailer and then walking out into the field to get reception on her cell phone. Those were trying times for everyone to say the least. During the most traumatic circumstances that I had ever experienced, my relationship with Diana and the support that she provided enabled me to maintain focus on my goals. At a time when everything in my life seemed to be a question mark, my relationship with my mentor was a source of stability and focus.

Two months after Katrina in October 2005, Diana extended an invitation to me to live with her while I transitioned to new housing. I would also (as a condition) work on my dissertation daily. I was once again shocked by her kindness and concern for my wellbeing. Thinking about her generosity, I still become emotional. It wasn't just her job; she *cared* about me. She *wanted* me to finish my doctorate. So I moved into her spare bedroom. Surrounded by debris and destruction in the streets of New Orleans we sat at her kitchen table, and I worked. In about a month I was able to clean up my old apartment and move into another one. All the while Diana was a steady influence, not pushing but gently suggesting that I should not lose focus. In May of 2007, without losing any time from my original plan, I graduated with my Ph.D. Diana went above and beyond; her commitment to my success was evident. She taught me everything I know about being a counselor educator and a mentor. The change in me was professional, but it was also personal. As I began working full-time in a tenure-track position she still supported me and encouraged me.

I always knew that I could ask her the tough questions. I have been so thankful for her influence. She taught me about how to work with clients, how to run groups, and how to teach. Through our professional relationship she taught me *so much more*. I had always been concerned about having solid relationships with people but now there was a new perspective for me: intentionality about focusing on relationships with people first, before anything else. Relationships like this one are enduring and personal, which is what differentiates mentoring from simply advising or teaching (Sangganjanavanich & Magnuson, 2009). Diana could have answered my questions, graded my papers and met the requirements of her job description to the fullest extent without doing many of the things that she chose to do—especially cultivating a relationship of trust and caring. During that time I also learned that I could be intentional about cultivating relationships with other professors and with supervisors; perhaps, if I asked for what I needed, they would be responsive. I began to see the counselor educator/student relationship in a completely different light.

My Experiences as a Counselor Educator

When I became a counselor educator I began developing relationships with my own students, using many of the methods that I learned from Diana. Organizing research groups, asking students to present at conferences, and becoming faculty advisor for Chi Sigma Iota, all contributed to my mentoring of students. In addition, I took the time to know each one personally. I wanted to know my students as human beings, not just as names on a paper or by the grades they earned in my courses. I felt surprisingly secure in my role as a new faculty member. Of course there was normal anxiety about balancing my time, scholarly production and tenure, but I knew what I needed to do: focus on building relationships with my students, co-workers, and administration. So that is what I did.

As counselor educators, we teach our students to stay in the moment with clients, to exhibit unconditional positive regard for them, to value cultural differences between and among themselves, and to use the relationship to promote a sense of peace, a comfortable environment to explore sometimes very uncomfortable concerns. The question follows then, how do we teach students to cultivate meaningful relationships with their clients? We teach ethical standards, the dos and don'ts of entering into professional relationships; we teach techniques, therapeutic factors of trust and safety. Still I have heard many conversations about how to teach students to have empathy for others and whether it is even possible to do so. I would argue that the best way to teach students about meaningful relationships is to *have one* with them.

Chung, Bemak and Talleyrand (2007) discussed the unique situation that counselor educator mentors encounter because of the similarities between the counseling and mentoring processes. It seems to me that those similarities make the relationship that much more important and effective for teaching. I am able to talk to students about the relationship that I have with them and how those boundaries in the relationship are both similar to and different from the counseling relationship. In addition, we are able to have conversations about how our relationships are cultivated and how similar things happen with clients. I believe that having a mentoring relationship with students provides the perfect experience for transfer of learning: students can take what they learn about our relationship and begin to understand how to have other professional relationships (with clients, for example) that produce personal growth and change.

There are many parallels between the counselor/client relationship and the teacher/supervisor/student relationship. When looking back over their educational careers, many might agree that the educators who really made a difference were the ones who fostered relationships with students and demonstrated that they cared about each one personally. I believe that this continues to be the case, perhaps even more so in higher education and specifically when a person is becoming a counselor.

The value of mentoring in the field of professional counseling is obvious when one considers that mentored students are often more confident in their professional identities (Elman, Illfelder-Kaye & Robiner, 2005). It is very clear to me that students become passionate about being counselors in part because they first see faculty being passionate about the profession. In addition, faculty mentors often provide the support needed for students who question their own abilities to be professional counselors, to stay in school, and to persist through student life's challenges. Personally, I want to send new counselors into the field who are confident, who know the value of being a mental health counselor, and who are proud of the profession they have chosen.

When I think of my students, there are many stories that I could share to highlight the power of relationships, but I will choose just one. I met a young woman in my multicultural counseling class two years ago. She had a friendly smile and disposition but spoke very quietly and infrequently. When I read her first assignments I saw that she had much to offer that she wasn't sharing with the class so I made a point to begin encouraging her. We got to know one another over the course of that semester. The following year, I saw her change and mature as a counselor. We began to have discussions about what she wanted to do with her career and how she could meet those goals. This year she began a doctoral program in counselor education, and I am so proud of her accomplishments. We are in frequent contact by email (she is now in another state), and our relationship will continue as she progresses through her doctoral study. It is my hope that she will begin to develop mentoring relationships with her faculty there. We have already begun discussions about how she might begin the process of creating such relationships.

Importance of Relationships with Colleagues

Beginning my fifth year as a counselor educator, I become more aware every day of the importance of fostering relationships with those around me including students, colleagues, and administrators. This is true personally and professionally. Academia is challenging and stressful at best. During my first two years as an assistant professor, I encountered many different disappointments, confusion, stress; at times I felt very isolated. The pressure to engage in scholarship, service and teaching, to do all of those things well and to have a personal life at the end of the day creates the need for an incredible juggling act. Again, what sustained me? My relationships with my colleagues carried me through those challenging times.

I can recall specifically one time (one of many, in fact) when I felt extremely overwhelmed with my professional commitments and with the politics of academia. I was sitting in my office at the university, inundated with work. Was I certain that this was for me? Was I fitting into the profession that I loved so dearly? At that moment my colleague and friend, Laura, came into the room. Of course she had no idea what was going through my mind, but she took the time to ask. Of course she was as busy, overworked and overwhelmed, as I had been that semester. She sat and talked with me. Again, I was reminded of moments of uncertainty from my past including my client in crisis and my own crisis as a doctoral student. Then I realized that what I needed was right there: my relationship with a friend and colleague who understood what I was going through. After having a good laugh and venting our frustrations we began talking about writing together and focusing on the parts of our chosen profession that we enjoyed. I again felt excited and committed to what we were doing there. I can think of countless other stories where we lifted one another up, sharing laughter and tears. Having now worked for two universities in tenure-track positions, I can say that my greatest resources were the colleagues who became my friends.

In my career there have also been tense moments in faculty meetings, in committee meetings, and other work activities. In those moments I find that my relationships with people are what make those moments just moments and not a way of life. I can focus on my genuine care for people and set aside the minor events of the day. Many times I am forcing myself to stay in the here and now—back to basics.

As a self-proclaimed existentialist, I admit that I believe that people need meaning in their lives and that we are all driven to find this meaning (Frankl, 1997). Although I would like to believe that my choice to be a counselor and counselor educator is truly altruistic, I know that I reap the benefits of the profession that I have chosen. I love teaching; I adore my students and—even with its faults—I love academia. At the end of the day, what matters most to me is that I have built relationships with those around me that will encourage them, that will sustain me and that will ultimately change the lives of the clients whom we serve.

Questions for Reflection

1. Which relationships are most important in your life, and how do you spend time nurturing them?
2. Did you have a mentor during the early stages of your career? If so, what did you learn from that relationship that you are currently using with your clients/students/supervisees?
3. What do you need from those around you in order to feel supported and successful? How do you ask for what you need?

References

Chung, R. C., Bemak, F. & Talleyrand, R. M. (2007). Mentoring within the field of counseling: A preliminary study of multicultural perspectives. *International Journal for the Advancement of Counseling, 29 (1)*, 21-32. doi: 10.1007/s10447-006-9025-2

Elman, N. S., Illfelder-Kaye, J., & Robiner, W. N. (2005). Professional development: Training for professionalism as a foundation for competent practice in psychology. *Professional Psychology: Research and Practice, 36*(4), 367-375. doi: 10.1037/0735-7028.36.4.367

Frankl, V. E. (1997). *Man's search for meaning.* New York, NY: Pocket Books. Gelso, C. J. (2010). *The real relationship in psychotherapy: The hidden foundation of change.* Washington, DC: American Psychological Association.

Sangganjanavanich, V. F., & Magnuson, S. (2009). Averting role confusion between doctoral students and major advisers: adviser disclosure statements. *Counselor Education and Supervision, 48*, 194-203.

Yalom, I. D. (2002). *The gift of therapy: An open letter to a new generation of therapists and their patients.* New York, NY: HarperCollins

Yalom, I. D. (1980). *Existential psychotherapy.* New York, NY: Basic Books.

Chapter 15

Weaving a Life Fabric—Faith, Family, and Career

ROSEMARIE SCOTTI HUGHES

Throughout my academic career, from the first day of entering my master's program, I operated on two tracks: an aspiration to learn how to incorporate faith with counseling, and the desire to help parents of children with disabilities. Thirty years later, I am still working out that spiritual paradigm, and helping parents of children with special needs has been interwoven with spirituality. What I thought so simple, in my initial enthusiasm, I have learned is relatively complex. I describe my journey here because I believe that the personal journey of the counselor is a core component both of the fabric of counseling for clients and to that taught to students.

My impetus to become a counselor came from my own frustrations in the process of securing educational, health, and community services for my second son, who has an intellectual disability. He was my inspiration for becoming a non-traditional graduate student, beginning graduate school at age 37, with four sons at home and a spouse in the military who was deployed often. My goal was to be able to help other parents move through the mazes that one encounters in the world of special needs children, and a counseling degree was the vehicle to attain my goal. I also wanted to learn how to help others incorporate their faith in meeting their family's needs.

Faith Background

Faith was always a part of my life, with Catholic grandparents from Italy and Sicily and all of the large extended family being Catholic. I had 16 years of Catholic schooling in Pittsburgh. After I married and left home, Mass on Sundays was always my priority. My children went to public schools but had religious education and received all of the sacraments. Faith was important but was something I took for granted, probably in the same way I took being American for granted. I found myself praying more when my husband was deployed and not paying prayer much attention when he was on shore duty and home.

However, a crisis in my life led me back to being faith-full. When my son with a disability was ten, I was at a point in my life where I was losing hope. He was difficult to manage, I had three other boys, and Dad was at sea. I had no relatives closer than 500 miles for support; I was feeling alone. I was on a Mother's Day picnic with a friend, also a Navy wife, who also had four boys. We had been support for each other through this cruise. I was somewhat frantic, as I could not get all of my children organized as we were attempting to get everyone appropriately paired to use the paddle boats at the lake. My son Chris, who has an intellectual disability, was 10 years old, and had been in a residential school. Changes were made in funding, and we could no longer afford the school. He was home, and was transitioning to public school. The other boys were 11, 6, and 2. Chris' level of ability and understanding at that time was just about that of a 3 or 4 year old. Together, they were more than I could handle, and my friend, concerned, told me that I looked as though I was "about to lose it." She was right. I was overwhelmed and unable to cope.

Not long after that disastrous outing, a friend from church told me about a group she had been attending on Monday nights. I asked her what was so special, and her reply was, "It is life-giving." At that same time, the ship's officers' wives were offering a Bible study, with free babysitting. I would go anywhere for free babysitting. I really did not think I needed to hear more about the Bible, as I had 16 years of Catholic education, but I was curious. One of the Navy wives asked me if I had ever considered praying for Chris. I thought that was ridiculous, as intellectual disability has no cure. I later thought about it, and realized I had nothing to lose, so I prayed for him. My answer, to my mind, soul, spirit—call it what you will—was a reassurance that God loved this child even more than I did and that he would always be provided for by God.

My absolute fear, for 10 years, was that my child would end his days as an uncared-for adult in an institution because I was no longer there. Through the Monday night group I learned that I could have a faith that was personal, adding to my church-based faith. My faith was rekindled through attending two different church/Bible study groups. The compassion and love shown to me in both, led me to realize that faith and trust in God were my only hope. I committed to living a life that included daily prayer, Bible study, and finding support from other Christians, not necessarily only Catholics. My world of faith expanded.

This is not a story of dramatic differences before and after. My sons were still active, busy, and noisy. Life as a Navy spouse was not instantly wonderful, but my attitude had changed. I was no longer in despair but had a sense of not being alone in my struggles. I read the entire Bible through each year for three years in a row. I wanted the ancient words to become part of my being. I wanted to rely on something besides my own grit and intelligence to get me through life. Choosing that road served me well through the many events of my life beyond those first years and into my career.

When I encountered students going through difficulties, often compounded by being far from home, I could understand and empathize. Roommate problems, a family death or medical emergency, marital problems, and finances were recurring concerns for students. To accommodate emergencies, I would help students by working with them or their faculty on class assignment submission deadlines. I still do that as an adjunct online faculty member. I had set a policy for all faculty in my school to meet with students not more than three times as a triage method for personal (non-academic) problems. When more help was needed, faculty were to refer them for outside counseling. This was designed to keep student-faculty boundaries clear. We put money into our budget that would allow four sessions of such outside counseling.

Becoming a Counselor Educator

My road to becoming a counselor began when I took a parenting course, *Systematic Training for Effective Parenting* (Dinkmeyer & McKay, 1967), and then became a facilitator. I was fascinated by the group process, and saw how peers helped facilitate change in families. The elementary school that hosted the classes was upper middle class. Most moms at that time were homemakers without outside jobs. They held themselves to high standards of perfection and expected the same in their children. We were able to give them permission to not expect perfection from their children or from themselves, erasing a lot of family conflict. Fathers, in general, at that time, were not skilled in positive disciplining, and one large gain was having both parents using the skills together, backing each other up and not allowing the children to rule. We also taught parents how to talk with their children about sex. One particularly humorous class was reviewing with both genders the proper anatomical terms for sexual organs. The atmosphere at the time was not like today, with everything out in the open for adults as well as children, and we had to help parents overcome their own embarrassment. I discovered that I really liked working with adults (I had been an elementary teacher), and perhaps I could use my skills to help other parents of kids with disabilities. So my road to graduate school began.

Graduate school introduced me to theories, techniques, skills, research, and other courses in a typical counseling program. My master's degree is from a Christian university, which gave me further Biblical knowledge. I chose to continue through a doctoral program at a local state university in order to achieve a new goal–being a university professor. I felt the spiritual sustenance allowing me to juggle classes, family, and working part time. When I became a university assistant professor and obtained my professional counseling license, I could not have been happier. I could counsel people and teach others to do so. I did a lot of presenting at conferences and offered workshops about children with disabilities and their families. I also secured two book contracts, one for professionals and one for parents, related to counseling families of children with disabilities (Cook, 1990, 1992).

I hit a speed bump when my 25-year marriage dissolved, but faith and counseling kept me focused. My counselor and I shared the same theological orientation, and the experience cemented for me the importance of being spiritual in the counseling room. Through the nine months of counseling, I struggled with the issue of why God would allow my marriage to end. I felt betrayed by God. I had prayed for my husband for 14 years. I was faithful in church attendance, in raising my children in the faith, and fulfilled obligations as a Christian spouse and Navy wife. I did everything my church required, and yet I could not save the marriage. I came to realize—as led by my counselor, through journaling, prayer, Scripture reading, and reflection—that I had to accept that which was not going to change. The counselor helped me focus on my gifts, talents, and character and upon the present calling in my life. We both spoke the same language of "vocation" rather than just a job. The therapy also helped me when I hit a block in writing my first book. When stuck, I had to first identify and resolve my anger at my husband about a certain point in my son's life before I could write the chapter on that particular developmental stage of children. The prayer my counselor prayed for me at the end of each session was significant to me; it helped sustain me between appointments.

A New Phase of Life

I was invited to take on administrative roles at the university, and I eventually became the first female academic dean of that university. I am now dean emerita after a 23-year career. I am currently in private practice and teaching online, and have come, full circle, back to my original goals. I work in a Christian practice, but not all of my clients are Christians. Many clients are children with disabilities and their parents. Some of my clients are adults with a disability. I am still refining how to be effective in counseling through employing my faith and the faith of my clients. I bring all of my years of teaching, researching, writing, and presenting as well as my own experience of hope and renewal to the counseling room.

I often find myself silently praying for help when I do not know where to go next with a client. I have clients who do some horrible things and yet I have to look at them as children of God who need compassion and understanding. I ask God to be in charge of who is on my schedule and even how many clients I have in a day. I pray to be able to accept people where they are, as they are. I believe that no one comes into my office by accident, but by purpose. I also have a strong work ethic so that I strive to follow office procedures and policies promptly to avoid adding to the staff's workload unnecessarily. I also strive to treat the staff with respect, even when some are much younger than I.

My approach is basically the same for all people, whether or not they have indicated on the intake form that they are practicing Christians. I help people clarify what gives them meaning in life, and what they can do to find that meaning. Even my clients who say they have no faith belief system, or do not want to discuss Christianity, are open to my approach. Active Christians have a wide variety of ways to practice their faith. I do ask clients if I can pray with them when the session has ended—

I do not do it at the beginning because I do not want that request to influence them in the session—and no one has ever refused, even those who have had "bad" experiences with church. The practice I work for has "Christian" in the title but that does not keep people without faith from our doors. I do not usually ask to pray with those who say God is not a factor in their life, but I do privately pray for all my clients each day. I am still on a journey and am privileged to walk alongside others as our lives intersect. I am daily called to accountability to "walk my talk." I am sure that there are days when I fall short of the standards I set out to attain. However, my goal is to match my actions to my faith.

I was privileged to be in an environment throughout my academic career where my desire to interweave spirituality with work was not only encouraged but required. The challenge was to have a good working knowledge of the Bible, be an expert in content, and spiritually aware of student and faculty needs. I am a person rarely satisfied with the status quo, and so I used our department's semi-annual retreats—which I would design—to teach faculty new ways of looking at and employing Scripture. We would also prayerfully plan for the department. I also provided retreats for other parts of the university. I believe that humor is part of our spirituality. For example, I began a retreat for the School of Divinity with *The Mississippi Squirrel Revival*, by Ray Stevens. I introduced it as "a spiritual song on which we will now meditate." After that event, a number of faculty bought Ray Stevens music. One never knows!

My faith has and does come into play as I advocate for children and adults with disabilities and their families. I have presented in parent groups, community organizations, and at local, state, and national conferences on the topic. I became a bit of a nuisance (and proud of it) at the university on accessibility issues and procedures for students who needed accommodations for their studies. I would remind people, over and over, that our doors needed automatic openers, and parking was not convenient for someone in a wheelchair. I would always raise the issue—in meetings to plan events—of how we could best accommodate those who do not see, hear, or ambulate normally. My guiding philosophy is that when we provide access on any level for those with disabilities, we make life easier for the rest of us: the temporarily able-bodied.

I now work with a local group, called the Faith Inclusion Network, to bring together all faiths to provide accommodations and programs for those with disabilities. I continue to be a consulting editor for the *Journal of Health, Religion, and Disability*.

A 21st Century Perspective on Spirituality

Faith is both dynamic and static. Surveys show that in America, over 90% of people believe in a power higher than themselves, and most people call that power God (Pew Research Center, 2009), who is generally considered as unchanging. About 75% of American people say that they pray often, asking for God's intervention in their lives, the dynamic factor (Pew Research Center, 2010). Within those percentages are a wide range of belief systems that counselors cannot ignore. People today "church shop," looking not so much at denomination, but seeking where their particular needs can be met. Going to church is not necessarily connected with having a faith—church attendance has remained stable in America since World War II, at about the 35% level (Campbell & Putnam, 2010). Faith does not require the same communal practices, or sacraments, for all.

Faith in America has changed since I was that cradle-roll Catholic child. Back then, one had to ask permission of the priest to be in a wedding not held in a Catholic church, or to send a child to public school. As a child, I was attuned to the numinous—the world of angels and saints, of Holy Days and pageants. That childhood interest was a base which launched my personal and professional interest in spirituality.

Academic Service and Spirituality

In my academic career I transitioned from one known as a Roman Catholic to one known as a United Methodist. I felt I had the best of both worlds, as I could "speak the language" of both faith traditions. I participated in ASERVIC (*Association for Spirituality, Ethics, and Religion in Counseling),* a division of the American Counseling Association (ACA), regularly because I wanted to bring inclusive perspectives of spirituality to my students. I found the "broadening" of my faith perspectives and their application to counseling and teaching to be exciting.

Some students entered the program wanting to know how to do "Biblical" counseling, which to most was defined as the ability to apply specific Scriptures to certain problems, like bandages. One of my hardest tasks as a counselor educator was to have students learn Biblical principles that are sound, time-tested, and able to contribute to a person's growth and development. For example, a favorite quote to support spanking is "Those who spare the rod of discipline hate their children." (Proverbs 13:24, New Believer's Bible). If that was an issue in class I would guide a student to look at the actual concept of "rod" in the Bible, which was one of leading and guiding, and not necessarily one of punishment. I would present several other passages that would support positive discipline, and then help students draw their conclusions on the meaning and purpose of discipline for children and the best way to accomplish it.

I began each class with a devotional of some kind, whether a reading from Scripture or other spiritual writing, drawing writings from various cultures and eras. I invited students to share the joys in their life that week as well as their concerns, and we would pray for them together. In some classes students would sign up to present devotionals.

As dean, I contributed to the department's weekly newsletter for our students through the "Dean's Desktop," a column to encourage students. This was another place to integrate faith and counseling. I had many words of thanks from students and staff alike about the columns and it was an enjoyable aspect of my job. As I became a team member and team leader of the Council on Accreditation for Counseling and Related Educational Programs (CACREP). I was often called upon to visit faith-based counseling programs, which was a wonderful opportunity to combine my CACREP knowledge with an understanding of how the particular program integrated faith issues. With experience in both Protestant and Catholic churches as well as evangelical and Pentecostal environments, I am "multilingual" on faith issues. I understand the goals set for students in faith-based programs and can appreciate various approaches to spirituality without having to compromise CACREP standards. At times I have had the privilege of attending Sunday worship with faculty when on a site visit.

ASERVIC and the Spiritual Competencies

My personal spiritual journey had a direct connection to my roles of counselor educator and professional counselor. I have been a member of Association for Spiritual, Ethical, and Religious Values in Counseling (ASERVIC) for many years, served on its board, and am currently on the editorial board for its official journal, *Counseling and Values*. My academic career has been spent working on integration of counseling and faith in the programs in which I have taught; and I suspect that will remain an ongoing theme of my life. I have come to the conclusion that integration of faith and attention to one's craft is the ultimate model for students. I believe that most counseling students are relational, and are looking for the role model, the inspiration, the person who will give them guidance in their professional and spiritual lives. Over the years students and I have published together, laughed and cried and prayed together, and have been concerned about each other's lives. In my current practice I am working with some people I have had in the classroom—which is wonderful. Also inspiring are some of those students with whom I had conflict, mostly over grades. Some have come back to me, years later, to apologize for how they acted and express appreciation that I held them to high standards. They often express that they are where they are now in their professions because of my actions. Those reconciliations have been deeply moving. I am sure, however, that my experiences of challenge and connection are probably not unique among counseling faculty.

I have found that it is one thing to list competencies which fully equip a spiritual counselor, and another to be able to live them out, teach them to students, and employ them in counseling. How do we measure how much sinks in? How do we know that students are employing these competencies in their professional lives? How do we know that they make a difference in the counseling room or the classroom? Where am I? Am I effective? Do my intentions match my results?

The following 14 items are the *Spiritual Competencies* (2009), from the ASERVIC website. For each competency, I reflect on my own perspectives and ongoing struggles as a counselor educator and a professional counselor, fully respecting all those who have brought these competencies this far. The views are purely my own, drawn from my own spiritual and professional journey.

1. The professional counselor can describe the similarities and differences between spirituality and religion, including the basic beliefs of various spiritual systems, major world religions, agnosticism, and atheism.

Descriptions often depend on what is in front of one's eyes at the moment. Even people who worship regularly in the same building have differing viewpoints on some tenets of their faith. The concept of a personalized faith is widespread. I had a student who was struggling because as she was learning about feminist perspectives in counseling; her former notions of man as head of the household were causing her conflict. With time and knowledge, she came to hold a balanced perspective. Perhaps the familiar quote, often attributed to St. Augustine, but also to others, is helpful: "In essentials, unity; in doubtful matters, liberty; in all things, charity."

2. The professional counselor recognizes that the client's beliefs (or absence of beliefs) about spirituality and/or religion are central to his or her worldview and can influence psychosocial functioning.

Recognition and the ability to raise the topic are two different skill sets. If I have not articulated my own belief system, can I invite another to do so? There is hesitancy, perhaps embarrassment, or perhaps fear of putting the client on the spot. Helping students, interns, and residents become comfortable in their own faith skin is an ongoing task, much like the acculturation levels we discuss in multicultural courses and competencies. Assigning students to make a spiritual life line, mark events that have contributed to both spiritual crises and growth, and then write reflections, can help produce that articulation.

3. The professional counselor actively explores his or her own attitudes, beliefs, and values about spirituality and/or religion.

There is a difference between exploring and honestly attempting to live by one's belief and value systems. I explore by reading about something; I live out my beliefs and values by actions. Our ethical codes contain much information about a value set, but the ethical codes are not where I look for the basic values of my life. It is because of my basic values that I choose to adhere to ethical codes. For example, I was once in a situation where revealing information about another faculty member would have changed students' opinion of what they wrongly thought had transpired and vindicated myself, but I ethically could not give out that information and keep to my own standards of integrity.

4. The professional counselor continuously evaluates the influence of his or her own spiritual and/or religious beliefs and values on the client and the counseling process.

Hopefully, during the practicum, internship, and residency time, a counselor has good supervision that will call this competency into play. However, the supervisor must first acknowledge and own personal beliefs and values to be able to be in an evaluative stance. Then one must act intentionally, just as though perfecting application of a theory, technique, or manualized treatment. Not knowing who one is or to what one subscribes can leave the supervisor without a compass.

Some students are unable to self-examine because of fear of confronting issues in their past or current life. In my programs, students who had this problem were strongly encouraged to get counseling. Sometimes they were required to step out of the program, engage with a licensed counselor, and present a letter from the counselor saying that their course of counseling had been completed and that they were suitable to continue in the program.

5. The professional counselor can identify the limits of his or her understanding of the client's spiritual and/or religious perspective and is acquainted with religious and spiritual resources and leaders who can be avenues for consultation and to whom the counselor can refer.

Finding a religious and spiritual resource and leader could prove difficult in a low-density population area without a variety of faiths represented, such as in the rural areas of my state where resources are sparse. Thankfully, there is the Internet. As content is increasing at exponential rates, counselor educators can steer their students into meaningful web searches to increase their learning in this area. University counseling departments can increase access for remote areas by creating compendia of web resources on their sites. This competency also tells me that I need to set aside my preconceived notions and biases and listen carefully to the client, allowing myself to be educated in the session, and in courses, by my students.

6. The professional counselor can describe and apply various models of spiritual and/or religious development and their relationship to human development.

Most theories and models are Western European/American. My ongoing quest is to learn more of belief systems that are not within my knowledge base. To learn of other religions, I recommend *God is Not One* (Prothero, 2010) and *God is Not a Christian* (Tutu, 2011).

7. The professional counselor responds to client communications about spirituality and/or religion with acceptance and sensitivity.

The active listening skills required for this competency are built into all counseling programs. However, the word "acceptance" poses a conundrum. Some of the students I have taught through the years think that acceptance is equivalent to denying their own faith, or condoning the client's belief set if it is radically opposed to their own. When reframed in acceptance of the person and sensitivity to the person, I believe a new paradigm emerges that is less threatening.

8. The professional counselor uses spiritual and/or religious concepts that are consistent with the client's spiritual and/or religious perspectives and are acceptable to the client.

I have limited experience in belief systems that are outside of Christianity and Judaism. My fear is of offending someone in a Muslim faith or in non-theistic belief systems because I do not know those spiritual concepts well enough to bring them into the session—or the classroom. Because I have not studied with any depth or seen that belief set in action I feel ill-equipped to use the concepts well. I have attended services in churches of several denominations as well as in Jewish synagogues. I have read a variety of fiction and nonfiction that deals with world religions. Travel around the world where I saw Buddhist monks chanting and Islamic worshippers praying; touring the Vatican; and learning the history of the Stave churches of Sweden, and many other such experiences, have helped me expand my understanding of various faiths. However, I have not lived for a lengthy time in any of those cultures, sharing the daily joys and struggles of their peoples. My own Sunday School class has been helpful, as we have explored major world religions through reading or videos. When we give students assignments of immersion in multicultural class, they are usually somewhat superficial and time limited. To be effective, I have to be open to allowing the client to do the "describing" that is in the first competency.

When clients tell me that they pray, I ask how they pray, when they pray, what their spiritual resources are, and if they have a faith community they find supportive. They describe their attendance habits and their families' religious backgrounds. You might think that I get downright nosey, but all of the information gives me a basis of understanding.

9. The professional counselor can recognize spiritual and/or religious themes in client communication and is able to address these with the client when they are therapeutically relevant.

I feel I am attuned to the spiritual and religious in general. For students, the supervision process is valuable in conveying how to bring these themes out to the student and the counselor. A serious issue for consideration is how to have the conversation with potential supervisors as to how religious/spiritual themes will be a part of their supervising. It might involve the faculty member conveying expectations that the student will be allowed to explore spiritual issues with the client and to be allowed to initiate the subject. Supervisors may need training, as some are hesitant in this area. In my program, we held once-a-year luncheons and provided continuing education events for all of our supervisors, where this skill was part of the content.

10. During the intake and assessment processes, the professional counselor strives to understand a client's spiritual and/or religious perspective by gathering information from the client and/or other sources.

When practicing in an office, initial assessment can be facilitated by a spiritual in-take form. Client responses on that form can then be used as starting points for discussion. Would it be helpful to have such an intake form for our students, to help instructors understand the students' concepts of religion and spirituality, or would that be invasive? Including course work in both designing an intake form and a self-disclosure form might be a good exercise for an ethics class.

11. When making a diagnosis, the professional counselor recognizes that the client's spiritual and/or religious perspectives

can a) enhance well-being; b) contribute to client problems; and/or c) exacerbate symptoms.

Once I recognize clients' belief systems and their functioning in one of the above ways, the challenge is a) help them to explore and use faith resources; or b) provide gentle confrontation; or b) and c). This is done without evangelizing or criticizing, bringing clients to a higher level of well-being within their framework. Clients' spiritual perspectives are easy to discover through use of the spiritual intake form and follow-up conversations about the role (or non-role) of their faith. Also, simply asking what is keeping the clients from making changes in their life usually gets an answer tied into the faith perspective that is informative. For example, consider a client who has multiple marriages and divorces because her moral standard is not to engage in sex outside of marriage. Having a "cafeteria" approach to the tenets of her religion, she has disregarded the fact that divorce is also disapproved by her church.

12. The professional counselor sets goals with the client that are consistent with the client's spiritual and/or religious perspectives.

The ACA code of ethics is clear on client autonomy. Also the market will dictate that people seeking counsel go where they feel they are being treated in an autonomous manner. When clients come in with multiple problems, as they inevitably do, I cannot push my agenda, even when my best professional judgment seems that I know the direction they need to take. I have to allow clients to choose the area for work, and be willing to help them set the goals they need. I then find that they are more likely, as counseling progresses, to be open to my offering them a few options to choose from on what to approach next and to commit to engagement.

13. The professional counselor is able to a) modify therapeutic techniques to include a client's spiritual and/or religious perspectives, and b) utilize spiritual and/or religious practices as techniques when appropriate and acceptable to a client's viewpoint.

I wholeheartedly agree, but with the reservations as to knowledge and authenticity I expressed earlier. For example, I keep a booklist for my clients, which has a mix of faith-oriented and secular titles. I always give them the whole list, but check off a few that may be beneficial to them given their beliefs. I have some printed prayers that transcend faiths— at least I believe they do—that I give out as I deem appropriate. I have never had anyone complain. The following is one illustration of faith and client issues: I recently had a discussion with a child and parent as to the child's desire to do an activity that would replace a weeknight church activity. I helped them sort through the pros and cons of the activity and what it meant to the child. The parent then reconsidered the original stance of requiring the child to attend the weeknight church activity.

14. The professional counselor can therapeutically apply theory and current research supporting the inclusion of a client's spiritual and/or religious perspectives and practices.

It was easier to keep up with current research as a full time academic than it is as a practicing clinician. Paperwork to get paid competes with time to read journals. I carry journals to the office to read when I have a no-show client. I also catch up at home when I am able. I no longer subscribe to as many journals as formerly, but being active in counselor education online also keeps me in the literature via student papers and discussion boards. When I have an issue with a client that requires more information, I access a variety of online sites and obtain specific information—a way of "keeping up" that is perhaps more efficient in the long run.

New Roles and New Opportunities

I have new roles in my life now—mother-in-law and grandma—which I deem just as important as my paid positions. Although my son with a disability does not live at home, I am still his advocate and maintain an active role in his life. With both parents and most of my aunts and uncles deceased, in my extended family I am now a member of the oldest generation. At the same time, I am moving toward the upper levels of age among counselor educators and therapists. There are sobering and yet satisfying thoughts of how I, as a female counselor educator, have traveled the various roads and roles of life to come to this point. Yet I know that there is still much more to accomplish and enjoy.

As to the years spent in the university, particularly those as an administrator, I do not miss the meetings, the memos, the ever-increasing paperwork and documentation. I have never been one to rest on my laurels (and am somewhat reluctant to talk about them), but I am satisfied with the part I had creating a $2.5 million chair in my department, the Rosemarie Scotti Hughes Endowed Chair in Christian Thought in Mental Health Practice—the largest single gift that had ever been received by my university—for the only named, funded chair. Our programs were and have been consistently CACREP and APA accredited. The department has met and exceeded annual budget requirements. The number of graduates from my department has continually grown as have staff and faculty. I am now dean emerita, the first also from that university, and I have no regrets about my university career.

In this new phase of my life, I want to write more; so I have joined a local writers' association and attended my first writers' conference. I hope to continue to travel, spend time with adult kids and grandkids as their schedules allow, volunteer in ministry, keep reading and learning, and be comfortable in my own skin. One of these days I may even organize my digital photos! I have had to come to terms with having a permanent physical disability in that a freak fall and several surgeries resulted in a loss of range of motion and strength in my right arm. I find that I have a number of limitations, but also have discovered some creativity in working around those limits. As we age, limits are part of life, but so are new opportunities and discoveries, and each one is a gift. As I age, I think about what my "bye" line would be ("obituary" to crossword puzzle fans) and I think I would like my life to be summed up as "She loved"— my major, overall, lifelong goal.

Questions for Reflection

1. How has your own spiritual life been a factor in your decision to enter the field of counseling?
2. What hinders you from being open about your spiritual beliefs and/or religious practices?
3. What would you like to do to incorporate spirituality in your counseling courses, and what do you need to do to make that happen?

References

Campbell D. E., & Putnam, R. D. (2010) *American Grace: How religion divides and unites us.* New York: Simon & Schuster.

Competencies for Addressing Spiritual and Religious Issues in Counseling (2009). Retrieved from www.aservic.org/resources/spiritual-competencies/)

Cook, R. S. (1990) *Counseling families of children with disabilities.* Irving, Texas: Word.

Cook, R. S. (1992) *Parenting a child with special needs.* Grand Rapids: Zondervan.

Dinkmeyer, D., & McKay, G. D. (1967) *The parent's handbook: Systematic training for effective parenting.* Circle Pine, MN: American Guidance Services.

New Believer's Bible, (2006). Carol Stream, IL: Tyndale House

Pew Research Center's Forum on Religion & Public Life (2009). Retrieved from http://pewforum.org/Age/Religion-Among-the-Millennials.aspx

Pew Research Center's Forum on Religion & Public Life (2010). Retrieved from http://pewresearch.org/pubs/1847/how-religion-divides-and-unites-us-david-campbell-conversation-transcript

Prothero, Stephen R., (2010) *God is not one: The eight rival religions that run the world.* New York: Harper One.

Tutu, Desmond, (2011) *God is not one.* New York: Harper Collins.

Chapter 16

Soul Work: Who Am I? What Do I Stand For? Where Am I Going?

MARY ALICE BRUCE

So many questions emerge as I work to nurture my soul and support my students and colleagues in promoting our collective dignity and soul connection. Drawing from the humanistic psychology movement (Maslow, 1998; May, 1953; Rogers, 1961) as well as works by Rose, Westefeld, and Ansley (2001) and Sperry and Shafranske (2005), soul work can be defined as both an internal and external process eliciting self-awareness and spiritual meaning that may provide a pathway to personal growth and self-actualization. Thus, the basic first steps for my personal soul work are to examine and increase my own self-awareness and self-knowledge.

Realizing who I am is a crucial foundation for my soul work as a woman, wife, mother, and professor of counselor education. Nurturing our own souls allows us to offer wholeness and healing in our counseling work, thus integrating the art and science of helping others. Indeed, the foundation of our professional identity draws upon the field of psychology, which ". . . literally means the study of the soul" (Duran, Firehammer, & Gonzalez, 2008, p. 289).

For a while, the counseling profession seemed to move away from soul healing. During the late 20th and early part of the 21st century, counseling seemed to swing more toward solution-focused, behavioral and cognitive perspectives rather than resonate specifically with soul work (Duran et al., 2008). With the emergence of managed care demands, perhaps counselors were responding to the impulses of immediate gratification and relief of pain rather than exploring inner voices and personal growth. Actually, I was feeling effective and successful with brief, solution-focused counseling as my theoretical foundation (Bruce, 1995; Bruce & Hopper, 1997). In keeping with the tenets of solution-focused work (Bruce, 1995), bringing forward strengths and possibilities in my counseling and supervision responsibilities seemed a good fit with my style. But, when watching myself, I noticed that it was as if I were sometimes just saying the effective words to ease others toward their goals, rather than being present in the moment. I believed that I strayed from the path and forgot that the process of counseling is soul work itself (Duran et al., 2008). I started to feel shallow in my connections, lacking meaningful interactions.

When I pay attention to being fully present in the moment and mindful, I am able to focus and clearly connect with each student or client. I observe myself sensing what is needed for each person and me to join into the moment. I can look around and send energy to support others, and I can respond to what is happening right now. Sometimes a moment of silence and a thoughtful nod of my head are needed to realize another's frustration or anger. Sometimes, a brief touch on the student's arm answers a need for sharing grief and pain.

For me, being present in the moment is particularly important when welcoming and starting a class with my students. We begin with students checking in and reflecting on their state of being that day. If someone brings forward surprising or tragic news, I am able to reach out and genuinely respond in a helpful manner. One day in class, a student revealed that his wife was just diagnosed with cancer and needed immediate intense treatment. Although I was swept into the devastating emotion, I grounded myself to be present and moved the focus to support him as he was with us in such a space. "Talk to us," and later, "How can we best support you right now?" I wanted to be with him, not be with myself in my own emotion. Being present allows me to be with others in the way I choose, rather than mindlessly distancing.

According to Duran (2006), the counseling profession itself, which had lost its soul (Beck, 2003), is now experiencing a spiritual infusion and is slowly steering away from the mechanistic medical model. I believe that when people were not experiencing meaning in their life's work, which may have eased too far into mechanistic operations, they realized that something needed to change. Ottens and Klein (2005) offered the idea of a spiritual soul as beyond superficial knowing, rather a deep grounding, the essence of which encompasses a person's morals, beliefs, values, culture, and faith. Nurturing of the soul is "a quest for transcendence beyond the limits of the self to a higher level of meaning that leads to authenticity, connectedness, compassion and oneness in and with the Universe" (Bruce, 2007, p. 188).

Being Present in the Moment

When I feel on a plateau in life, or even stuck or down in the dumps and need to nurture my soul, I return to my basic first step of being present and mindful. Rather than operating on automatic, I slow myself and observe myself, living each moment. For example, I drive my car to the parking lot and instead of parking in a comfortable spot, I park in a different area, taking notice and making a mental note to myself of a new spot. I watch myself step out of a habitual pattern and do something different to avoid my usual behavior. It is such a small step, and yet it reminds me to observe myself, step out of myself, be with myself. As I walk out to my car, I smile to myself and realize that I am not in a rut; I watch myself and enjoy this small pleasure of surprising myself out of a pattern, out of autopilot and into the rich present. I feel grounded.

Another reminder to myself to be truly present, comes when the phone rings. The ring itself reminds me to stop, pause, and then pick up the phone, watching how I respond rather than grabbing the phone and greeting the caller. Again, such a small reminder helps me stay present more and more. Day to day situations offer many opportunities for reminders to be present and observe myself. When working at the computer, I stop every 15 minutes, stand, throw back my shoulders and breathe deeply. Also, when others stop by my office or even greet me from the hallway, I watch myself smile and stand to acknowledge them, shifting into a genuine presence.

I find all this fairly easy to do when I am not experiencing anxiety or worry. A key point for me is to be able to step a bit away from myself when I start to feel emotions overwhelming me. The slight shift of perspective with a step away can let me take charge, rather than the emotion taking charge of me. I take a huge slow breath—a belly-breath. Additional slow, monitored breathing with a physical stretch starts to calm and ground me. For me, the grounding allows the emotion to flow through and down. The emotion might ripple through several times; then as I stand on it, I take charge. I am not ignoring the emotion. It gathers, sometimes in my stomach, sometimes in my chest or head. Whether positive or negative emotion, I gather it, focus and name it, rather than let it fragment me. Even happiness can get out of hand with effusive, regrettable behaviors. And I'll say it: sometimes it is very hard to step away. Then I need solitude and a physical shift out of the surrounding context where the emotion is grabbing me in order to return to a grounded presence.

When I am present and mindful, I can respond quickly with thoughtfulness to situations that emerge. I don't become so caught in impulse or emotion. Being present keeps me open to possibilities and opportunities. I can say "Yes, let's think about that idea," rather than being stumped or negatively reactive when the unexpected zooms in front of me. I can adapt and operate with flexibility. I can remember when we welcomed a new dean into our college. At our initial lunch meeting together, she stated, "Great to think that your department may merge with departments xxx and xxx with you as the head." I had not previously heard or contemplated this idea. Initially, I felt shock. And then, as I took a breath to keep grounded and present, I nodded and said, "Something to consider," which indeed it was!

Actually, I feel better about myself when I can respond with an open stance. Even if my heart/intuition initially tells me "NO," I am pleased that instead of automatically responding negatively, I can offer respectful acknowledgement of an idea or proposal and then consider possibilities as well as perspectives of others. And sometimes I realize that I leap to a NO when I really do not have all the information, insight and wisdom to make a thoughtful comment or decision. Although I may leap to a NO when something is catching me from my past of which I may be unaware, upon reflection I step away and consider possibilities when I am wide eyed, rather than blinded by my baggage. In summary, when present and aware, my energy is positive, allowing me to act thoughtfully and be my best.

Connections with Others

Engaging with others can bring powerful growth in soul work. Sometimes, I sense positive energy and easy connection with others. What a joy to intuitively appreciate someone. When I am open and in a good space, I can easily welcome others. I care and want to understand how a person thinks, feels, and acts. I try to truly understand and step into the shoes of another person. I continually work on genuine, focused listening and not jumping into how I want to respond.

My real test comes when someone approaches me with anger or blame. As a school counselor, teachers often asked me to be with them during parent conferences due to worry about strong emotions and parental reactions. I was able to provide support and help when needed. But it is different when I am the one attacked. I have to concentrate and focus to watch what is happening, calm myself and then recognize and accept the strong feelings of someone else. In the moment, I must work hard to put myself into that person's shoes and move into empathy to understand what might be really going on underneath everything, the true meaning of the situation. Sometimes, I just cannot join with that person's values or beliefs, but I can acknowledge the person and possible emotions that we may each be experiencing.

For example, at our institution, we have a university technology department that has not been responsive to our department's website needs. Thus, our recruiting efforts have been stymied by lack of updates of application deadlines, current interview dates, pictures and even the addition of new faculty members. How difficult it was to listen carefully as the head technology man talked with me about his frustrations. Yet I calmed myself, really listened to him (it helped that it was via phone), and acknowledged him. I feel satisfied that I offered understanding rather than anger.

Currently, I am exploring other strategies for website changes. Sometimes very serious conflicts occur, and I work hard to experience the feeling without having the feeling grab ahold of me. Thus I am able to express myself appropriately and offer a clear, congruent message. Bringing forward my concern, I wonder about the situation, and ask that we find a solution or disengage from our agreement. However, it is still difficult for me to be consistently caring of others when we are involved in emotionally charged interaction that creates a negative energy. Observing myself and keeping compassion all around is hard work.

One of my best friends and I sometimes do have run-ins. One of us will say to the other, "Seems we are off balance. What do we need to sort out?" Since we do work so closely together, political implications can be devastating. Thus, working through problems by bringing them forward to understanding and processing without jumping to hasty solutions, can offer hope for collaboration and healing in a dynamic, humanistic way. It can be scary too. Sometimes I can feel something come between me and a colleague or student when I do not know the person well enough to be sure that there is adequate mutual trust to explore the source of tension. I just wonder aloud, "Is everything OK? Seems there is a little bit of weirdness with us today." It takes courage for me to reach out, but I bolster myself, since I feel the bad energy when things are wrong. On occasion, I approach someone —from the one-down position—wondering how it is with us, and find the other person is not ready or does not need to talk about our connection. At least, I have reached out and done my best in a respectful manner. The door is open for the future.

Appropriate self-disclosure can also be helpful in building relationships. Sometimes I find myself offering a very brief story of my own to emphasize a connection or commonality that we share. Our department often has students returning to higher education after some years away. Students usually worry if their brains will work again, if they will be able to manage graduate school, or if they will be able to connect with the other students in their cohort group. Upon learning that I was a stay-at-home mother for eleven years who then began earning her graduate degrees, students usually express some relief that they will be understood, and that it is possible to move forward with some degree of confidence regarding their graduate program with others appreciative of the diversity they bring.

A Way of Being in the World

As I nurture my own soul for healing and harmony, I know that social injustices continue to wound diverse cultures and marginalized peoples. Oppression is often inadvertently perpetuated by means of well-intentioned mental health professionals who guide clients toward behaviors in keeping with the ethnocentric practices of dominant U.S. society and the existing power structures. However, I believe that counselors recognize that they have an ethical responsibility to become culturally sensitive, employ culturally appropriate helping interventions, and advocate against social injustices.

As a counselor educator, I continue to take small steps to urge humanistic consideration of diversity and soul-healing practices that can lead to increasing professional proficiency. In my college, I was honored to head the diversity task force, appointed by the dean and charged with bringing forward a conceptual framework to underlie our vision of diversity. Our task force also was successful in proposing a formal Diversity Council in the college to address cultural competencies of faculty, staff and students relating to education, research, and practice. The proposal, and its inclusion in the college's by-laws, was a challenge with some faculty members stating, "I am tired of spending time and money on diversity when we need technology upgrades." "Are we done yet? I have heard enough about multiculturalism. Let's move on." Surprisingly to me, faculty members of color, who were task force members, were negative about much positive movement. I learned that those particular faculty members often commented, "Those Whites are giving us lip service again." I believe years of covert oppression and unacknowledged pain still plague us.

Especially as a White woman, I know it is the time to stand up for what is right and good for all. And I realize the change must first happen with me. Watching myself to catch stereotypes and prejudices of my own is essential. Just last week, our department was approached to consider a spousal hire, the hiring of the partner of a potential faculty member whom the university really desires to hire. Since the desired faculty member was African American, I assumed that his partner was African American too. Wait, I caught myself and realized what an assumption I was making. I may have good intentions but stumble and bumble. At such times, I need to reach out for help and be willing to stand in a vulnerable position. My soul work takes place in just that space of vulnerability. Bringing issues forward and wondering how I can support a community of careful listening, understanding and forgiveness takes courage. The question is: How we can engage in more soulful activities to promote diversity and multiculturalism?

During my sabbatical, I was fortunate to be supported by my university and a Fulbright grant to collaborate with psychology faculty members of the Universidad del Valle de Guatemala. The collaboration included teaching a counseling course for master's students intending to be school counselors. It also offered the national teachers various workshops that presented communication and relationship ideas for connecting with their students. How my eyes were opened with the support and collaboration each student, teacher and faculty offered!

In this Latino culture, the idea of collective work was demonstrated in genuine ways. During the weekend of spiritual growth which I facilitated for the female faculty, the theme of *Women helping Women* emerged due to the numerous bonds and heartfelt experiences shared. I still have a lot to learn about how to support others and myself in bringing forward generous welcoming of diversity and responsiveness to others.

Self Awareness and Self Knowledge

Realizing who I am and knowing my limitations and strengths, seems to be of utmost importance to my soul work. I must watch myself, quiet negative self talk, recognize my psychological issues and deal with them as they emerge. Asking trusted others for feedback is a good way to realize work that needs to be done. Once, I was asked to present at a staff meeting of our college. I arrived and listened while the business meeting was conducted before my presentation. Afterward, I asked my office associate for feedback. She responded that during the business items, I was sitting back in my chair, almost slumped, and thus seemed uninterested in being with the staff. Although my passion and content eventually engaged the participants, she worried that my initial posture affected that audience and their feelings of connection with me. I had not thought anyone was paying much attention while I was deep in thought, running through my presentation to come. What an insight regarding the importance of being present and mindful in connecting with others.

As I know myself better, I realize the kind of small treasured times that are available in day-to-day life to nurture my soul. Walking in the early morning to breathe the fresh air and glimpse the mountains, running my finger over a crystal placed on my office desk, listening to a piece of music that brings fond memories to mind and thrills my entire being, receiving a surprise call from my son to tell me his daughter is taking her first steps, such gifts bring me hope in our world.

Caring for myself each day by mindfully noticing its small joys gives me energy to surge with my intuition and creativity. I am more likely to try something different in teaching, learning and supervision when my imagination is freed. Once, during live supervision in our onsite clinic, one of our students was trying to find ways to support the client and celebrate her achievements. Those of us in the observation room decided to write a note to the client to join the counselor in recognizing the client's hard work and the progress she had made. We slipped the note under the door of the counseling room. The counselor was surprised and pleased to present the client with the note. The client was touched with emotion that the team cared enough to write a note detailing some of the appreciation they had of her powerful work. This seemingly small gesture was significant to the client. She returned to the clinic the next year to thank everyone for our care and affirmation. Small, day-to-day actions can make a world of difference by giving encouragement and hope.

Conclusion

As I focus on my soul work, my values and beliefs, as well as strengths and limitations, become clear to me through self-reflection. I can increasingly accept myself and live authentically. Increasing my inner strength and nurturing my soul pushes me forward. I believe that I can approach others and share my thoughts and feelings in a caring manner with appropriate boundaries, thus offering compassion and kindness as I better connect with myself and others. Such living brings me into glimpses of oneness and awe. As I continue on my journey, I realize that being in the world and moving through life in a thoughtful, present manner enhances my self-awareness and knowing this helps me support my students and grow.

Questions for Reflection

1. How do you help yourself be present in your daily life?
2. What lessons are others offering to you that support your soul work?
3. How are you an advocate?
4. Where are you going? Are you on the path?

References

Beck, J. (2003). Self and soul: Exploring the boundary between psychotherapy and spiritual formation. *Journal of Psychology and Theology, 31*(1), 24-36.

Bruce, M. A. (2007). Nurturing the spirituality of our youth. In O. Morgan (Ed.) *Counseling and spirituality: Views from the profession* (pp. 187-201). Boston, MA: Lahaska Press.

Bruce, M. A. (1995). Brief Counseling: An effective model for change. *The School Counselor, 42*, 353-363.

Bruce, M. A., & Hopper, G. (1997). Brief counseling versus traditional counseling: A comparison of effectiveness. *The School Counselor, 44*, 171-184.

Duran, E. (2006). *Healing the soul wound: Counseling with American Indians and other Native peoples.* New York: Teachers College Press.

Duran, E., Firehammer, J., & Gonzalez, J. (2008). Liberation psychology as the path toward healing cultural social wounds. *Journal of Counseling and Development, 86*(3), 288-295.

Maslow, A. H. (1998). *Toward a psychology of being (3rd ed.)* New York: Wiley.

May, R. (1953). *Man's search for himself.* New York: W. W. Norton.

Ottens, A., & Klein, J. (2005). Common factors: Where the soul of counseling and psychotherapy resides. *Journal of Humanistic Counseling, Education and Development, 44*, 32-45.

Rogers, C. (1961). *On Becoming a Person: A therapist's view of psychotherapy.* New York: Mariner Books.

Rose, E., Westefeld, J., & Ansley, T. (2001). Spiritual issues in counseling: Clients' beliefs and preferences. *Journal of Counseling Psychology, 48*(1), 61-71.

Sperry, L., & Shafranske, E. (2005). *Spiritually oriented psychotherapy.* Washington, DC American Psychological Association.

Index

About the Authors

Ellen S. Amatea is a professor in the Counselor Education Program in the College of Education at the University of Florida. She is a psychologist and a marriage and family therapist and maintains a private practice specializing in counseling children and adolescents and their families. Ellen's research interests include the processes and outcomes of family involvement for the development of children and youth, particularly underserved low-income children; interventions for children and adolescents with behavior problems; and the preparation of educators in family involvement in education. Ellen teaches graduate courses in school counseling and in marriage and family counseling. In addition, she has taught an undergraduate course in teacher education on family and community involvement in education for the past 10 years.

Mary Alice Bruce is a professor of counseling and the school counseling program coordinator in the Department of Professional Studies, of which she is chair, at the University of Wyoming. She has served as a member and chair of the CACREP Board, co-chair of the ACA International Committee, Peace Corps volunteer in East Africa, and Fulbright Scholar in Guatemala. Mary Alice's research interests include spirituality across the lifespan, mentoring relationships and mentoring programs, as well as group work and the creation of caring learning communities. She enjoys golf and cross country skiing with her husband and friends.

Rebekah J. Byrd is an assistant professor of counseling and school counseling program coordinator in the Department of Human Development and Learning at East Tennessee State University. She serves on many regional, national, and state wide committees. She has also written multiple refereed journal articles and book chapters. Her research specialization falls primarily in issues pertaining to children and adolescents, school counseling, and LGBTQ concerns. Other major research interests include play therapy, human rights and social justice, group work, self-injury in adolescents, women's wellness and Adlerian theory. Rebekah has been a faculty member at ETSU since 2010 and currently lives in Asheville, NC with her partner Alex, and their 3 dogs (Neptune, Gemini, and Joe) and 2 cats (Adhara and Faun).

Marion Cavallaro is an associate professor and coordinator of the community and clinical mental health counseling programs in the Department of Counselor Education at The College of New Jersey. She is a Licensed Professional Counselor and a National Certified Counselor. Marion enjoys teaching counseling theory, career counseling and clinical internship courses and her research interests focus on curriculum strategies in teaching these courses, the career counseling needs of diverse populations and counselor education faculty development. Marion enjoys yoga, reading, traveling and spending time with her husband and family.

Katrina Cook is an assistant professor in the Department of Educational Leadership and Counseling at Texas A&M University—San Antonio. She is a Licensed Professional Counselor, a Licensed Marriage & Family Therapist, and a certified school counselor who also provides supervision for counseling interns and marriage and family therapy associates. She enjoys her relatively new career as a counselor educator where she focuses on multicultural counseling and professional identity development of student counselors. She is also interested in creative interventions in counseling and serves on the editorial board for the Journal of Creativity in Mental Health. Katrina spends much of her personal time restoring a 1929 cottage and creating and binding books by hand.

Penny Dahlen received her Master's degree from Colorado State University in Counseling and her Doctorate from Idaho State University in Counselor Education and Supervision. She is a licensed professional counselor in Colorado. She has held faculty positions at a variety of institutions and is currently the Director of the Training Clinic at Argosy University, Denver. Penny received the 2010 ACES Mentor of the Year

Award for her work with doctoral students at Argosy University. She also has a private practice in Evergreen, Colorado.

Christine Ebrahim is an Assistant Professor in the Department of Counseling at Loyola University New Orleans. She received a Master of Science degree from Loyola and a Ph.D. in Counselor Education from the University of New Orleans. She is a Licensed Professional Counselor Supervisor and a National Certified Counselor. Christine is the President of the Louisiana Association of Counselor Education and Supervision and also has a private practice. Her research interests are in the areas of professional school counselor preparation, the use of play therapy by school counselors, supervision, legal and ethical issues, and peer consultation.

Kelly Emelianchik-Key is an assistant professor in the Counseling Department at Argosy University - Atlanta. She is a Licensed Professional Counselor and a National Certified Counselor. Her clinical, teaching, and research interests include: counseling adolescents and families, intimate partner violence intervention and prevention, assessment in counselor education and working with marginalized populations. Kelly is a member of several professional organizations and has presented at multiple national and state counseling conferences. Kelly and her husband stay busy with their newborn baby, Owen, and are excited for many new adventures in their role as parents.

Lori Ellison is an Assistant Professor in the Counseling Department of Marshall University. She is a Licensed Professional Counselor and Approved Licensed Professional Supervisor in West Virginia. Her research interests include supervision, ethics, spirituality, academic integrity in higher education, and college student issues. She has been an active clinical professional in the mental health field for more than 20 years working in community mental health and college and university settings. She and her husband have raised twins, Emmalee and Hunter, who will be seniors in high school in the 2012-2013 school year. They both enjoy participating in their children's activities at school, church, and in the community as much as possible.

Nancy Forth is an Associate Professor in the Counselor Education Program at the University of Central Missouri. In addition to coordinating the Community Counseling Concentration, Nancy teaches content and clinical courses as well as provides supervision to master's level counselors-in-training. Her research interests include using creativity in counseling and supervision and counselor development. Nancy is a licensed professional counselor and a National Certified Counselor with varied clinical experience. She has worked with diverse clients (individual, groups, couples, and families), children and adults, families, single parents, those who have been victimized and who have perpetrated crimes, and collaborated with K-12 school systems.

Stephanie Hall is an assistant professor in the Department of Psychological Counseling at Monmouth University. She is a licensed professional counselor in both New Jersey and Louisiana and a National Certified Counselor. Her interests include multicultural counseling, women's issues in counseling, counselor professional identity, grief counseling, and group work.

Rosemarie Scotti Hughes is Dean Emerita of the School of Psychology and Counseling of Regent University. She is also a Licensed Professional Counselor and a Licensed Marriage and Family Therapist in Virginia and a National Certified Counselor and National Certified School Counselor. Her academic, clinical, and publishing career of over 25 years encompasses a wide range of topics generic to counseling, with a particular focus on adults and children with disabilities and their families, ethics, and spirituality in counseling. Personal interests include being a Stephen Minister, world traveling, and visiting the grandchildren (currently nine). She continues to be on journal editorial boards and is currently writing and hoping to publish in various genres.

Carol Klose Smith is a clinical assistant professor at the University of Iowa in the Department of Rehabilitation and Counselor Education. Carol received her master's degree at Western Illinois University and worked for 10 years as a Licensed Profession Counselor. Upon graduation Carol worked as an assistant professor at Winona State University, returning to the University of Iowa in order to pursue her research agenda and coordinate clinical training for the school counseling program. Her research areas include career development issues in the schools, counselor preparation and supervision, and women's issues. Carol enjoys spending time with her family, playing the viola, summers at the lake and running.

A manda C. LaGuardia is a counselor educator at Sam Houston State University. Her research interests include applications of Adlerian and Feminist theories, family and adolescent issues, group counseling, and professionally identity development.

C hristina M. Rosen is an assistant professor in the Human Development and Psychological Counseling Department in the College of Education at Appalachian State University. She is a Licensed Professional Counselor Supervisor and Licensed Clinical Addictions Specialist in the state of North Carolina, and a National Certified Counselor. Her professional career as a counselor started in 1988. Her teaching, clinical and research focus is on dual diagnosis, supervision and mentoring, and advocacy. In addition she explores the impact of culture (including a global perspective) and belief systems on the counseling and client relationship, and the supervisor and supervisee relationship. Her spare time is spent traveling, playing with her dog, and exploring nature with family and friends.

A tsuko Seto is an associate professor in the Department of Counselor Education at The College of New Jersey. She is a Licensed Professional Counselor and a registered Disaster Response Crisis Counselor in New Jersey, NBCC Approved Clinical Supervisor, and a National Certified Counselor. Her clinical, teaching and scholarship interests include counseling with intercultural couples and families of Asian heritages, multicultural counselor education preparation and supervision, and creative interventions in counseling. Atsuko and her husband spend much of their personal time playing in water and at parks, or doing lots of pretend plays with their three-year old daughter, Emma.

M ichelle Shuler is an assistant professor in the Department of Psychology and Counseling at Northeastern State University (NSU) in Oklahoma. She is currently the Program Chair of the Masters in Substance Abuse Counseling track at NSU where she is interested in increasing counselor competence in the use of recovery interventions. Her clinical and scholarship interests include working with individuals and families in recovery and use of ritual as an intervention when working with addictions. She is currently seeking training through the Celebrant Foundation and Institute to become a Celebrant. In the near future she hopes to be engaging individuals, families, and groups in the use of ritual to increase their positive mental health.

Sondra Smith-Adcock is Associate Professor in Counselor Education at the University of Florida (with specializations in School and Mental Health Counseling). Sondra has been a counselor educator for 15 years, and at the University of Florida for 11 years. She has published numerous book chapters and journal articles on counseling children and adolescents. Her current research interests include play therapy, adolescent reputation enhancement, prevention of delinquency and bullying (including relational aggression), and school-family-community collaboration. Since beginning her tenure at UF, Sondra has married and had two sons. She received tenure and promotion in the same month as her youngest child was born. Balancing motherhood and academia has been her life's pursuit for the past 10 years.

Carol M. Smith is a nationally board certified licensed professional counselor. She holds a Master's in Mental Health Counseling and a Ph.D. in Counselor Education and Supervision from Kent State University. She has a Master's in Biomedical Clinical Ethics from the University of Virginia Medical School. Her major research interests include end-of-life issues; grief, loss and trauma counseling; creativity and resilience; and the interface between biomedical ethics and the mental health needs of those involved in health care dilemmas.

LeAnne Steen is the Chair & Associate Professor in the Department of Counseling at Loyola University New Orleans. She completed her Masters of Arts in Counseling at Texas State University, and her Ph.D. in Counseling at the University of North Texas where she specialized in play therapy, counselor supervision, filial therapy, and activity therapy. LeAnne's research interests include parenting populations, diversity and spirituality in play therapy, trauma and healing related to Hurricane Katrina, hospitalized children, siblings of hospitalized children, beginning counselors, and experiences of junior faculty. She also has a private practice.

Barbara C. Trolley is a Professor in, and the Buffalo Center Campus Coordinator for, the St. Bonaventure University's Counselor Education program. As chair of her university's disability committee and the past coordinator of the autism training program, Barbara is committed to working with youth and diverse populations. She is the lead author of five books on cyberbullying and school counseling, and has written numerous professional articles in the rehabilitation and grief counseling areas. Barbara was the creator, first editor of the New York State School Counseling Journal. She has conducted countless professional workshops at the local, state and national levels. Her prior work includes a decade working as a therapist and administrator, addressing family issues, especially around child abuse and grief.

Anna Viviani is an assistant professor in the Clinical Mental Health Counseling Program at Indiana State University. She is a Licensed Clinical Professional Counselor in Illinois, NBCC Approved Clinical Supervisor, and a National Certified Counselor. Her clinical and research interests involve childhood sexual abuse and other trauma survivors, understanding trauma and unresolved grief, the impact of trauma on growth and development, and counselor education preparation and supervision. Teaching interests include theory, group, growth and development, and supervision. While Anna and her husband continue a commuter lifestyle, they enjoy traveling and entertaining family and friends whenever possible.

Laurie L. Williamson is a Professor and the Director of the Professional School Counseling Program in the Department of Human Development and Psychological Counseling at Appalachian State University in Boone, North Carolina. Teaching and research interests include life and career planning, hybrid course development, experiential education, and international studies.

Cirecie West-Olatunji serves as Associate Professor and coordinator of the Counseling Program at the University of Cincinnati and is president-elect of the American Counseling Association. Cirecie has initiated several clinical research projects that focus on culture-centered community counseling, systemic oppression, and traumatic stress. Her publications include two co-authored books, Future Vision, Present Work, and Counseling African Americans, several book chapters, and numerous articles in peer-reviewed journals. Cirecie has provided consultation internationally in Asia, Africa, and Europe in the area of multicultural counseling and education. Additionally, she provided consultation in a PBS initiative to create a children's television show focusing on diversity through KCET-TV in Los Angeles, CA ("Puzzle Place").